HAMPTON WICK

BRICK BY BR

The Building and Buildings of Hampton Wick 1750 - 2012

Volume 1: Lower Teddington Road and environs

Ray Elmitt

HAMPTON WICK HISTORY SEPTEMBER 2012

For Vicky

I am always grateful for the help and encouragement I receive from fellow local history enthusiasts especially Kelvin Adams, Paul Barnfield, Ken Howe, Colin and Richard Pain, John Shaef. Thanks also for the particular help I have had in the preparation of this volume from local residents including Robert Cruickshank, Elsa Day, Kenneth Hayman-Stephens, Andrew and Magdalen Miles, David Pratt, Guy and Margaret Raynes, Michael and Pandi Stepan, Peter and Sally Thwaite, John and David Turner, Sue Williams. Finally I am pleased to acknowledge the assistance I have received from the staff of the Local Study Rooms in both Richmond upon Thames and Kingston upon Thames.

First published 2012 by
Hampton Wick History
1 The Grove, 24 Lower Teddington Road
Hampton Wick, Surrey KT1 4HJ
website: www.hamptonwickhistory.org.uk
email: ray@hamptonwickhistory.org.uk

ISBN 978-0-9571679-3-3

Contents

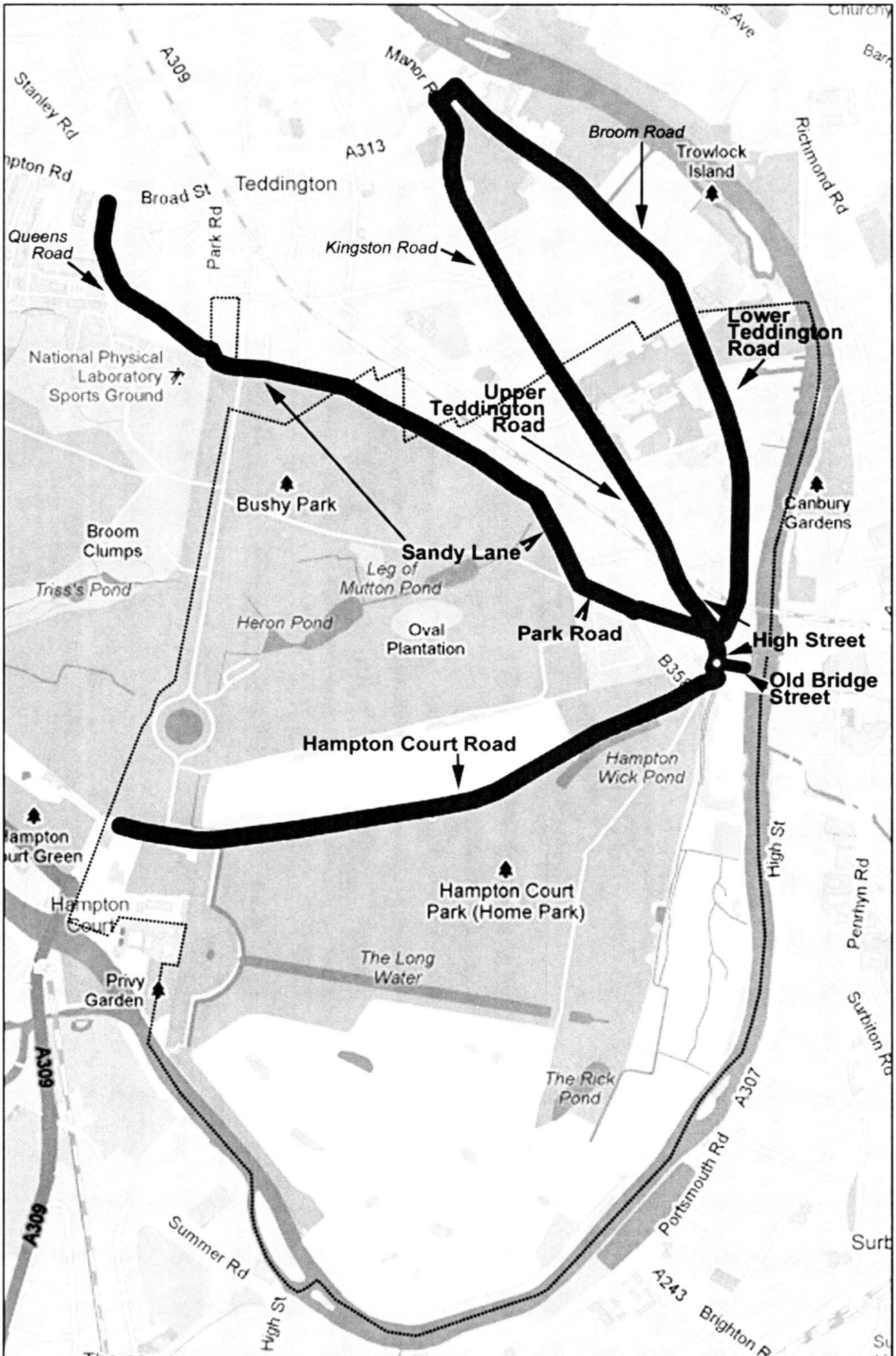

Hampton Wick in 2011 showing the Parish Boundary (marked with a dotted line) and principal roads.
(courtesy of Google Maps)

Series Introduction

Hampton Wick owes its importance to three factors: one geographic and two historic. First, it is located on the River Thames at a point where the riverbed provided a fordable crossing. Second, it is immediately opposite Kingston, historically an important market town where seven Saxon Kings were crowned. Third, it is close to (and was part of) the Manor of Hampton Court which was in existence from the time of the Domesday Book and which became increasingly prominent once Henry VIII had appropriated it from Cardinal Wolsey in 1528.

These three factors worked in combination with each other. The juxtaposition of both the town and the manor created a natural flow of traffic between the two, which necessarily passed through the hamlet of Hampton Wick to use the ford and - from the end of 12th century - the bridge. Travellers from further afield whose journey involved crossing the river were also funnelled through the hamlet because for five centuries this was the only bridge crossing between London Bridge to the east and Staines Bridge to the west.

However, while it enjoyed this unique position, Hampton Wick lacked autonomy because it fell within the larger parish of Hampton. This subservience was significant because the Wick and the Town (as the local population referred to the two entities) were physically separated by 900 acres of Royal Park. The long walk to St Mary's church, Hampton on Sundays and Feast days was a constant physical reminder of the Wick's lesser status. The division of proceeds from the Poor Rates - two-thirds to the Town and one-third to the Wick - was also a long-running grievance.

Around 1830 Hampton Wick was able to make its first bid for freedom. The fear of unrest within the growing population following the end of the Napoleonic Wars led the Government to fund the building of several new churches. St John the Baptist Church in the Wick was originally opened in November 1830 as a chapel-at-ease for St Mary's, Hampton but the Bishop of London upgraded it to a full parish in July 1831, with its own vicar and its own precisely defined boundary (see page 8). The only setback was the stipulation that the existing split of the Poor Rate proceeds between the two communities must be maintained.

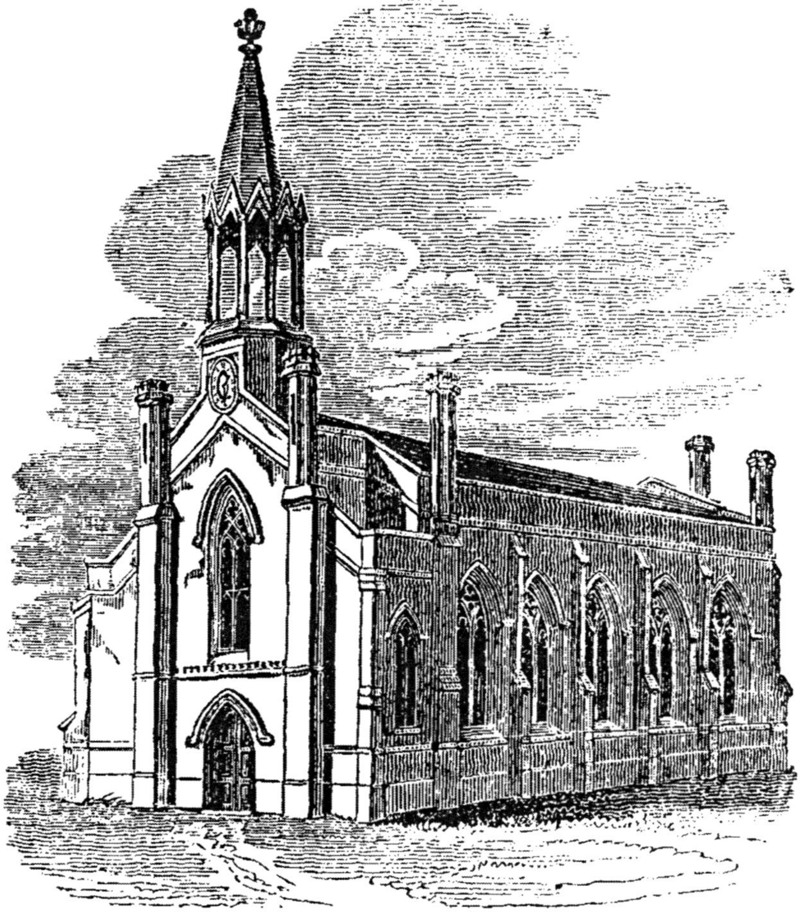

The establishment of the Parish Church of St John the Baptist, opened in 1830, gave Hampton Wick its own identity.

In 1863, the railway came to Hampton Wick via a branch line from Twickenham to Kingston. The following year Hampton received its railway connection but this was on the separate spur line out to Shepperton. Four stations and a change of train at Strawberry Hill now separated the "neighbours". This separation must have had an impact on the two communities as well as being a real consideration in the minds of the new generation of commuters.

The third and decisive break with Hampton also came in 1863 when the new Local Government Act allowed the Wick to establish its own Local Board that, amongst other powers, enabled it to retain and spend the proceeds of its own Poor Rate. By now Hampton Wick was experiencing an explosive growth both in population and in house-building, and the new-found independence of The Local Board empowered it to direct this more effectively. It was the practical question of how to dispose of the sewage - one of their direct responsibilities - that would prove the greatest challenge for the Board.

--oOo--

The physical layout of Hampton Wick reflects its origins. The river crossing made the bridge and its approach the focus of the village. (Old) Bridge Street and its junction with the High Street became the most densely populated area and at this point converged the four roads used by travellers passing through the Wick or using the crossing. The layout and road system is evident on the 1740 map (see page 8) on which the junction of the High Street with the road to the bridge is marked with an arrow.

Immediately north of this point, the High Street divided into three routes shaped like the head of a trident. The left prong headed north west towards Hounslow Heath passing the western boundary of Teddington. The central prong proceeded north towards Twickenham, passing the eastern end of Teddington High Street. The right prong stayed close to the river and eventually rejoined the central road at its junction with Teddington High Street. South of the focal point, the High Street soon turned south west as it headed between the walls of the two Royal Parks on its way to the palace and Hampton Court Green. The road system had probably been unchanged for centuries. The first new road (Church Grove) was built in 1830 to provide access to the new church of St John the Baptist.

When St John's became the local Parish Church, the authorities used the River Thames to define the eastern and southern parish boundary (see page 4) while the western border skirted the front of Hampton Court Palace and then almost exactly followed the line of Chestnut Avenue in Bushy Park. Only the northern limits lay close to an existing community and the irregular path of the

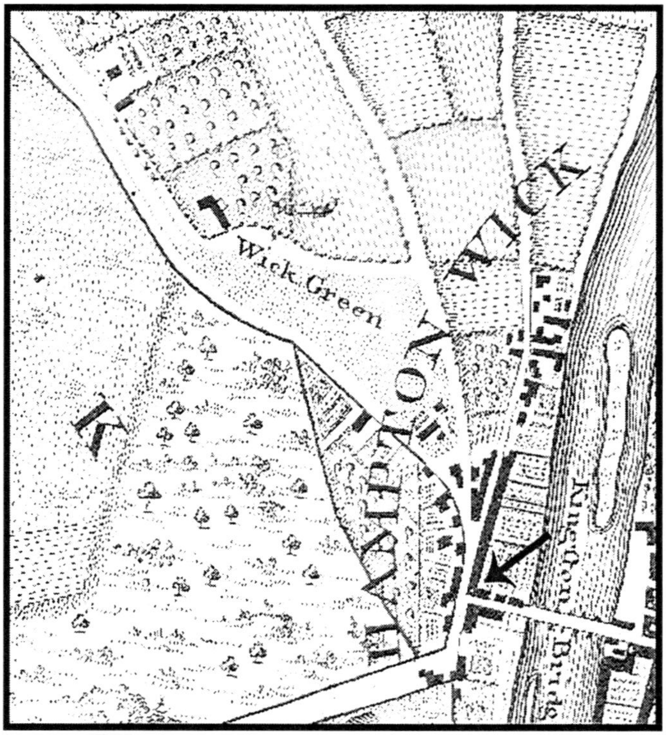

above Detail from Jean Rocque's Map of Hampton Court and Surrounds c1740. The arrow marks the junction of the main street and the road to the bridge from which the road system radiates.
below Description of the Boundary of Hampton Wick Parish published in The London Gazette. The line of the boundary as described is marked by a dotted line on the map on page 4.

Numb. 18828. [1501]

The London Gazette.

Published by Authority.

TUESDAY, JULY 26, 1831.

The boundary to commence in the centre of the river Thames, at Kingston-bridge, where the hamlet of Hampton-wick joins the parish of Kingston, and to comprise the west side of the river, along the whole extent of the parish of Kingston to the parish of Thames-Ditton, where the river takes a direction westward; and the boundary then comprises the north side of the river, separating the district of Hampton-wick, from the parishes of Thames-Ditton and East Molesey, till it comes opposite to Hampton-court-palace, where it joins the town division of Hampton, and leaving the river goes up the centre of the Privy-gardens to the south front of the Palace, along which it proceeds eastward, and thence along the east front of the Palace northward, and returns westward up the Office-yard, and along the south wall of the Kitchen-garden, to within fifteen feet of the west wall of the same, at which distance from the wall it continues in a northerly direction till it comes to the high road leading to Hampton, which it crosses, and passing through a house, the property of Mr. Evans, proceeds in a straight line to an oak tree in Bushy-park, and thence to a tree on the west side of the avenue leading from Hampton-court to Teddington, up which avenue it continues nearly to the end of the park, where it leaves the town division, and joining the parish of Teddington, proceeds in an easterly direction to a tree close to the foot-path leading from Teddington-park-gate to Hampton-wick, whence it goes out of Bushy-park, and crossing a road, called Sandy-lane, passes round two pieces of land, called the Pepper-pieces, and again enters the park for a short distance; it then again leaves the park, and proceeds eastward till it reaches the river Thames, where, leaving the parish of Teddington, and rejoining that of Kingston, it continues along the centre of the river till it reaches Kingston-bridge where the boundary commenced; an isolated portion at the north western extremity of the district is bounded on the east and north by the parish of Teddington, and on the west and south by the town division of Hampton, which district is more particularly described in the accompanying plan, and is therein surrounded by a red line.

boundary at this point shows how existing arrangements with the neighbouring parish of Teddington were accommodated.

--oOo---

There are no direct records of population numbers in Hampton Wick before 1800. However, it is probable that the historical population trend would broadly mirror that of London itself - which grew from 600,000 to one million over the course of the 1700's. On this basis, the population of Hampton Wick in 1700 was probably around 350.

The first national Census of 1801 shows the population of Hampton Wick itself (i.e. excluding the Palace) had grown to around 600. By 1861 this had become 2,000 and by 1891 around 2,400. The population peaked in 1951 at 3,400.

To cater for this more than five-fold increase, the infrastructure of the village underwent dramatic changes in several distinct phases. The early stages of growth took place along the existing road system. Open fields disappeared under housing and by 1850, many of the available roadside plots were full: cottages and tenements for the workers, substantial villa blocks for the middle class and extensive mansions with gardens to the river for the wealthy. The schools for girls and boys were built in 1837 and 1843 respectively - the latter included a public library room. Twenty three shops and eight pubs served the population.

The next phase of development - fuelled by both the accelerating birth rate and the arrival of the railway in 1863 - required the release of more land and the provision of new roads to access it. East of the High Street, Station Road and Seymour Road were laid out in the 1860's followed by Glamorgan Road in the 1880's. West of the High Street, St John's Road linked to Church Grove in the 1860's, while Vicarage Road and Cedars Road arrived in the 1880's, followed by Warwick Road in the 1890's. By 1900, the High Street had fifty one shops and seven pubs. The Local Board had built its offices on the High Street in 1884 and Assembly Rooms were opened on Park Road in 1889. Both schools were expanded in the 1880's and several small private academies flourished in the village. The Roman Catholic Church opened in 1893 and the Baptist Chapel in 1905.

The start of the new century in fact saw a small temporary reduction in available housing when preparation for the arrival of the trams required a programme of demolition on the High Street, mainly of older run-down housing stock. Not only did this prompt higher quality replacement building, but also meant that the High Street itself gained a wood-block surface for the benefit of pedestrians and the increasing number of cyclists. The constraints of the river and parks surrounding the village dictated that further housing provision could only be achieved with higher density redevelopment of the existing sites. In the 1930's, some of the mansions and almost all the cottages gave way to developments like Ingram House, Park Court and Jubilee Court. The only new roads were Monmouth Avenue in the 1930's, Beverley Road and Woffington Close in the 1950's.

Due to the decreasing size of households, the population had actually declined to 2,400 by 1991 - the same figure as a hundred years earlier. Nevertheless, the last 50 years has still seen significant new major developments such as Broom Park and Elton Close (1960's), Beckett's Place (1980's), Spinnaker Court (1990's) and recently Marina Place (2010) and Sandy Lane (started in 2011). It is perhaps a sign of the times that most recent large-scale developments since 1980 have been on land previously used for commercial purposes.

--oOo--

As the two elements of this book's title - The **Building** *and* **Buildings** of Hampton Wick - suggests, this material falls into two parts:

- The first half recounts the <u>history</u> of the way in which the village has developed from 1750 to the present day. It answers the obvious questions: who owned the land? who built the roads and houses? who lived in them? how have the buildings been altered and extended over time?
- The second half is designed as a **<u>walking guide</u>**, to help those interested in going out and exploring the attraction and fascination of today's Hampton Wick buildings for themselves.

The first half has drawn on the wide range of sources that is available covering different time-frames. These include Hampton Court Manor records (1640 - 1936), Land Tax Assessment Books (1767 - 1832), Poor Rate books (1808 - 1915), Street Directories (1850 - 1940), historical maps (1650 - 1956), Census Returns (1841 - 1911), Council Planning Applications (1880 - date), Telephone Directories (1925 - 1984) and Electoral Registers (1847 - 2012) as well as English Heritage's descriptions of the 23 listed buildings in Hampton Wick.

Given that there are over 800 properties in Hampton Wick, the size of the overall task and the volume of information available have led to two pragmatic decisions for the project:

1. The material is to be split into three separate books covering different parts of the village. This table shows both the sequence in which the volumes will be published and what streets each will cover:

Volume 1 - East	Volume 2 - West	Volume 2 - Central
Lower Teddington Road	**Park Road**	**High Street**
Aspen Close Baygrove Mews Glamorgan Road Lexington Place Monmouth Avenue Normansfield Avenue Raeburn Close Seymour Road Station Road	Bennet Close Cedars Road Church Grove Park Court Saddlers Mews St John's Road Sandy Lane School Lane School Road Vicarage Road Vineyard Row	Barge Walk Beverley Road Bushy Park Hampton Court Road Home Park Home Park Terrace Marina Place Old Bridge Street Upper Teddington Road Warwick Road Woffington Close

2. In parallel with the books, a web site has been created (see page 166) containing a page for each residential property providing, as a minimum, a list of occupants and (if built before 1911) a link to the Census returns for that property. The web page also includes links to other relevant material where available such as Estate Agent Sale Particulars, recent and historic Planning Applications and any other archive material.

The books have a common structure and, within the specific geographic area of the village covered, are self-contained. They begin with a geographic and historic overview, then give a snapshot taken around 1850 using the first accurate map and descriptions available to us, followed by a number of chapters detailing the listed and significant buildings - and their occupants - as captured in this snapshot.

Each book then traces the subsequent housing developments that took place decade by decade from the 1850's to the current day, highlighting the fascinating - and often lively - interactions between the developers and the planning authorities. Finally, there are a set of guided walks along each individual street with illustrations and a brief background of every single property on either side of the road.

The intention is that this material - viewed alongside the web page for each property (described in the Appendix starting on page 166) - will enable the reader to trace the origin and explore the richness of all the buildings of Hampton Wick ... brick by brick.

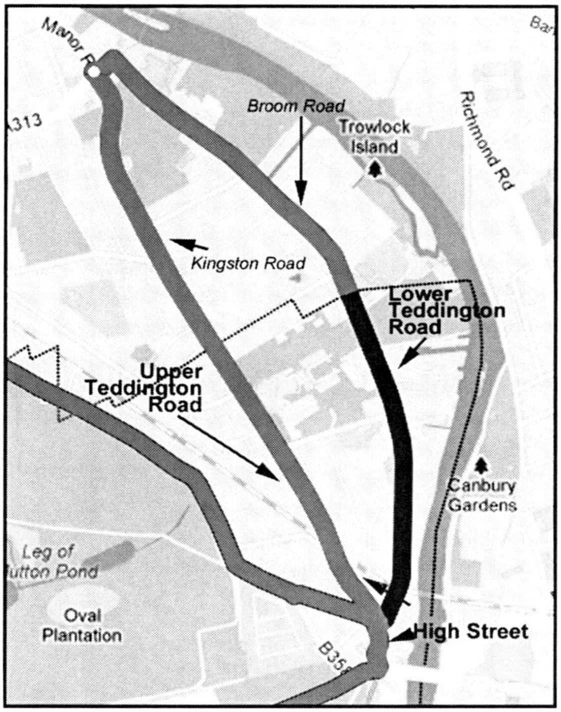

above: Lower Teddington Road becomes Broom Road as it crosses the Parish Boundary (shown as a dotted line).
(courtesy of Google Maps)
below: Downstream of Kingston Old Bridge from the Surrey shore.
(Water Colour by Thomas Rowlandson 1756 - 1827)
(courtesy of Kingston Museum and Heritage Service)

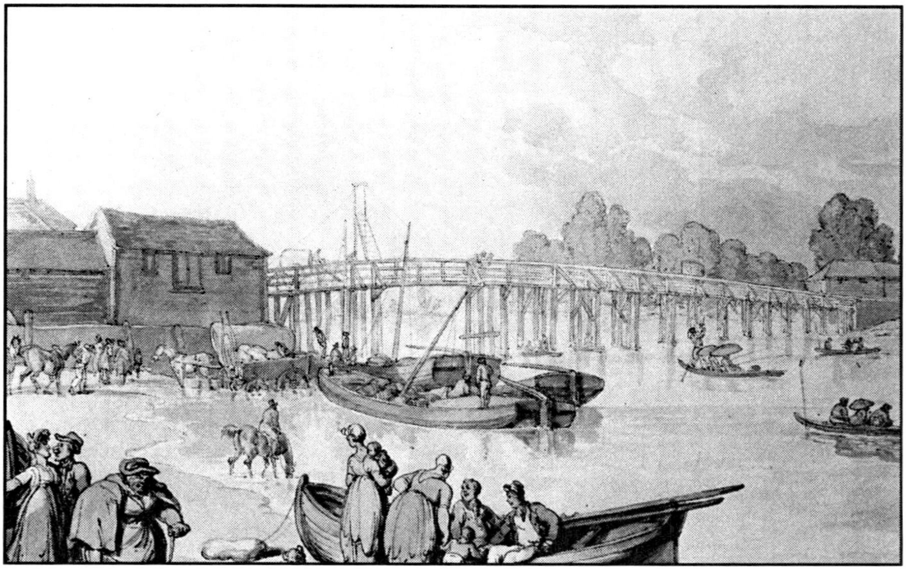

PART ONE: DISCOVERING THE PAST

Lower Teddington Road

Lower Teddington Road (together with its northern extension called Broom Road) runs for 2000 metres from its junction with Hampton Wick High Street (in the south) to its northern end where it rejoins the continuation of the High Street (now called Kingston Road). On this stretch the River Thames describes an arc as it flows initially due north from Kingston Bridge and then north west towards the present-day Teddington Lock. Lower Teddington Road/Broom Road runs broadly parallel with the river but with a lesser arc so that it is within 50 - 100 metres of it at the bottom and top ends and around 350 metres distant at the midpoint. At various times this thoroughfare has been called the Green Lane to Teddington, Wick Lane, Swan Lane and the Lower Road to Kingston. It was definitively named Lower Teddington Road as one of the first decrees of the Local Board in 1864.

In his excellent book "Hampton Wick: The Story of a Thames-side Village", Paul Barnfield recounts suggestions that originally this was the one and only road to Teddington but that frequent flooding in mediaeval times required an alternative route further west and away from the river. This latter (called Upper Teddington Road) runs as a straight-line between the two ends of Lower Teddington Road/Broom Road.

Until the first Teddington Lock was built in 1810, the Thames was tidal as far as Walton and sometimes even Staines. There had been a ford across the river (probably at low tide) from at least Roman times. Thomas Rowlandson's late 18th century watercolour (see opposite) of the Kingston shore just downstream of the old bridge, with its horse and cart standing in the water unloading a barge and a punt in midstream, shows just how shallow the river could be at low tide.

Both lower and upper roads are already clearly shown in Jean Rocque's Map of Middlesex c1740 (see page 8). It also shows the buildings on both sides of Lower Teddington Road near the centre of the village around The Swan. Further north the buildings are mainly on the east (river) side of the road only for, despite the risk of flooding, these were associated with the malting industry for which easy river access was important.

Between the Lower and Upper Teddington Roads was an area called the Wick Field. Originally this would have been divided into strips and farmed by tenants but this traditional arrangement had disappeared many centuries before. Paul Barnfield explains how the land had been absorbed into Hampton Court Manor. He cites several examples where illegal enclosures of formerly common land had been legitimised by the Manor Court and establishes that most of the land either side of Lower Teddington Road passed into the ownership of Charles Montagu, 1st Earl of Halifax in 1710. Montagu had purchased the position of Keeper of Bushy Park the previous year. The Upper Lodge in the park had been wrecked by a great storm a few years before. In return for rebuilding the lodge at his own expense, Montagu had successfully negotiated with the Treasury that he and his heirs should retain the position of Keeper "for three lives" - a fairly common, though restrictive, form of Mediaeval tenure. With effective ownership of the Park thus secured for a reasonable term, Montagu saw the additional land in Hampton Wick as a logical and viable investment. The first of the three lives did not last long for Charles Montagu himself died in 1715. The inheritance passed to his nephew George Montagu who was clearly as proprietorial as his uncle. Amongst many other "improvements" to the estate, in 1734 he ordered the building of the brick wall around the northern and eastern boundary of the Park from Hampton to the Wick. This was completed in 1737, the year of his death. A contemporary described George as "a squanderer of his money so that it is said that his daughters will have a very small fortune". This proved to be an accurate assessment. There were five marriageable daughters to be provided for and, to fast-track the provision of dowries for each, Montagu's Executors (including his own son George) successfully promoted a Private Act of Parliament to allow a fire sale of assets.

The records of Hampton Court Manor for 13 June 1741 show that John Tilson of Watlington Park in Oxfordshire took up ownership of much of the Hampton Wick land and property. He held the investment for thirty years before selling on the estate in 1771 to Dr Robert James whose family retained it until it was finally sold in 1850 to John Guy, a wealthy local Solicitor, significant landowner and serial property developer. The full extent and content of the estate is included in a detailed description contained in a Sale Catalogue of 1810 (which is available to view online in the web pages for *Moiravale/Thameside Place* on www.hamptonwickhistory.org.uk).

As will be seen later (page 57), the subsequent subdivision and sale of this land provided the basis not only for the development of Lower Teddington Road but also the creation of all other housing development east of the High Street/Upper Teddington Road including Seymour Road, Station Road, Glamorgan Road and Monmouth Avenue.

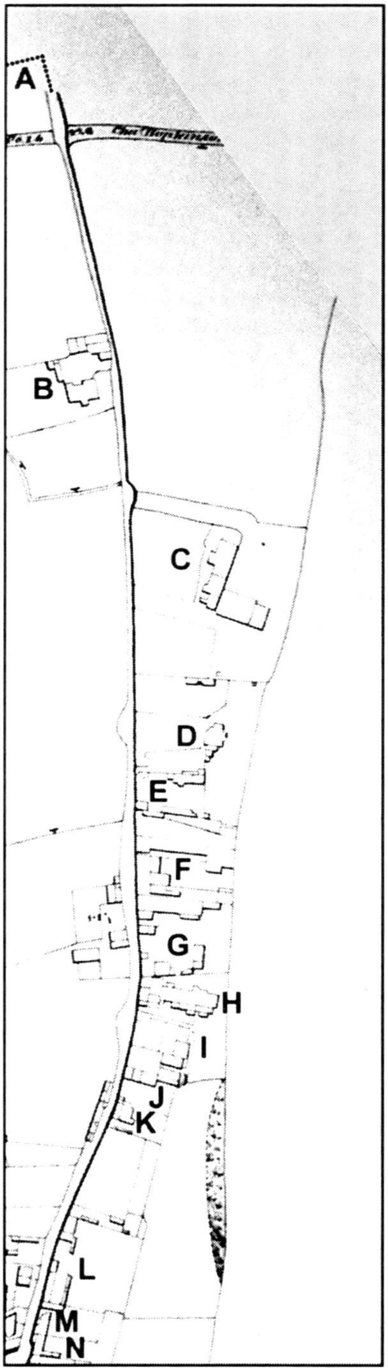

Locations in Ayliffe's account

(shown on the 1828 Enclosure Act map)

A - footpath to the upper road (now Normansfield Avenue)

B - Mr. John Guy (*The Elms*, destroyed by enemy bombing 1944)

C - The starch factory (later *Moiravale* now *Thameside Place*)

D - *The Grove* (called *Grove House* in 1850)

E - Mr. Brewer (demolished 1860, now site of *Wick Lodge*)

F - Mr. Fortnum (*Walnut Tree House*)

G - The Smiths (house demolished in 1870's, site now occupied by *Thames Bank* and *Woodlands*)

H - Mr. John Horne (*Riverside*)

I - Malthouses (burned down in WWII now *Burgoine Quay*)

J Sweet Stuff Manufactury - demolished for railway

K - Mrs. Gee's house (Ivy Cottage demolished around 1870, now the site of *Aquilla House*)

L - Mr. Winter's palatial residence - (*Rivermead*)

M - Mr. Macfarlane (*Wolsey's Cottage*)

N - Mrs. Norton (*River Cottage*)

Lower Teddington Road in 1850

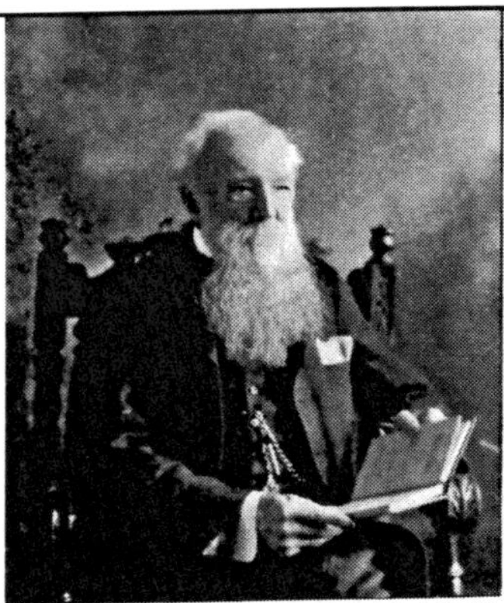

Photo] [J. S. Catford, Kingston.

Mr. George William Ayliffe.
Born at Hampton Wick, 1828.

Before continuing to explore the development of Lower Teddington Road, it is worth spending time studying this remarkable snapshot of the properties and residents as they existed around 1850. The following account of his childhood reminiscences was recorded in the **Surrey Comet** by George William Ayliffe around 1914 under the title 'Recollections of an Octogenarian'.

"Commencing the perambulation of the village from the parish boundary in the Lower Teddington-road, and coming towards Kingston Bridge was a footpath (A on map opposite) leading from the Lower Teddington-road to the upper road, near the parish pound and boundary. Mr. Ayliffe said there were open fields as far as the residence (B) of Mr. John Guy, solicitor, who was the founder of the firm known in later years as Guy and Wilkinson, and in more recent times as Wilkinson, Howlett and Wilkinson.

"Then came Hart's starch factory (C), in which Mr. Hart, a quiet old gentleman, worked with his family.

"The next house (D) was *The Grove*, which was the residence of Mr. Edward Lapidge, the architect of Kingston Bridge, which was commenced in 1825 and completed and opened in 1828. Mr. Lapidge was also the architect of Hampton, Hampton Wick and Ham churches. He gave the site upon which Hampton Wick church stands, and was the first builder of the Terrace facing Kingston Bridge. He was a tall and erect gentleman, usually dressed in black with a tall hat with tassels, wore hessian boots and was exceedingly active. *The Grove* had a large garden extending to the Thames, with a splendid lawn furnished with noble trees. The property is still owned by members of the family, who continue to reside in the village.

"The next cottage (E) was occupied by Mr. Brewer, a maltman, a very hard working man with a large family. Next was the residence (F) of Mr. Fortnum, a tea dealer who carried on a very large business opposite the White Horse Cellars in Piccadilly in the name of Fortnum and Mason. Then came a range of malthouses leading up to the residence (G) of Messrs. Henry and Richard Smith and their sister, eccentric but very charitable people who did a flourishing trade in malt. Some more cottages were followed by the residence (H) of Mr. John Horne, standing near the river; these premises are now occupied by Mr. Burgoine, and included an extensive range of malthouses (I) reaching to the Thames, with a large landing for barges. Mr. John Durham's sweet stuff manufactory came next (J) and was noted especially for sugared almonds. Mrs. Gee resided in the adjoining house (K) which had an extensive garden; she was a very eccentric lady, rich and charitable. This house was occupied for some years by Mr. William Woods, the creator of Surbiton Park Estate. For many years Mr. Woods would not allow anyone except Mr. Ayliffe to shave him.

"The next house (L) was the palatial residence of Mr. Winter, who had a son about the age of young Ayliffe, who was allowed to go in every day to play with Johnny Winter, and whatever toys, or books, were given to one, the like were also given to the other. This house was for many years the residence of Captain Gordon, a relative of Lady Albinia Cumberland, of Hampton Court Palace. He was succeeded by Mr. Aubrey Paul, a famous banker of his day, whose family were very much respected in the village. Next was the residence (M) of Mr. Macfarlane, a retired Naval officer, who had a Scotch servant. Both were very eccentric, but lived a very quiet life. This property was subsequently acquired and occupied by Mr. James Gridley.

"In the adjoining house (N) lived Mrs. Norton, her son and a lady named Dean."

Field by field, plot by plot

This next section of the book traces the development of Lower Teddington Road from the earliest recorded buildings to the present day. It shows how each field sale and each release (or redevelopment) of land from an existing plot led to the gradual (and now almost complete) infilling of the whole road on both sides.

The account starts with those properties that were in existence before 1850 and included in Ayliffe's account. These are described in the order in which they are mentioned by Ayliffe (i.e. north to south). The narrative then explores at length what happened as a result of a major release of new land for building in the 1850's.

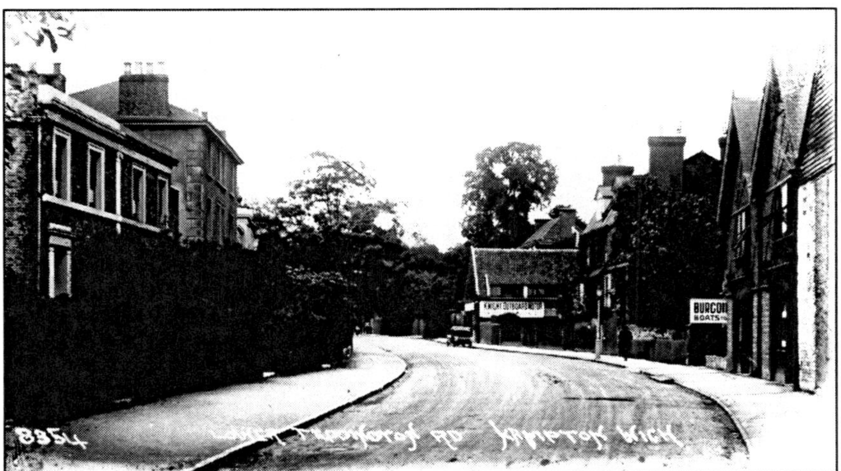

A postcard view of Lower Teddington Road around 1920. Three malthouses are seen on the extreme right and a fourth is in the middle distance.

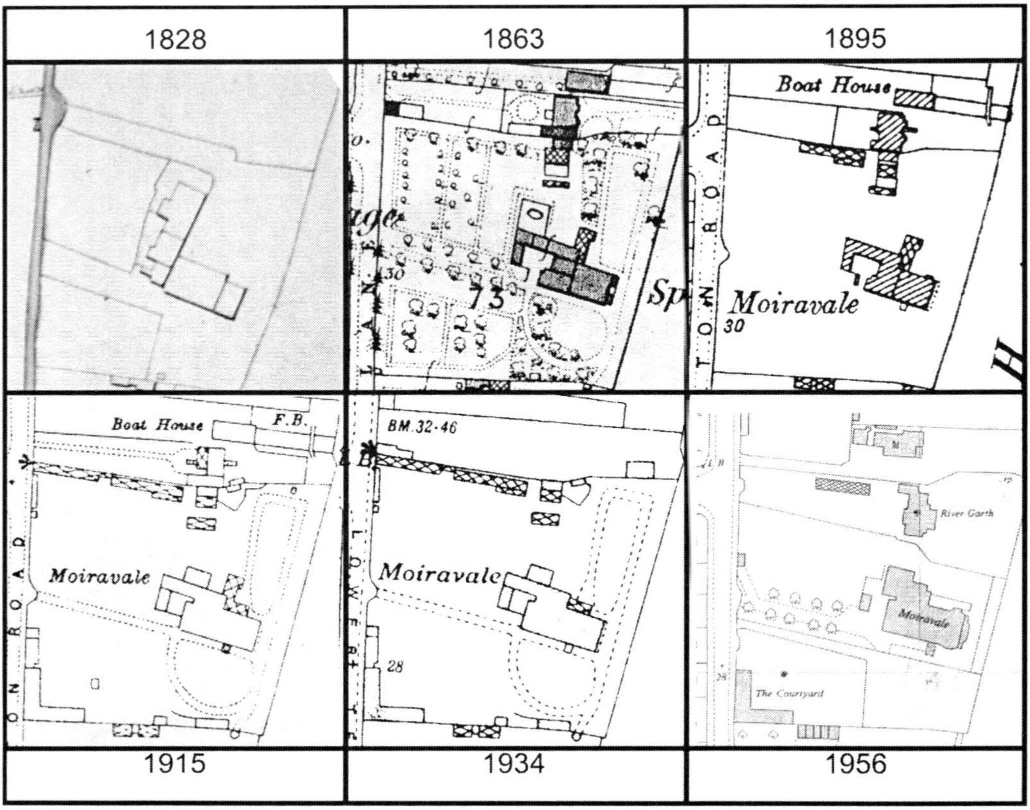

above: The earliest plan shows the starch factory occupying the north of the site. This had been demolished by 1863 when the property had become purely residential. The *porte-cochère* entrance porch has been added by 1895 and the stables by 1915. The 1956 map shows four separate properties occupying the original site.
below: *Moiravale*'s turn-of-the-century elegance

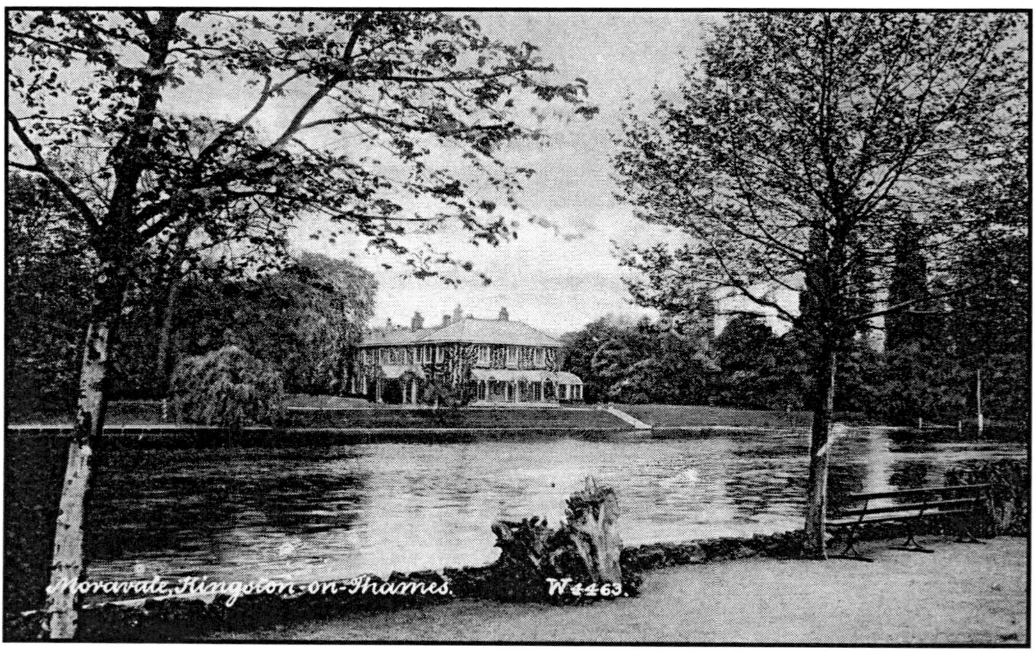

Moiravale (now Thameside Place)

Ayliffe Location C (page 16) - now 26 Lower Teddington Road

Moiravale is probably one of the best-known properties in Hampton Wick. For fifty years it was a Council-run residential care home and many village families would visit their elderly relatives there. It closed in 1998 and lay empty and increasingly dilapidated.

The building was sold in 2003, converted into 13 high-class properties restricted to those aged over 55, renamed *Thameside Place* and reopened in 2006. And in their marketing publicity, the developers Beechcroft could not resist repeating one of the village's most favourite rumours concerning the house - that Edward VII (when Prince of Wales) installed his mistress Lillie Langtry in *Moiravale*. Sadly this myth is just that ... a myth. Edward and Lillie did have a love nest but it was in Bournemouth not Hampton Wick. Nevertheless, the fact remains that this property has indeed had a colourful history.

The earliest recorded reference to the property occurs in the Roll of the Hampton Court Manor proceedings of 13 June 1741 when a "customary messuage formerly in the occupation of Joseph Hart and then late of George late Earl of Halifax ... containing by estimation 20 acres" is mentioned as part of the "fire sale" needed to pay the debts of George Montagu, 2nd Earl of Halifax. This is the first mention of the Hart family who were associated with the property on and off for around 130 years.

The Harts were mainly starch-makers. However, one exception was Anthony Hart (later Sir Anthony) who was a lawyer and diplomat. He was born in 1754 on the Island of St Kitts in the West Indies where his father was Governor. He was educated in the UK, qualified as a barrister and became a KC in 1807. He was appointed solicitor general to Queen Charlotte in 1816 two years before her death at Kew Palace. In later life he became a Privy Councillor and ended his public career as Chancellor of Ireland 1827-30.

Sir Anthony's 21-year lease on the *Moiravale* site (which also included the six-acres of the Cold Harbour field) was signed on 12 February 1799 and is included in the *Moiravale* webpages on www.hamptonwickhistory.org.uk . The agreement allowed him to "vary the present nature and situations of the buildings as he shall think fit". The document went on to note "it (was) his intention to convert part of the Buildings which at present are used for malting into the Dwelling part of the premises and to convert other parts of the present Buildings to the use of malting." He started exercising this option immediately by building a new section on the river side of the plot and by 1810 had created (according to a contemporary sale catalogue also on the website) "A Genteel Villa (On a small scale) containing a handsome Drawing Room and Eating Room communicating by folding Doors, Three principal Bed Chambers, Two Dressing Rooms and Three other Chambers exclusive of the Garrets."

However, a valuation conducted in 1813 noted "the two principal rooms were erected ... without any elevation from the level of the Ground to make it correspond with the old part of the House which is the reason the Dry rot in some degree has taken the Wainscott in several parts ... which occasionally will want to be repaired."

At this stage the site also contained "a large Malting of Two Floors" which, although part of the same overall lease, was sublet to the maltster. The 1841 census referred to the property as Skinners Hall and recorded 72-year old Roger Forster as the tenant. By 1844, the maltings was converted to use as a starch factory when Sir Anthony's descendant 62-year old Pleasant Hart moved in with his wife and three spinster daughters. When the landowner sold the estate in 1850 (see Page 57), the title to the main property was bought by the Harts for £1,500 (around £3.8m today) and transferred to the three daughters. A strip of land on the north side was set aside for building a retirement property for Pleasant Hart. In time the starch factory was pulled down and the whole family moved into retirement.

In 1862 the property was sold to Frederick Christopher Leader for £5,500 (around £9m today) and he renamed it *Springfield*. Leader describes himself in the 1871 census as a Wine Merchant but soon after he became Manager of the Alhambra Theatre built on the site occupied since 1936 by the Odeon, Leicester Square. He took over the licence for the theatre from 4 February 1876 and ran it until 3 July 1877. This relatively short period may be explained by the number of mortgages and further advances he took out on *Springfield* such that, when it was sold in 1887 for £5,975, Leader's share was down to £975.

By 1890 the property was acquired by Frank Williams Jones a 48-year old American from New Hartford, Connecticut. The story of the acquisition and the subsequent renaming of the house is both extraordinary and poignant. Jones was born into a wealthy high society family - his bride's family invited US President Grover Cleveland to their wedding. The President accepted! Jones trained as a lawyer and was admitted to the American bar. In 1880 he had joined the newly-founded Bell Telephone Company and in December 1881 was sent to South America where he established lines on the east and west coasts. He then moved to London to set up the Bell Telephone European HQ. Married in 1885, Frank and his bride initially lived in Victoria Road, Surbiton where their daughter Moira Vail was born. Their second child, a son, was born in the Grand Hotel in New York in 1888. Frank's wife Jeannie died later that year after they had returned to London and was buried in St Mark's churchyard, Surbiton. On moving into Hampton Wick two years later, Jones immediately renamed his new home for his daughter and almost certainly in memory of his late wife. He retained the property through to his own death in 1914 although in practice he was seldom at home - the 1911 Census records the housekeeper home alone in a building with 24 rooms!

In 1914 *Moiravale* was sold to James Willing for £4,000 (now about £2.4m) and the conveyance document included a plan showing the wonderfully rambling layout of the house and its extensive glasshouses, garden, stables and boathouse. The same plan was included in the documentation of the sale concluded in 1947 for £10,000 with no apparent changes having taken place in the ensuing 30 years.

The purchaser was Harold Victor Venables who had ambitious plans for the site. In 1949 he applied to the Borough of Twickenham for three major changes. First, he got permission to convert the stables into a

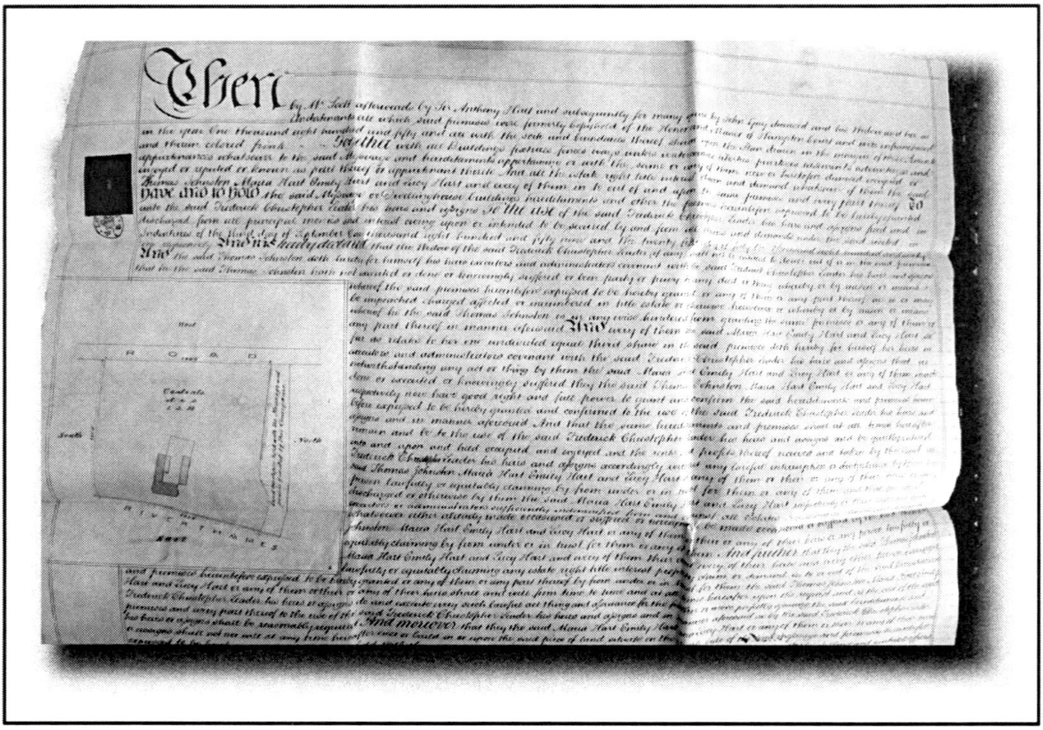

The Capon, Campbell, Clare and Clare Collection

The London Metropolitan Archives has a collection of documents deposited into archives by this firm of solicitors which covers all title transfers as well as valuations and inventories of *Springfield/Moiravale* for the years 1862 - 1947. It also includes sale catalogue from 1810 detailing the entirety of Dr. James' estate in Hampton Wick and Teddington. Images of many of these fascinating documents are included on the website www.hamptonwickhistory.org.uk which accompanies this book.
below left to right: *Moiravale* (1970) *Thameside Place* (2004)

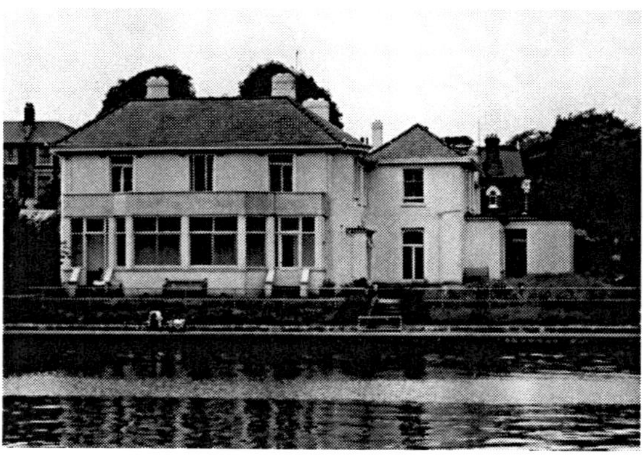

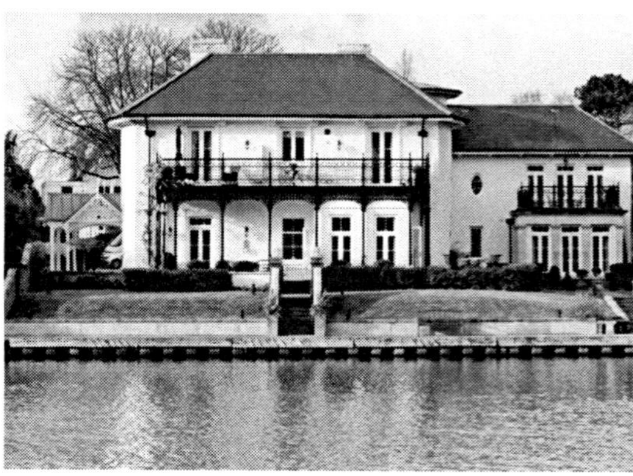

5-bedroom detached house which is now known as The Courtyard. For 30 years this was lived in successively by Tommy Steele and then by Justin Hayward of The Moody Blues. Venables' second application, also successful, was for a three-bedroom house - which he called *Garden Close* (now known as *River Garth*) - which was built on the site of the kitchen garden and lawns on the northern section of the plot, retaining some of the original glasshouses. Venables' third application, to convert the main house into 6 flats appears to have been refused permission by the Borough of Richmond, but he seemingly turned this adversity into opportunism by then selling the house to the Council themselves who converted it into a Care Home for up to 37 residents. The last piece of Venables' jig-saw involved a plot on the south-east corner where the boathouse had been and which would be reached using a long narrow strip of land alongside the original drive. His 1950 application for a modest 2-bedroom bungalow was never built and it was not until 1959 that the current development of three flats was built and named *Thames Reach.*

The recorded history of this property traces a progression from fifty years being a malthouse/starch-factory with workers accommodation, through almost exactly a century of use as a single opulent family house and garden and finally sixty years of development culminating in the site now supporting no fewer than eighteen separate residential units. Throughout all this, the house itself has retained two clearly visible links with its origins: the east-facing facade built over two hundred years ago still rises up gracefully from the riverbank, and the charming *porte-cochère* entrance which for the last 150 years has sheltered and welcomed visitors alighting at the front door of this remarkable property.

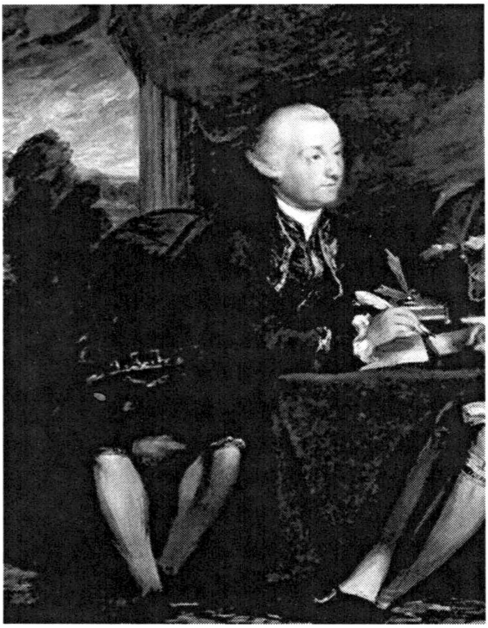

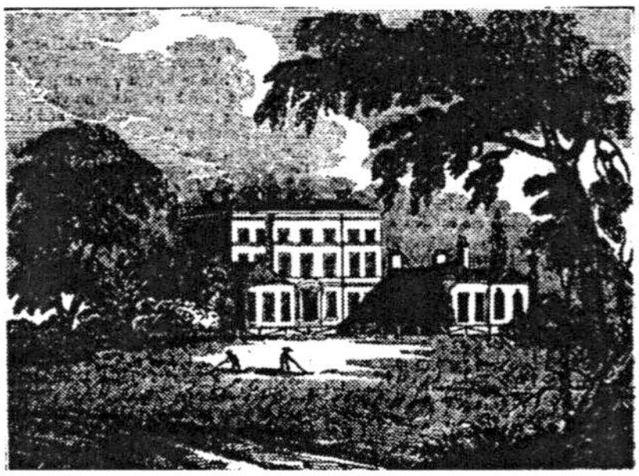

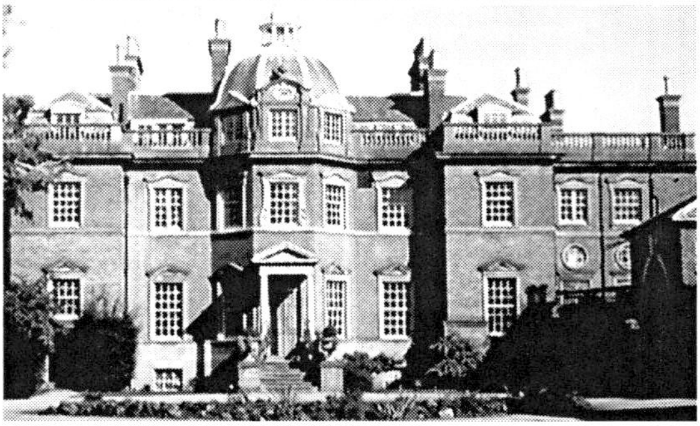

George-Montagu Dunk, 2nd Earl of Halifax with his three local properties: Bushy House, his official residence (top right), Hampton Court House which he built for his mistress (above right) and *Grove House*, now known *The Grove* (below)

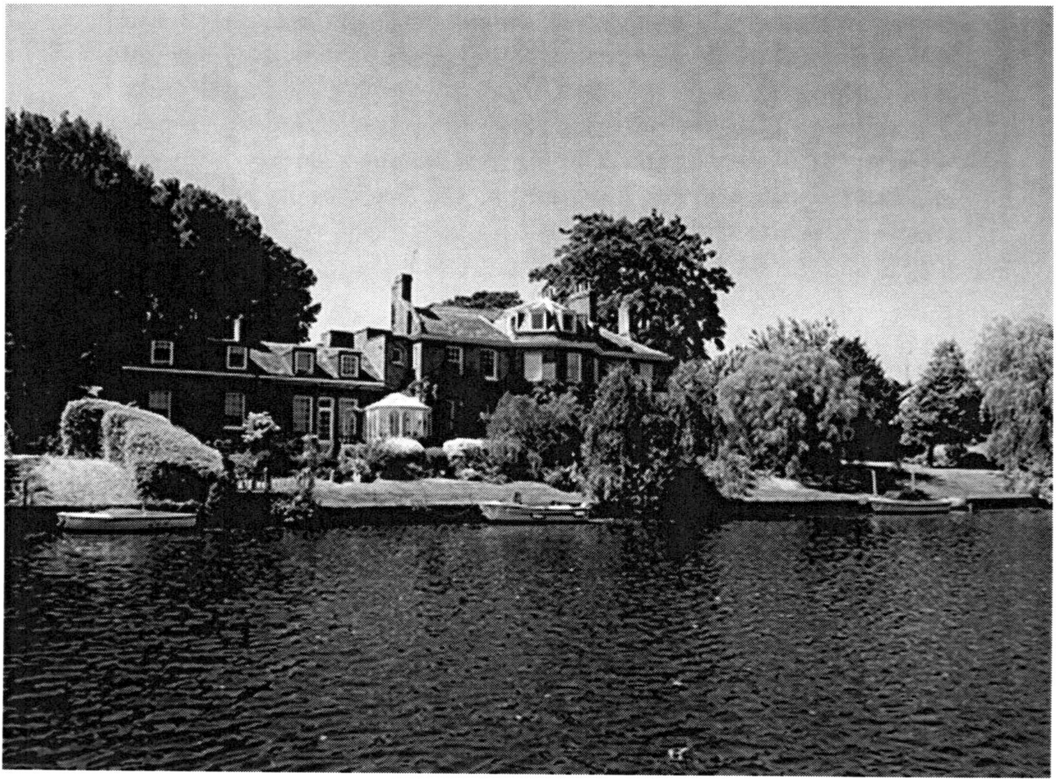

Grove House (now known as The Grove)

Ayliffe Location D (page 16) - now 24 Lower Teddington Road

English Heritage Grade II Listing (June 1983):
Large, late C18, house. Two storeys with attics. Brown brick front, 7 bays wide with 3 centre bays set slightly forward. Modillion cornice. Slated mansard roof behind shallow parapet. Central entrance contained in later front extension. River front also of 7 bays with the 3 centre bays forming canted bar. Brick faced with band at first floor level and modillion cornice which supports a shallow parapet over the centre bays and eaves at the side. Slated mansard over the centre bays only.

Grove House was amongst the few properties recorded on the 1828 map of Lower Teddington Road which existed purely for pleasure rather than as an adjunct to a malthouse or farm-holding. The pleasure in this case was that of George, 2nd Earl of Halifax who built the house around 1750.

George Montagu-Dunk, second Earl of Halifax, was Minister of Trade and Plantations (after whom Halifax, Nova Scotia was named). He owned extensive estates in Northamptonshire and opportunistically appended his wife's family name "Dunk" to his own "Montagu" in order to qualify him to inherit her family fortune. He was also Steward of Hampton Court Manor, living with his wife and young family in *Bushy House*, a large mansion within Bushy Park. Around 1750 George commissioned the Montagu family architect Thomas Wright to build *Hampton Court House* on the opposite side of Bushy Park where he installed his mistress and their daughter. It seems likely that he used the same architect for *Grove House* which he was building at the same time. As to why he built it, one can but speculate that a quiet secluded place by the river only a short horse (or carriage) ride away from both his wife and his mistress was too tempting a prospect for such a wealthy and compulsive philanderer.

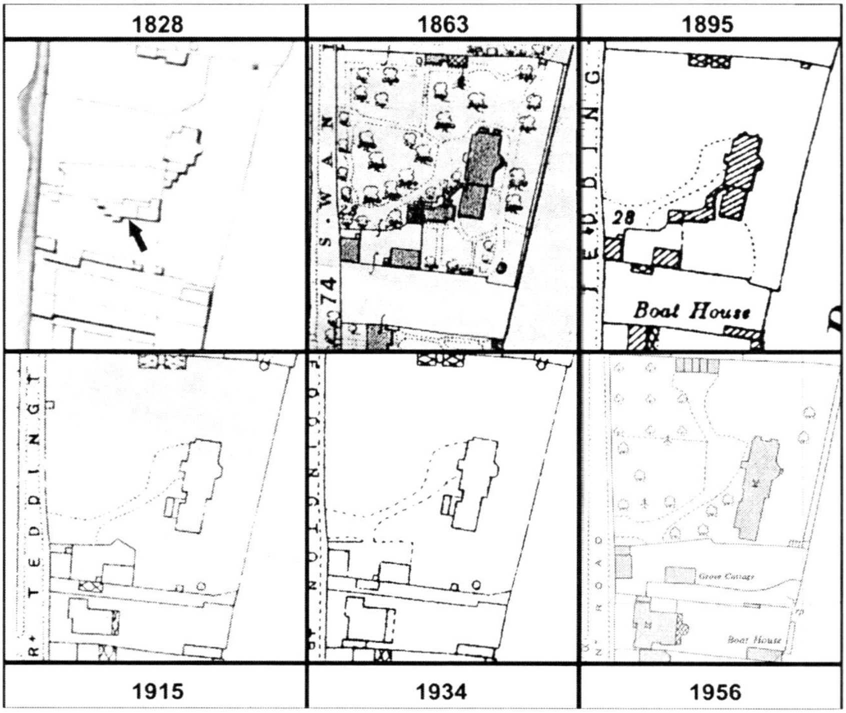

above: the earliest map shows Steele's Hovel (arrowed) in the grounds of *Grove House*. It was later incorporated into the footprint before disappearing altogether around 1900.

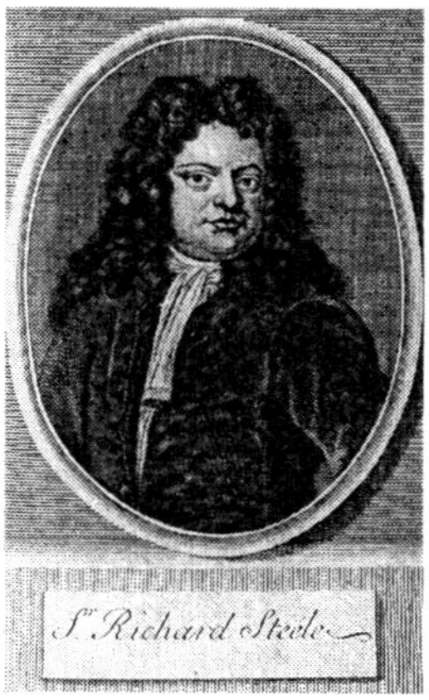

The Hovel, Hampton Wick
April 7th 1711

My Lord Halifax

When I first resolved upon doing myself this honour, I could not but indulge a certain vanity in dating from this little covert, where I have frequently had your Lordship's company, and received from you many obligations. The elegant solitude of this place, and the greatest pleasures of it, I owe to its being so near those beautiful manors wherein you sometimes reside: it's not retiring from the world, but enjoying its most valuable blessings when a man is permitted to share in your Lordship's conversations in the country.

With the above flowery letter, Richard Steele, co-founder of *The Tatler* magazine dedicated the fourth volume to 'Charles, Lord Halifax'. He sent it from 'The Hovel' which may very well have been built on land the Earl had given or leased him.

However he later rented out the house (possibly because his wife's death in 1753 removed his need for a secret bolt-hole).

The second resident was George Lowe who had been appointed the King's Gardener at Hampton Court around 1738, a post he held until his death at *The Grove* in 1758. He had been a predecessor to Lancelot 'Capability' Brown who was appointed Master Gardener in 1764. It was Brown who planted the great vine at Hampton Court - using a cutting from a vine at Valentine's House in Ilford previously tended by George Lowe. George was succeeded at *Grove House* by his nephew Robert Lowe who was a highly successful seedsman and nurseryman with extensive grounds on the site of what is now Vicarage and Cedars Roads. The scale of his operation can be gauged by the list of plants sent from his Nursery to William de Grey, First Baron Walsingham at Merton Hall, Norfolk in 1775 which included 500 Spanish chestnuts, 200 horse chestnuts, 400 Italian poplars, 500 laburnums and 1,000 green hollies. Soon after his death in 1790, *Grove House* acquired a new owner and occupier in the person of Samuel Lapidge.

Lapidge was employed by Lancelot 'Capability' Brown as one of his surveyors and assistants. The two men became close friends and Lancelot was godfather to Samuel's first child Edward. Following Brown's death in 1783, Samuel took over responsibility for completing several of Brown's outstanding projects as well as becoming Head Gardener at Hampton Court itself. Samuel had married George Lowe's daughter Sarah Clara in 1778 and they had seven children, all but one born before Samuel and Sarah moved into *Grove House* in 1793.

On Samuel's death in 1807, his eldest son Edward Lapidge became head of the household which also included his mother and five siblings as well as his own wife and child. Unsurprisingly, Edward started some significant alterations and expansions to the original building as well as adding a single-storey extension at the south end to house a billiard room. To increase servant accommodation, he also connected a cottage in the grounds to the main house with a long covered passage. This cottage, known as "The Hovel", was once the home of Sir Richard Steele (see article opposite). Finally, he also built a substantial coach-house and separate stable block in the south-west part of the grounds.

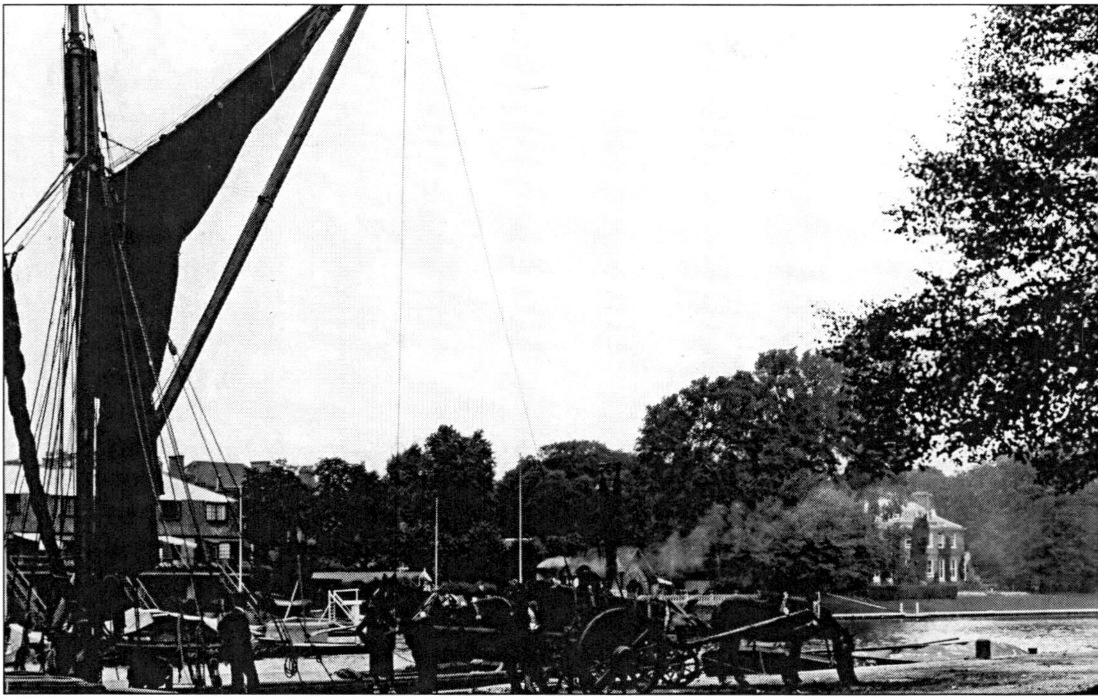

above: Coal being delivered to the original Kingston Power Station in the late 1920's with *The Grove* just visible on the extreme right.
(photo: John Dixon-Scott, courtesy The National Archives)
below: *The Grove* with *Moiravale* in the background, photographed from Canbury Gardens on the Kingston bank.

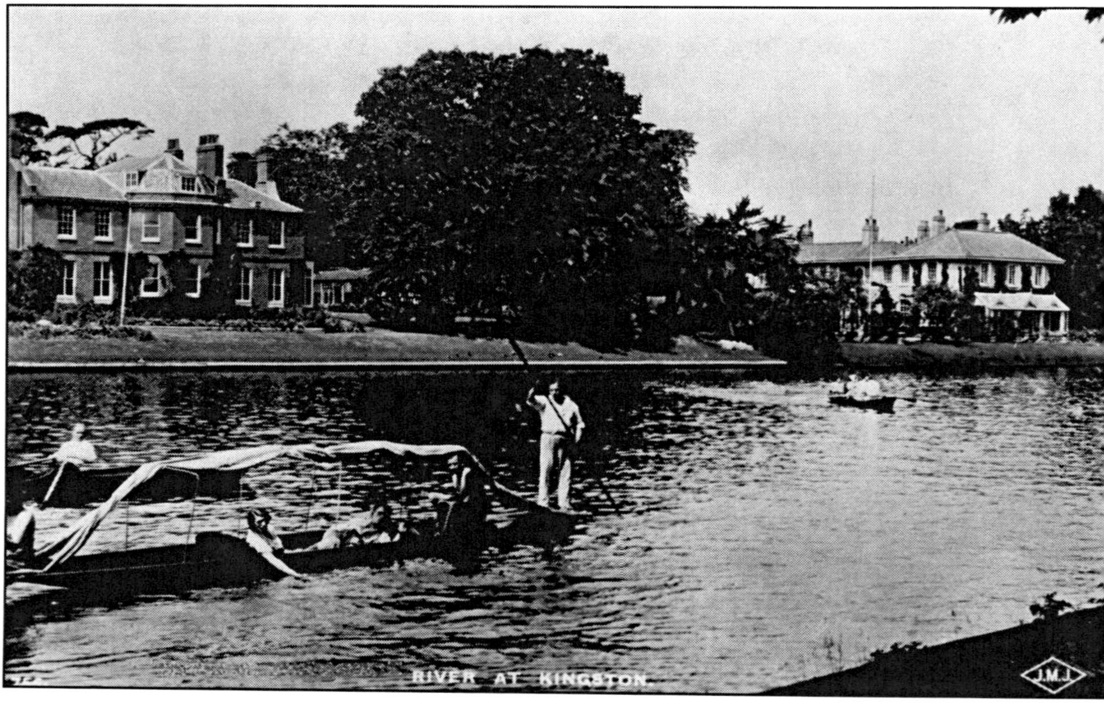

Lapidge was an architect so would have produced the plans for the various building works himself. He also completed several other major local projects included the new Kingston Bridge (1828), St John the Baptist church Hampton Wick (1830), the replacement of St Mary's Hampton (1831), St Andrews Ham (1832), The Terrace opposite the entrance to Home Park (c 1840) and The Endowed School (1844). His architectural practice was actually based at Green Street in London's West End (where he also had a house) and he was working on several housing redevelopment schemes in that area. He was dividing his time between the two locations but the pre-railway commute must have been time-consuming and unsurprisingly, he finally moved out of *Grove House* when his mother died in 1831, although ownership stayed in the family until the death of Lapidge's nephew Macdonald Henry Lapidge as late as 1945.

For the next thirty years *Grove House* was subject to several short-term lets. One of the most colourful lessees in this period was Colonel the Hon. Charles Henry Maynard - only son and heir of 3rd Viscount Maynard - to give him his full credentials. Quite why he came to live at *Grove House* for two years from 1851 is still an intriguing mystery: was he perhaps hiding from a scandal? He renamed the house "Steele's Villa" but its name reverted after he left.

In 1862, Thomas James Nelson moved with his wife and family of eight children into *Grove House*, which he then renamed "The Grove". The rent was £130 per annum (present value £85,000). Nelson was soon to be appointed Solicitor to the City of London, a post he held until his death - with the present-day equivalent of a seven-figure salary. In that capacity, his two greatest achievements were the preservation of Epping Forest as public access land (1871) and the freeing of all bridges on the Thames from tolls (1878).

Nelson used all his City knowledge, experience and contacts to the benefit of the local community and its institutions. On moving to Hampton Wick in 1862, one of his first acts was to persuade his fellow parishioners to set up a Local Board to determine their own affairs and maintain their independence from neighbouring Hampton and Kingston. He was one of the first elected Board members and chaired it for eighteen years until his death in 1885. He was also a governor of the Hampton

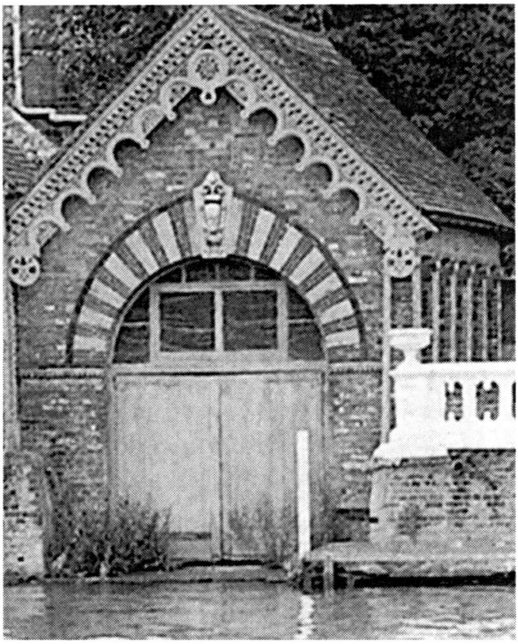

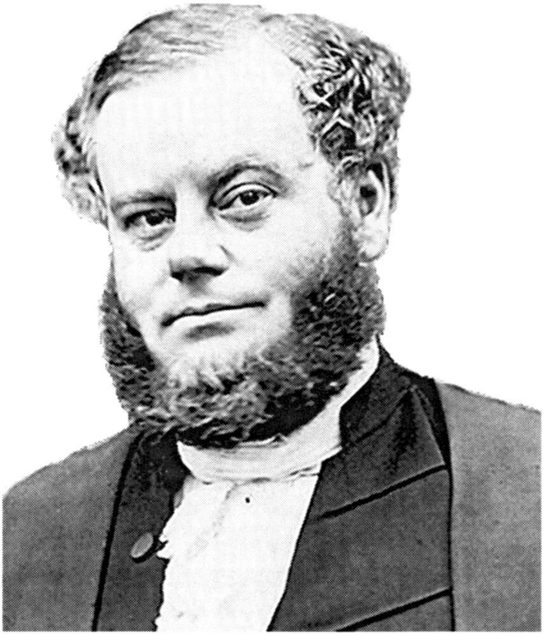

above, right and left: Sir Thomas James Nelson and the boathouse he built for *The Grove*

below: Nelson took great interest in the Annual Kingston Regatta whose finishing line was opposite *The Grove*. This view was taken in Canbury Gardens on the Kingston bank.

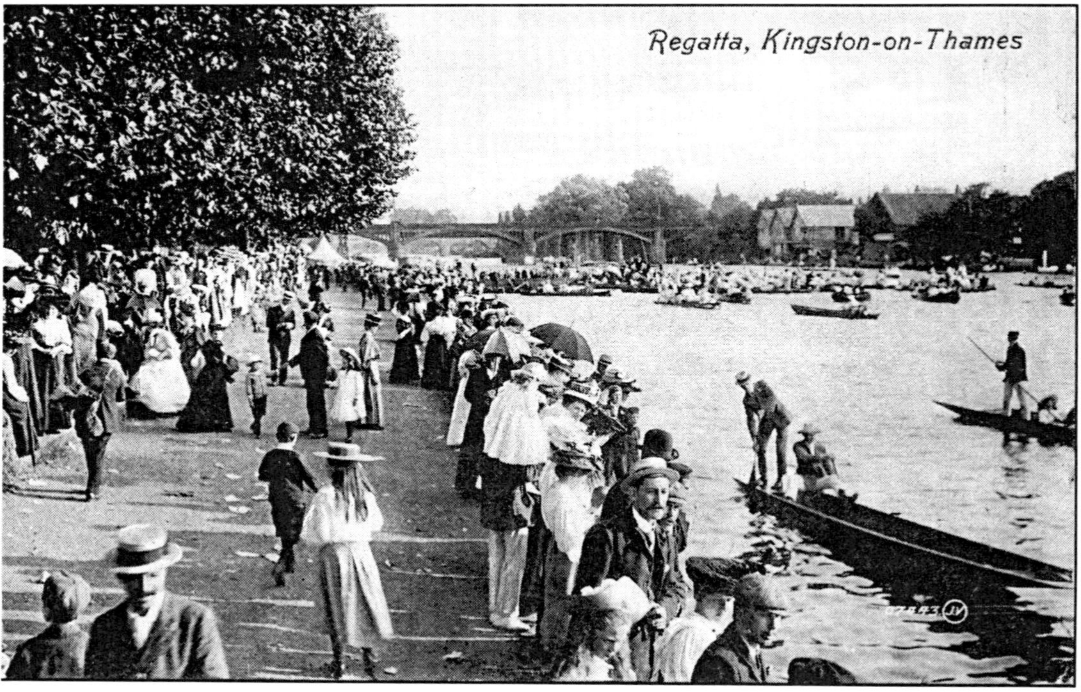

Wick Endowed School and took a very deep interest in the Teddington and Hampton Wick Cottage Hospital.

When time could be snatched from his many roles, Nelson delighted in the pleasures of the river - he held the office of President of the Junior Kingston Rowing Club and took a great interest in the annual regattas. He bought the plot of land between *The Grove* and *Walnut Tree House* which had contained a disused malthouse. This he demolished and built a magnificent polychrome brick boat house in which he kept his handsome steam launch *Peri.* This land was sold in 1912 as the site first for the bungalow known as Wick Lodge and most recently the house of the same name completed in 2012. The boat-house still exists.

Around 1900, the drive-side extension was demolished but no further alterations were made to *The Grove* for the next 50 years.

When the last member of the Lapidge family died in 1945, his executors split *The Grove* into two lots: the southern end of the plot with the stables and coach-house were converted into today's Grove Cottage while the main house and garden were sold for £5,000 for conversion into five apartments. The only visible changes at the time were an extension to the original billiard room and a new garage block on the north wall. In 2003, the southern extension was converted into two-storey residence.

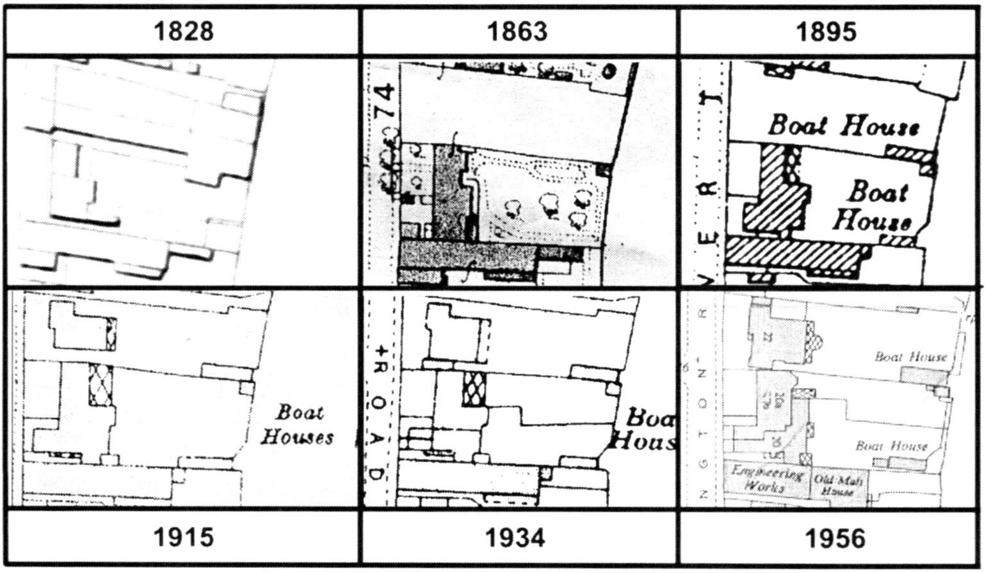

above; maps showing the development of *Walnut Tree House* and its curtilage.

below: Main facade of *Walnut Tree House*

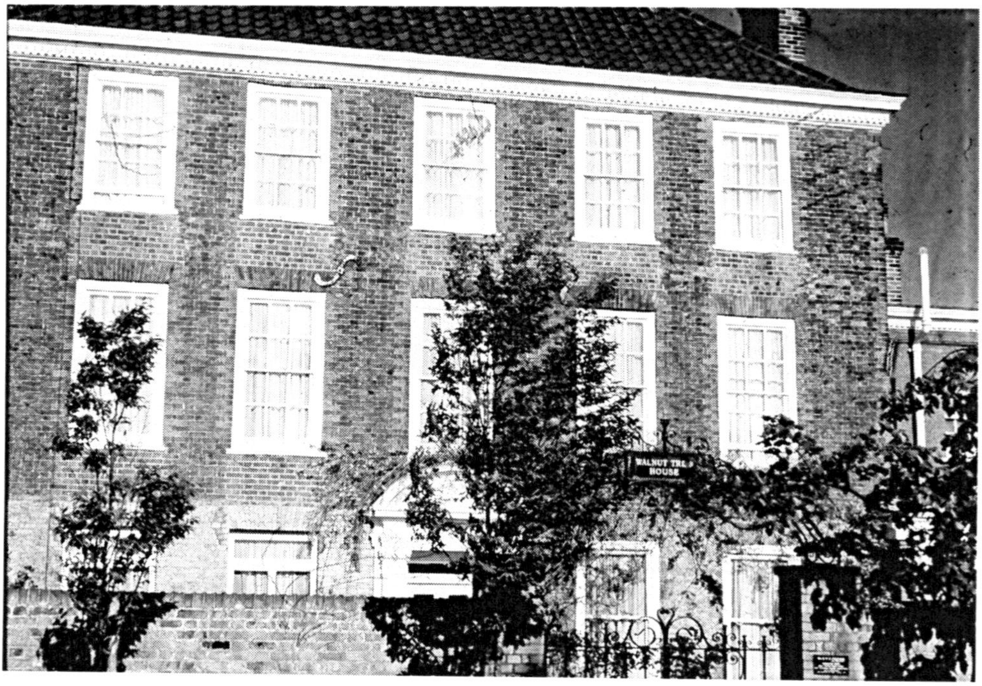

Walnut Tree House

Ayliffe Location F (page 16) - now 20 Lower Teddington Road

> **English Heritage Grade II Listing (September 1952):**
> Early C18. Three storeys, 5 windows, brown brick, red dressings. Dentilled eaves cornice, hipped pantiled roof. Sash windows in nearly flush frames on upper floors altered on ground floor. Central door with bowed pediment and broken cornice above Corinthian pilasters.

It is generally held that *Walnut Tree House* was built in 1728, probably by Elliott Bishop of Lincoln's Inn, to provide accommodation for the proprietor of the brewhouse (later converted to a malthouse) built to the north of it. The original accommodation consisted of six rooms arranged on three floors with a central staircase and chimneys at either end. There were also cellars. Bishop had the leasehold of the property and sublet it to the maltster, who was initially Thomas Wood and later William Smith. In 1752 both the leasehold rights and occupancy passed to John Wornham Penfold a maltster from Kingston. The rights remained in the Penfold family for over 100 years but at some stage they moved out and started letting the accommodation and the malthouse separately. The room to the left of the front door was given a significant increase in ceiling height by lowering the floor and at the same time lengthening the room towards the river.

Later the house was extended southwards until, by 1828, its footprint was similar to today's. However, these extensions were probably more utilitarian than residential and were replaced by a more substantial structure in the 1880's which also included a coach-house. Meanwhile the malthouse building itself had been demolished around 1862 and its land sold.

Walnut Tree House was further re-arranged in the mid-1930's when the house and garden were divided to form three separate apartments known as Numbers 20, 20a and 20b Lower Teddington Road. From then until now the process of division has progressively been reversed. In 1956 Numbers

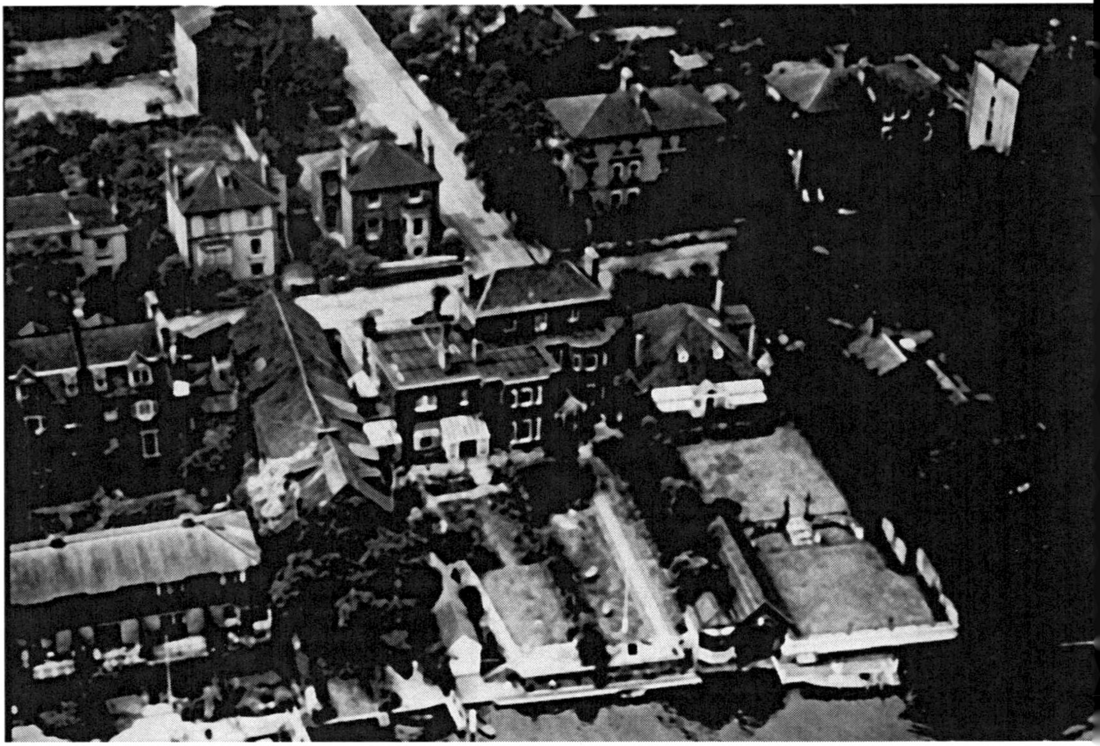

above: aerial view of *Walnut Tree House* showing the original house and the substantial extensions to the south dating from the 1880's. Note the bungalow on the site of the former malthouse.
below: The roof of *Walnut Tree House* was devastated by fire in 1988.

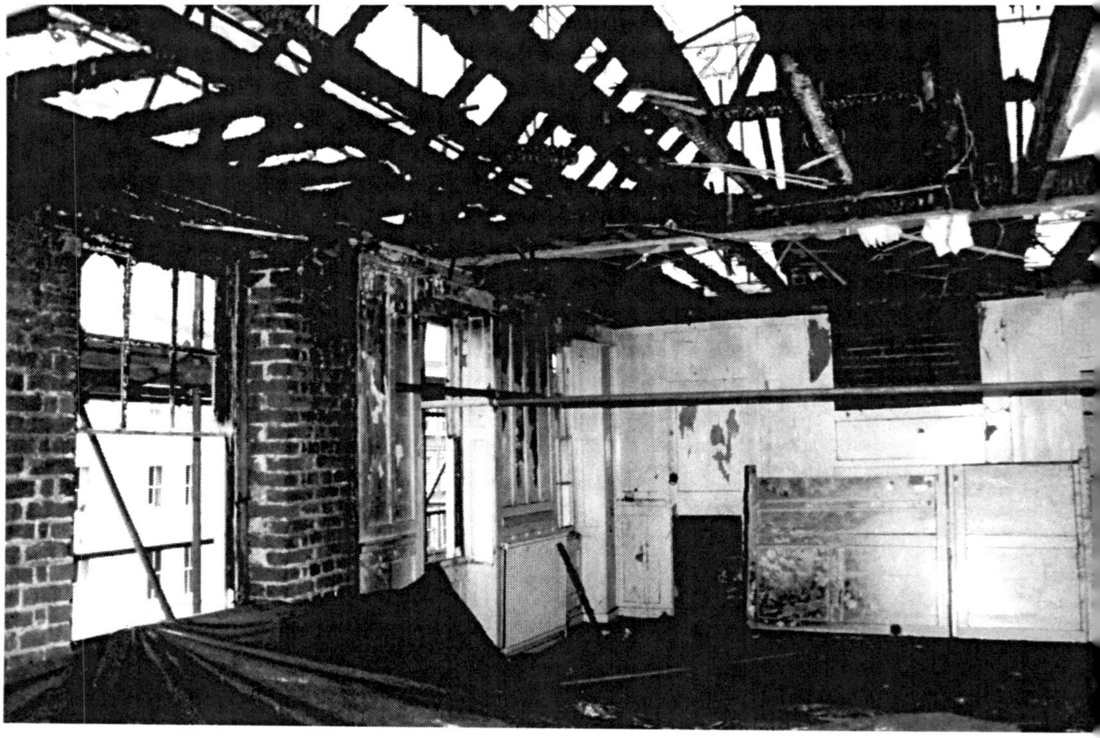

20a and b were brought together into what was effectively the original early eighteenth century layout and served as house and surgery for a local doctor.

Amongst past residents perhaps the most well-known nationally was Richard Fortnum son of the founder of Fortnum and Mason grocers and tea dealers. Richard inherited the business in 1815 and ran it until his death in 1845, building the foundations of Fortnum and Mason's reputation as provision merchants. For much of this period Richard divided his time between his apartment above the shop in Piccadilly and *Walnut Tree House.* In both premises he lived with his unmarried sister Ann. The Hampton Wick property was listed in Richard's name until 1836 and thereafter as Ann Fortnum's though Richard continued to live part-time at *Walnut Tree House* where he died on 5th December 1845. Ann retained the house until her own death two years later.

In more recent times, Dr. Gordon Feltham was a much-loved and highly colourful resident of *Walnut Tree House.* His surgery was located in the small, un-soundproofed conservatory at the back of the house. The waiting area consisted of a limited row of chairs in the hall just inside the front door. Dr. Feltham's nature was always out-going - and out loud - and he obviously felt it his duty to provide occasional humorous outbursts from within to embarrass his current patient and entertain the patiently waiting line in the hall.

The present owners had a catastrophic start when, just before they were due to move in, there was a major roof fire which destroyed most of the original timbers and severely damaged the upper storeys. They have since gradually expanded their property, first being offered two rooms from Number 20 and then finally the balance of that building. Now very sensitively reintegrated, *Walnut Tree House* has returned to its origins of being a single - albeit now substantially enlarged - family house.

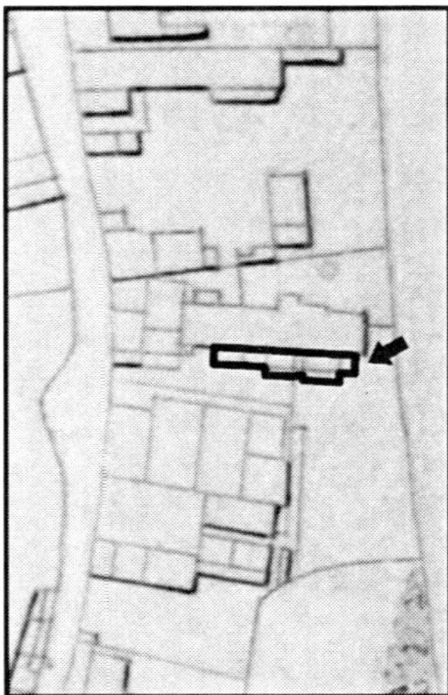

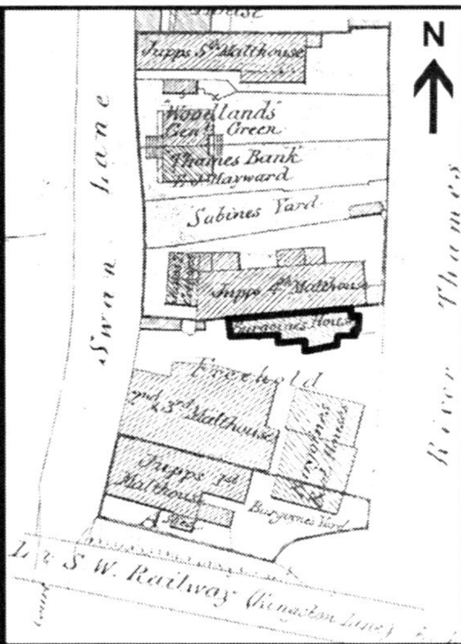

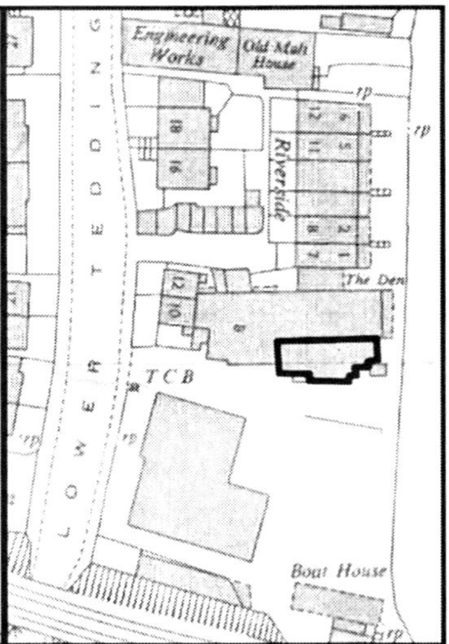

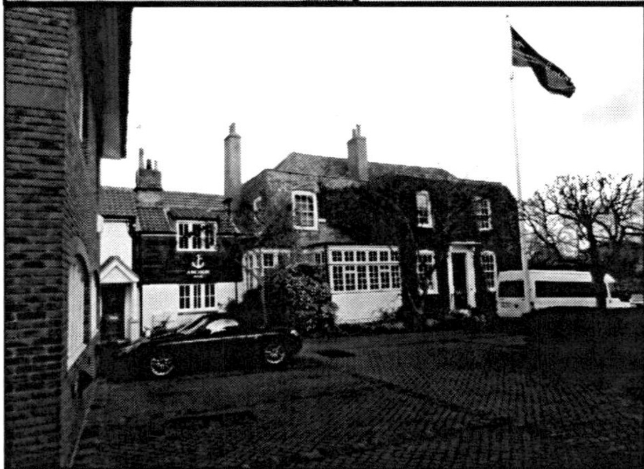

above left to right: *Riverside* (arrowed) and its environs in 1828, 1884 and 1956
Left: view from the south
below: river front (east) around 1900. Note the three malthouses behind the boat- and club-houses and a fourth malthouse next to *Riverside* house itself (all arrowed).

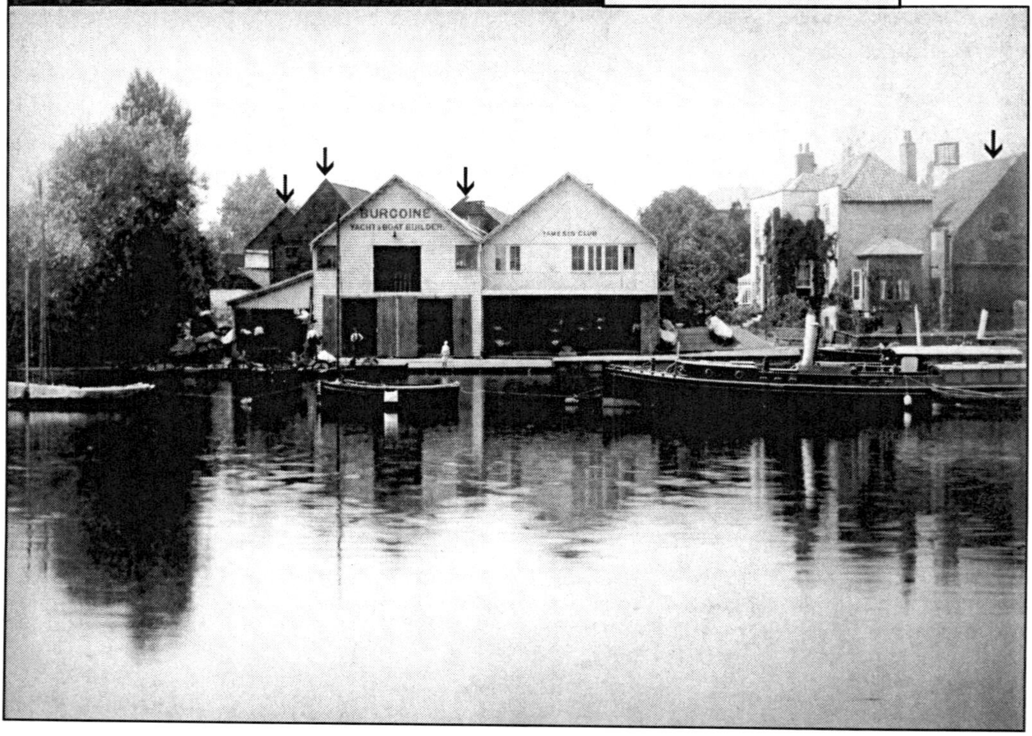

Riverside

Ayliffe Location H (page 16) - now 8 Lower Teddington Road

English Heritage Grade II Listing (June 1983):
On river bank off road. Early C18, altered. Two storeys and basement, brick with old pantile hipped roof. Four windows, with projecting 2-window centre. Central door up steps has modillion cornice on large consoles. Several windows altered. At back, with gable end towards river, is brick and tiled building (possibly originally barn) with modern wooden verandah with balcony in front. Various other accretions. The former outbuildings between the house and the road have been altered and added to make three small houses

Riverside was one of three properties on this stretch of Lower Teddington Road that were closely associated with the malting industry (historically one of the principal activities of the village along with market gardening and employment at Hampton Court Palace). By 1800, there were six malthouses in close proximity here: three adjacent at the south end, one adjoining *Riverside* itself (these four and the house itself being owned by the Lawes family) and two further to the north, located one each side of *Walnut Tree House*, (owned, like the house itself, by the Penfolds - see page 35). From 1809 onwards, there are records telling which maltsters were associated with which malthouses. The three southerly units (with a combined capacity of 25,000 litres) were originally operated by Robert Tosley who lived in *Riverside*. (Toseley also operated the malthouse at *Springfield*/Moiravale at the same time). Some of his workers lived in a pair of cottages just west of *Riverside* (now Numbers 10 and 12 Lower Teddington Road). The other three malthouses (of 30,000 litres combined capacity) were run by George Keane whose house stood near the south end of what is now *Salamander Quay*. One of his workers lived in a cottage by the northernmost malthouse whilst the others probably had modest living quarters on the opposite side of Lower Teddington Road.

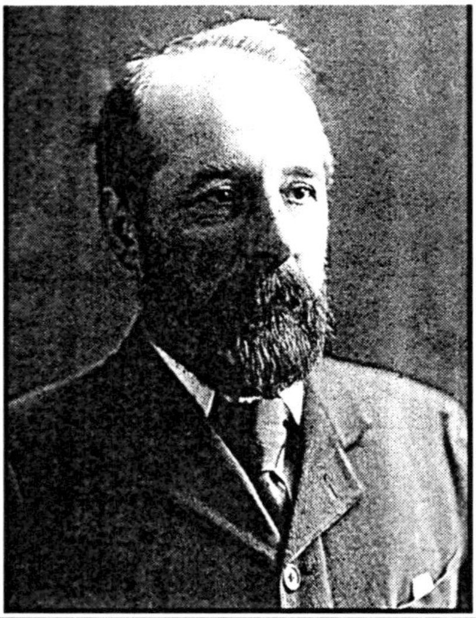

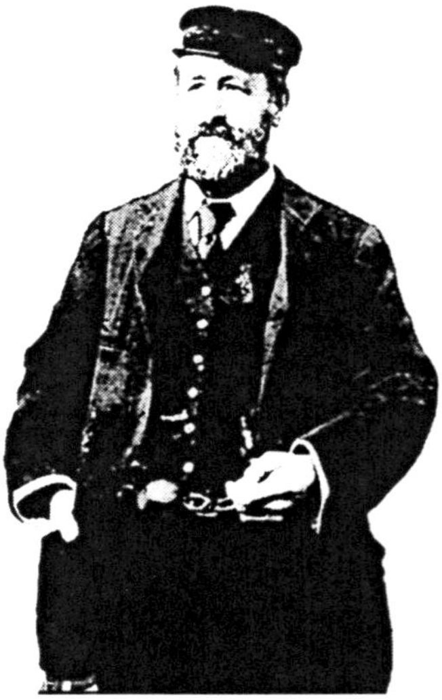

above left and right: Charles William Burgoine (1836 - 1910) and Alfred Thomas Burgoine (1846 - 1927). The two brothers established their yard at *Riverside* in 1872.

below clockwise from left: boat-building frames (a drawing by Lucy Millett of the view from her studio at Old Castle Wharf), camping punts for hire, Thames A-raters designed by Alfred Burgoine are still raced at Thames Sailing Club, The *Sunbury Belle,* a rival's craft, moored opposite Burgoine's yard

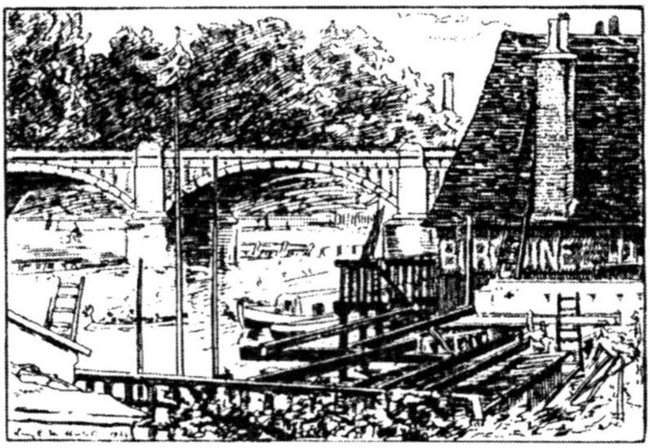

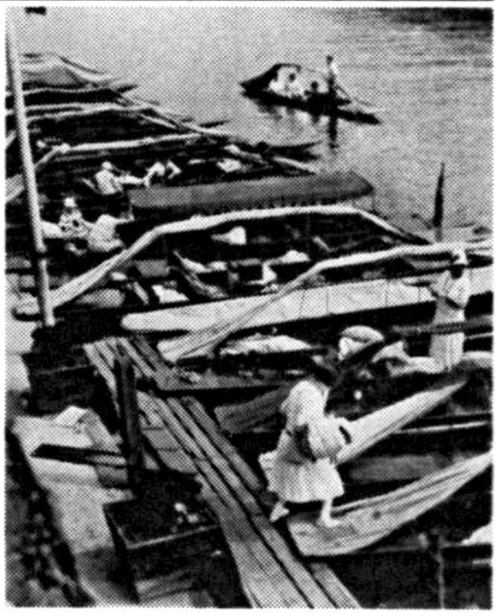

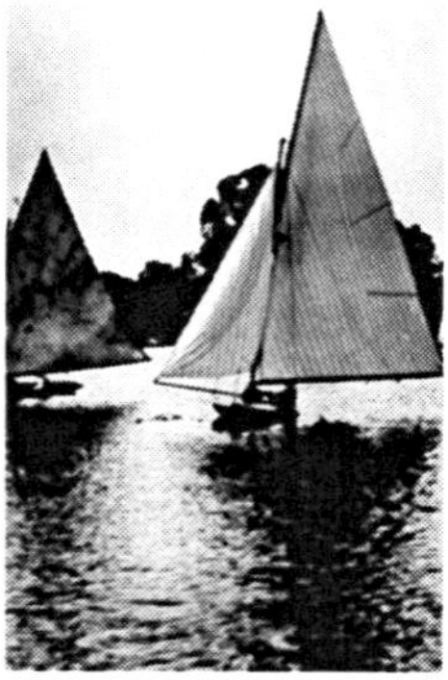

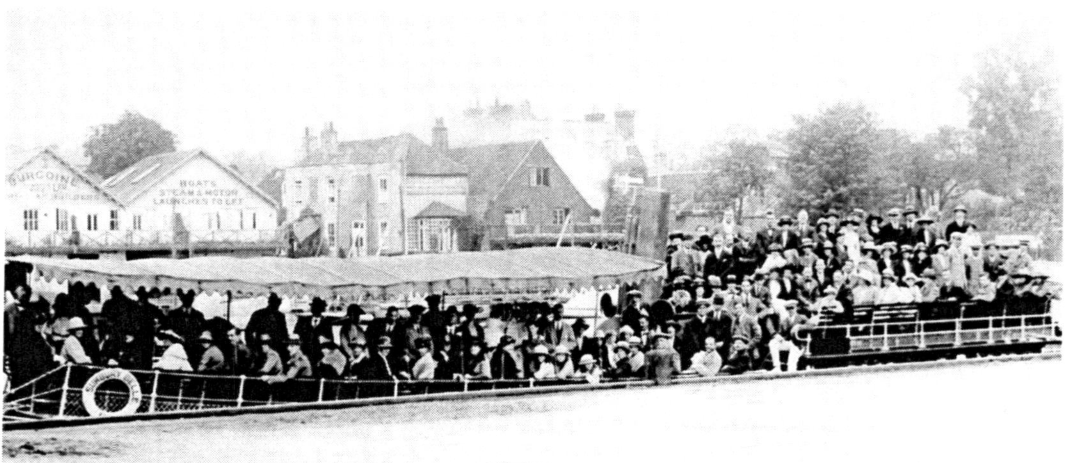

Robert Tosley was followed at *Riverside* by Mrs Elizabeth Galley (from 1830-1845) and Keene by the Smith family (mentioned by Ayliffe in his reminiscences - see page 23). When Mrs Galley retired in 1845 at the age of 70, John Horne took over her three malthouses as well as the accommodation in *Riverside*. Soon after, he was also operating the two Penfold-owned malthouses. The Smiths had retired but remained living in the maltster's house.

Things began to change in the early 1860's. John Horne, now in his 70's, retired and moved out of *Riverside* into the recently-built *Gomer House* across the road at Number 25. William Ford succeeded him at *Riverside* and operated the three southernmost malthouses. Meanwhile the Penfold family sold their two malthouses: the one on the north side of *Walnut Tree House* (together with its malt-worker's cottage) was demolished and the land sold to their neighbour, a tenant at *The Grove*. The other unit became part of the remaining group of five malthouses, now all owned by Mrs Eliza Wilson (née Lawes).

By the mid-1860's, all five units were being operated by David and Joseph Jupp. Part of a Brentford-based family of 14 children, these two brothers operated a large business (under the name of French and Jupps) with further maltings at Kingston, Spitalfield in the City and at Stanstead Abbots near Ware in Hertfordshire. On arriving in Hampton Wick, David Jupp lodged with the retired maltster John Horne at *Gomer House*. Later he moved round the corner to become one of the first residents in the newly-created Station Road. His younger brother Joseph is shown in the Hampton Wick Electors Register as being resident in Ware, so presumably he was running the Maltings there (which as of 2012 is still in operation under the same name of French and Jupp). With the two Jupp brothers thus accommodated elsewhere, *Riverside* become available and was let to the Burgoine brothers - Charles and Alfred - who had already set up a Thames boat-building business on the opposite bank in Kingston upon Thames, just south of the Hogsmill River. At first it was older brother Charles who moved into *Riverside* whilst Alfred lived in The Terrace (opposite Kingston Bridge). However in 1882 Charles' wife committed suicide and the following year he married a 19-year-old bride, walked out of the Thames-based business and began a new life as a boat-builder in Lowestoft. He and his second wife went on to have eight children.

Meanwhile Alfred moved into *Riverside* and continued to expand the business. The 1884 Hampton Court Manor plan (see map at top centre on page 38) shows the changes that had taken place: Burgoine's had erected two boathouses between the malthouses and the river; Jupps were now leasing all five malthouses together with the pair of malt-workers cottages; the house in which the Smith's had lived (see above) was now demolished and replaced by a pair of

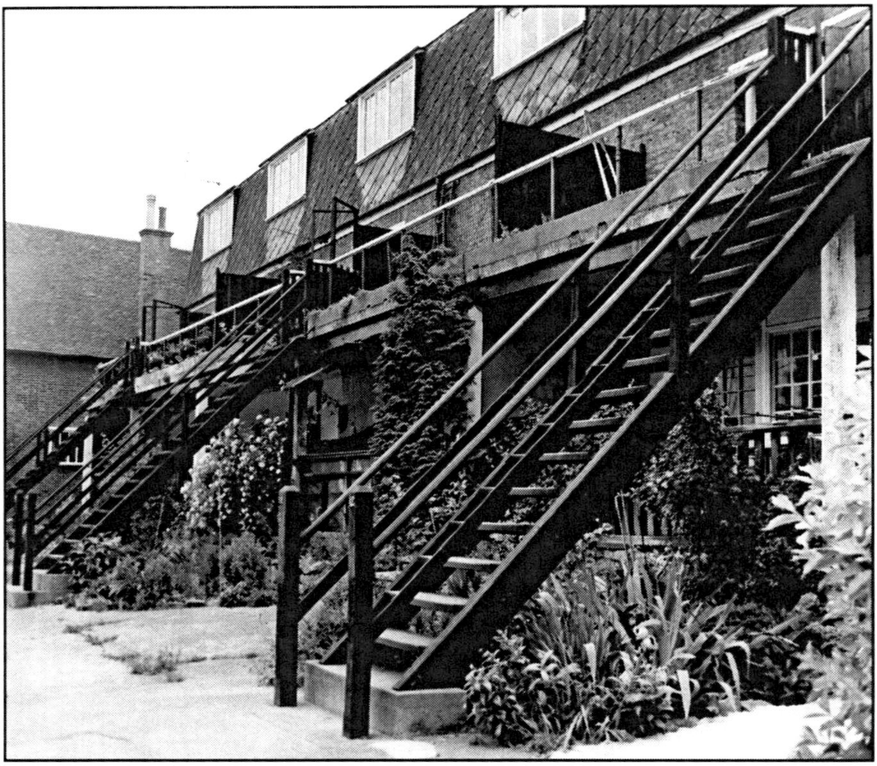

above: The original *Riverside* development dating from 1925. They were remodelled in 1979.
below: The AVA Thames Works was built after WWII, and is seen here in the 1960's. The building was demolished in 1990 to make way for the present Burgoine Quay development.

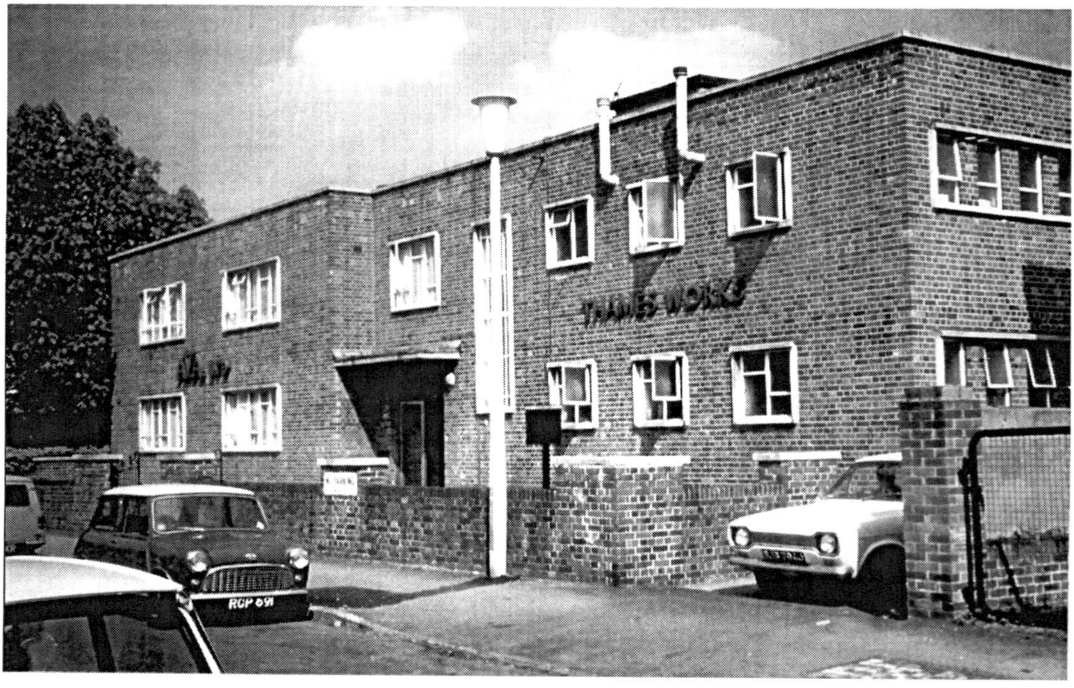

semi-detached 3-storey houses (now Numbers 16 and 18 Lower Teddington Road).

Ten years further on and malting came to an end in this part of Hampton Wick; Burgoine now took over the leases of three malthouse buildings and was busy designing and building large numbers of boats - both steam and sail. Amongst the latter was the famous Thames A-rater, a design produced for the Thames Sailing Club. Several of these still operate out of the Club's premises on Portsmouth Road, Surbiton. In 1888, the Tamesis Sailing Club was formed with its first clubhouse at the *Riverside* yard. In 1910, however, Burgoine's company went bankrupt. The Kingston premises were sold first, then the lease of the *Riverside* campus along with 55 boats. This lease was bought by Harry Offer, Alfred Burgoine's son-in-law, and has remained in the Offer family ever since. This was the end of boat-building as such although slipway repairs and hiring of boats continued, especially in the summer season. The new company diversified into property development with Timothy Offer, Alfred Burgoine's great-great-grandson, now at the helm.

A development of 12 flats (also called *Riverside*) was erected on the former boat-building yard. These were remodelled in 1977 and renamed *Salamander Quay.* The original Jupps 4th and 5th malthouses have been progressively converted into a combination of flats, offices, small workshops and artists studios. The original boathouses and three malthouses (Jupps 1st, 2nd and 3rd) were demolished and replaced by an office block and a factory. In 1990, the current Burgoine House replaced both of these latter developments together with the original Hampton Wick village morgue which had been located alongside the railway embankment since the 1880's.

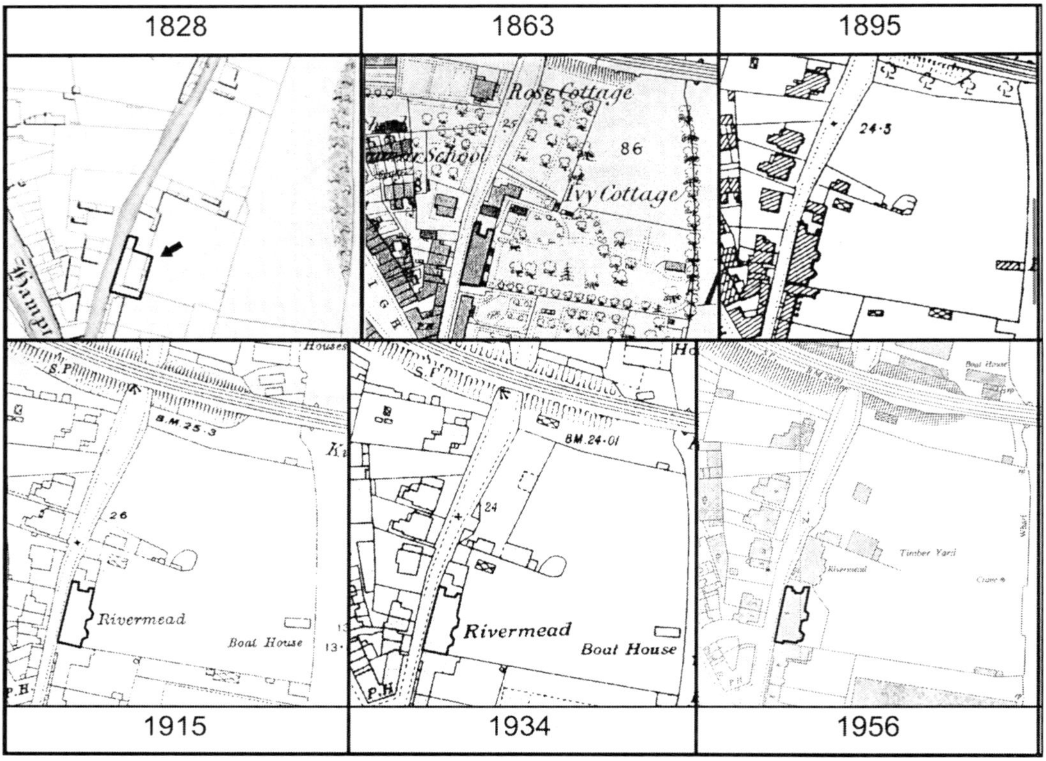

above: *Rivermead* and its extensive gardens. This was the last area on Lower Teddington Road to be developed in the 1980's.
below: The front facade of the house as seen from the office car park. The facade is relieved by the canted bays and the unusual central recess. Note in the background the Arts and Crafts wing of *Wolsey's Cottage*.

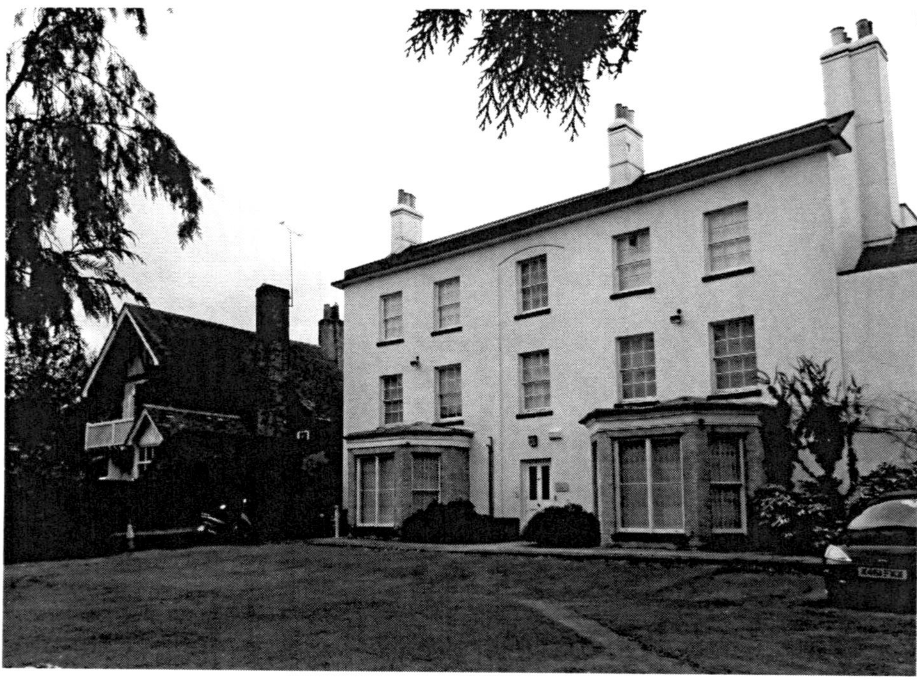

Rivermead

Ayliffe Location L (page 16) - now 6 Lower Teddington Road

> English Heritage Grade II Listing (June 1983):
> Early C19 house. Stuccoed; slate roof to parapet. Lower front is 3 storeys, 5 windows wide (2:1:2) with centre bay set in 3-storey segmental-arched recess. Outer pairs with broad single storey canted bay window to ground floor. Slate roof with eaves. Road front is irregular with various extensions. To the right a doorpiece with 4 Ionic pilasters.

Like its two neighbours to the south, *Rivermead* has its back to the road but, unlike the other two, it is relatively easy to see the front facade by walking round into Becketts Place. Before being turned into offices in 1978, *Rivermead* was a private residence with a substantial garden and adjoining meadow amounting to almost two acres, stretching down to the river and northwards almost to the railway. Somewhat surprisingly it is only in the last thirty years that this prime site has been built on.

The first known resident was William Eatwell who, despite his jovial surname, seems to have had a really tragic life. The only son of a Wiltshire couple, his father died before William was two. He joined the Bombay Marine (the fighting - as opposed to mercantile - navy of the East India Company in Asian waters) where he was involved in several hair-raising escapades. He married the daughter of a fellow marine and their first child was born in Bombay (Mumbai) before he and his wife returned to England and went to live in Hampton. They had a further five children, two of whom died in childhood (along with their mother) and three died young - one fell overboard whilst yachting in India and was taken by a crocodile; a second was shot in battle in the Punjab and the third died of hepatitis when she was eighteen. Only his first-born son remained as company during Eatwell's 32 years of widowhood.

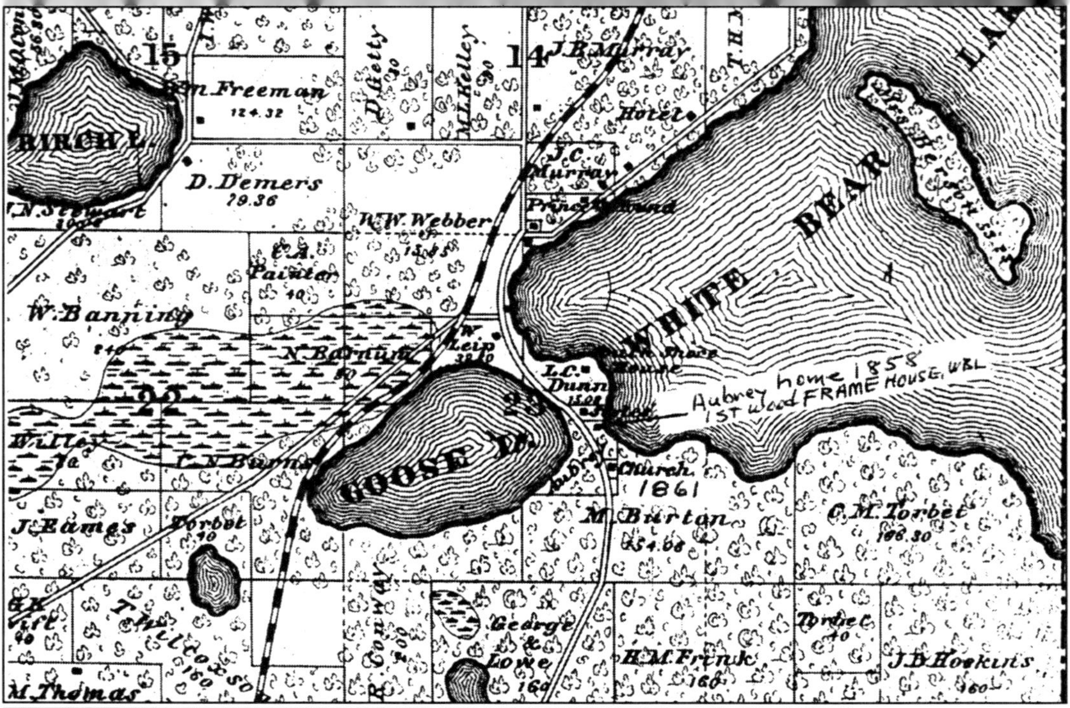

above: Ruined banker Aubrey Paul fled from Hampton Wick and started a new life in the remote north of the USA.
below: Louisa, Lady Paul, was known to her Minnesota neighbours only as Mrs. Aubrey, the local schoolmistress and devout churchwoman.

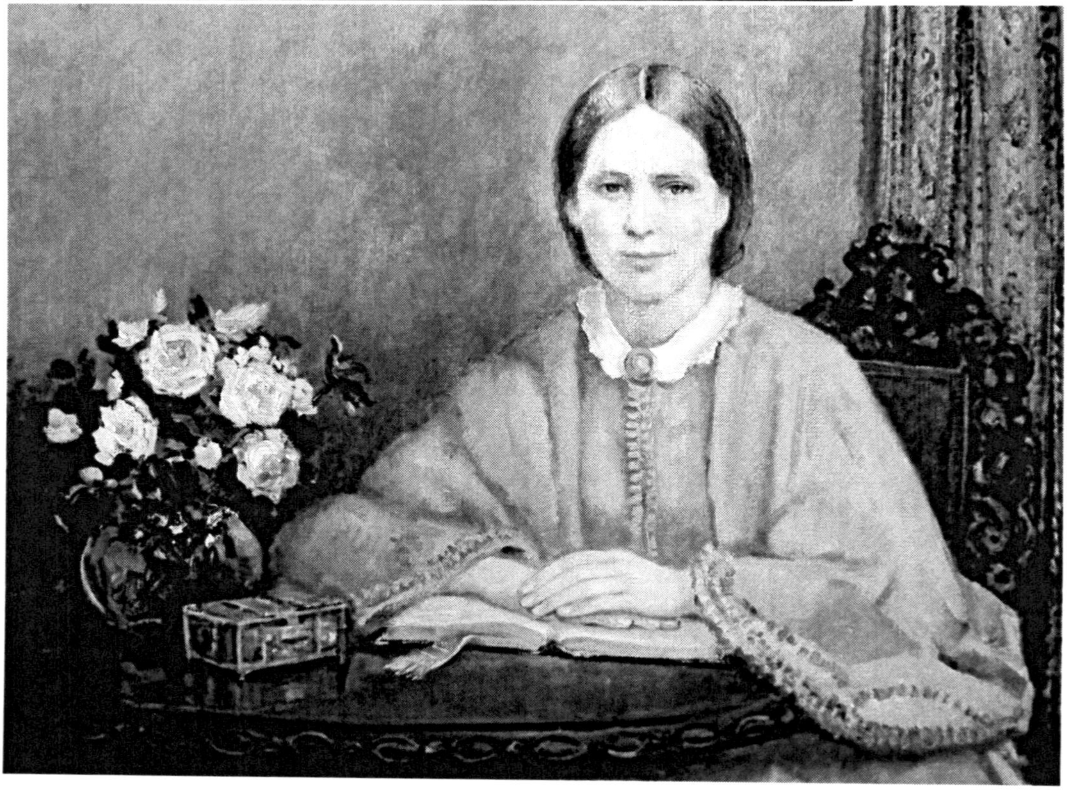

He moved to *Rivermead* after the death of his wife and stayed for five years. He died aged 83 in Cheltenham and is buried in Hampton with his wife and three of their children.

Misfortune of a different kind - but one which resulted in an amazing story of self reinvention - befell the residents of *Rivermead* a few years later. Sir Aubrey John Dean Paul *Bart.* was a member of a wealthy banking family. He arrived at *Rivermead* with his new bride at the beginning of 1851 and, with a safe job and good prospects at the bank, life seemed rosy ...

In 1855 his father and two partners in the bank were convicted of fraud and the bank collapsed with debts amounting to around £1bn. They were sentenced to fourteen year's transportation to Australia. With his own career and prospects ruined, Paul and his wife Louisa left Hampton Wick and apparently simply "disappeared". In fact it emerges that, changing their name to John and Louisa Aubrey, the couple had travelled via Canada into Minnesota and become one of the first settlers at White Bear Lake. Rich land, abundant game, and scenic lakes attracted the early pioneers to this area. Aubrey was quite content to live a rough frontier life – hunting, trapping and competing with the Indians in the pursuit of game. Locals spoke of him roaming the country accompanied by "Powder" and "Shot" his hunting dogs. He also took up boat-building and photography. Mrs. Aubrey received a regular income from her family and added to it by teaching the children of other pioneers, who remained unaware of the couple's aristocratic origins. One day a letter came to John Aubrey announcing that his father had returned to England (released early through ill-health) and had again taken his title and some of his possessions. When word was received of Sir John's death on Sept. 7, 1868, it was time for the eldest son to return England and assume the baronetcy.

The couple now moved to Putney where he set up as a photographer with studios at Thames Place, near The Hard. In 1875 the couple retired to north-west Italy, close to the Monegasque border where Sir Aubrey died in 1890. His indomitable wife outlasted him by a further 35 years.

---oOo--

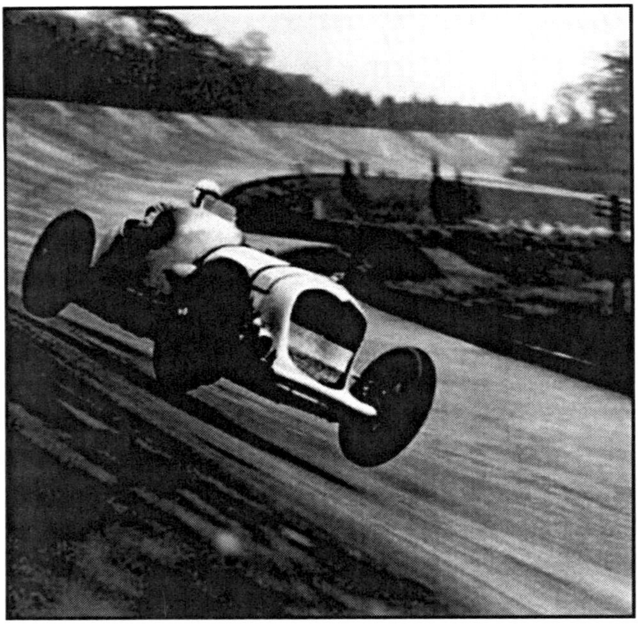

above: John Cobb, grandson of *Rivermead* resident Rhodes Cobb held the all-time Brooklands speed record at 143.44mph. Here he is seen with all four wheels off the ground.
below: Frederick Cornes' company pioneered Japanese trade in the 1860's and is still flourishing.

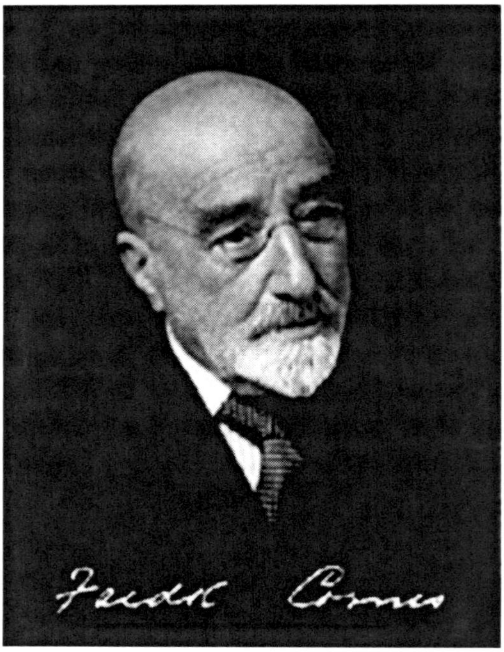

Rhodes Cobb, a fur broker, lived at *Rivermead* from 1855 to 1861. He was the grandfather of John Rhodes Cobb, racing driver and world speed record holder.

The next resident was Charles James Weale who was managing director of the family wine merchant firm Bull & Weale. He had married the daughter of the firm's co-founder and they moved into Hampton Wick in 1862. Unfortunately the *Rivermead* jinx struck yet again and he declared bankruptcy in 1874 and committed suicide the following year. His widow then married John Arthur Buckley, another Lower Teddington Road resident.

Meanwhile, Weale's sister-in-law Henrietta Alice Bull had married Frederick Cornes, a merchant, and they were living in Broom Road (the continuation of Lower Teddington Road). Cornes was involved when Japan very first ended its 200-year trading isolation in 1858. He had been born in 1837 in Macclesfield, one of the main centres of the British silk trade, where his father owned a small silk mill. After learning the family business, he left England in 1858 for Shanghai to act as a silk buyer for a Manchester based importer. The opening up of Japan made available new sources of silk and Frederick Cornes moved to Yokohama early in 1861 where he established a partnership with a young tea trader, to export silk and green tea. In 1863, the company secured the agency of the P&O steamship line. In 1868 they were appointed the first Lloyd's agent in Japan - a position that Cornes and Company still holds to this day. Frederick and Henrietta moved into *Rivermead* in 1881 where the last two of their seven children were born. They remained there until Cornes' death in 1927. He left a legacy equivalent to almost £100m.

---oOo--

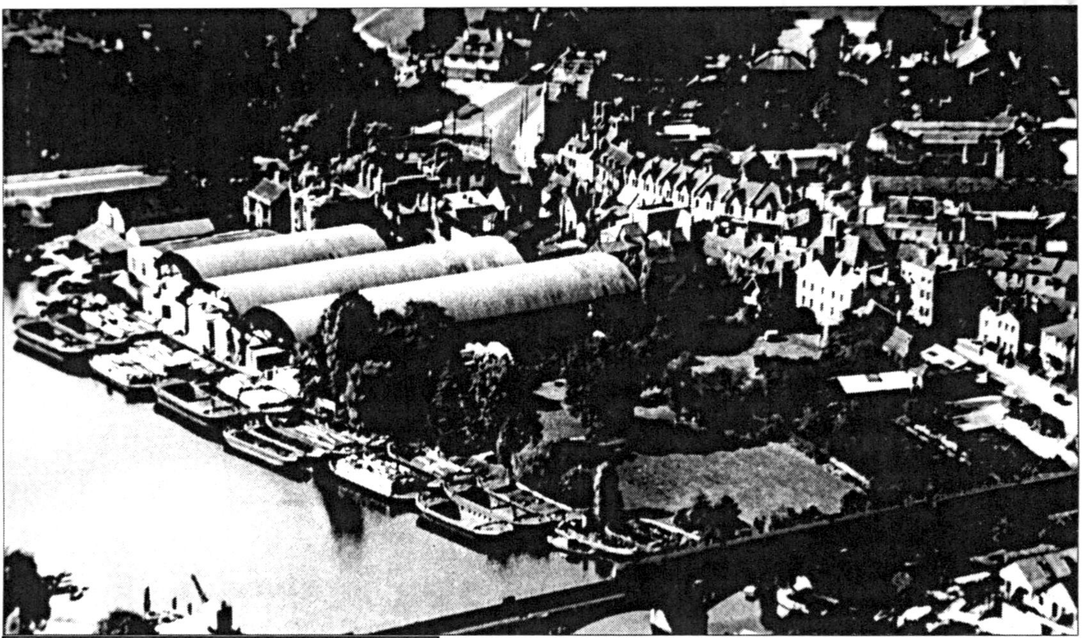

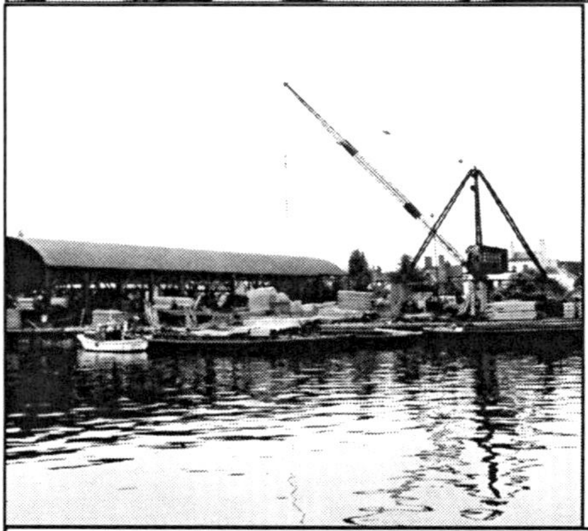

Top: *Rivermead* in the 1930's with its tree-lined garden in the foreground.
Left: The garden became a timber and building materials yard in the 1950's
Bottom: By the 1980's it was home to the Parman Marine Brokerage. When this operation closed, the site was redeveloped as Becketts Place, Spinnaker Court and most recently Becketts Wharf.

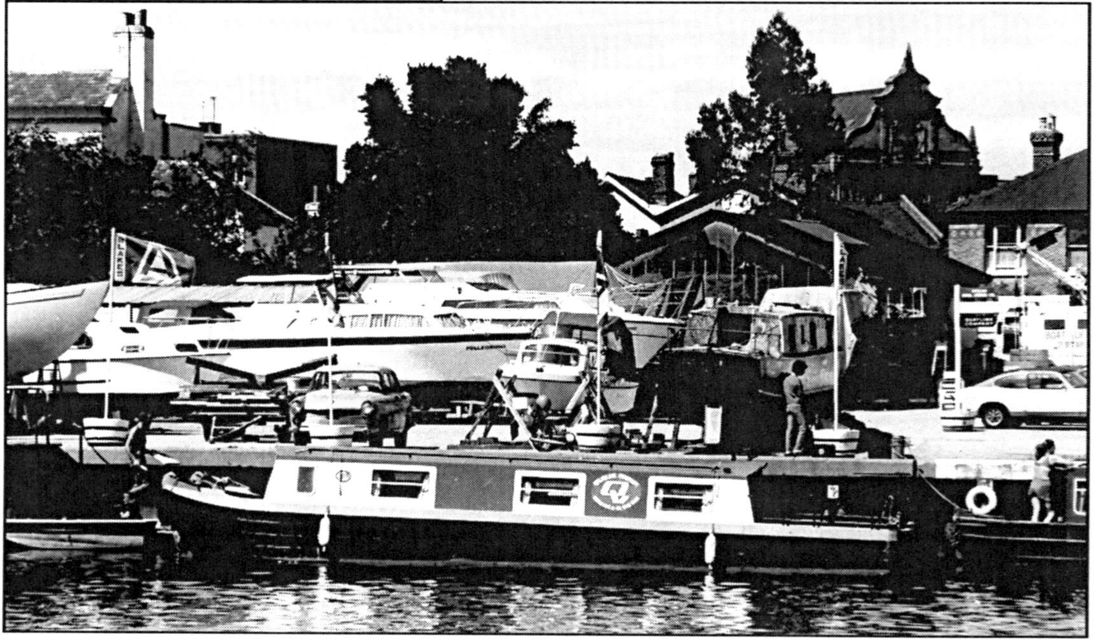

The last private residents of *Rivermead*, Charles Walter Beckett and his son of the same name, were seemingly the first to exploit the land for commercial use. Beckett was a lighterman who had the contract to deliver coal for the Hampton Court Gas Works on Sandy Lane. The wharf was on York Terrace, just upstream of Kingston Bridge from whence the coal was taken by horse and cart to the works. For a short while he leased a shop unit in Home Park Parade as his office. When he moved into *Rivermead* in 1929, he transferred his office there but continued to unload by the bridge. However once road deliveries started, it seems likely that the Becketts started using the land on Lower Teddington Road as a wharf. Their tugs would make the run up to the East India docks to collect cargo, mainly wood and other building materials. Unlike Gridley Miskin at the next door wharf where the workers would unload the planks off the barge by sliding them onto their shoulders and manhandling them into the sheds, Beckett installed a crane (later two cranes) to speed up the work. An ex-employee recently related how he would arrive in his tug back from the docks and immediately climb into the crane to unload his own barges. When the lighterage operation closed down, a boatyard took over the site. By the late 1970's *Rivermead* had become an office building, the Becketts had moved into a bungalow next door and what was once a rich man's private garden and meadow was destined to become home to hundreds of residents and office workers.

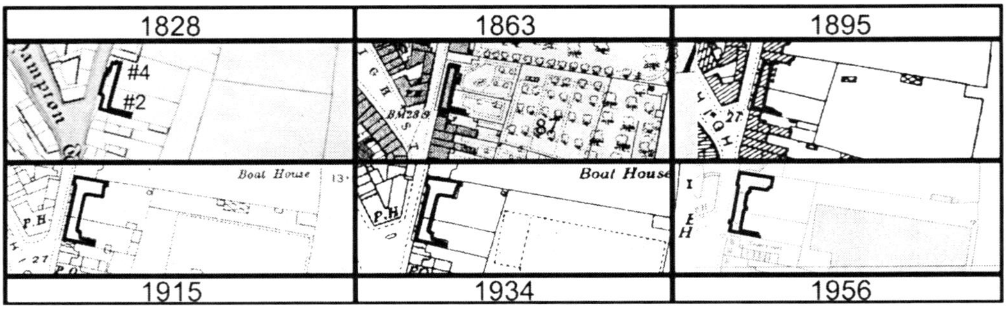

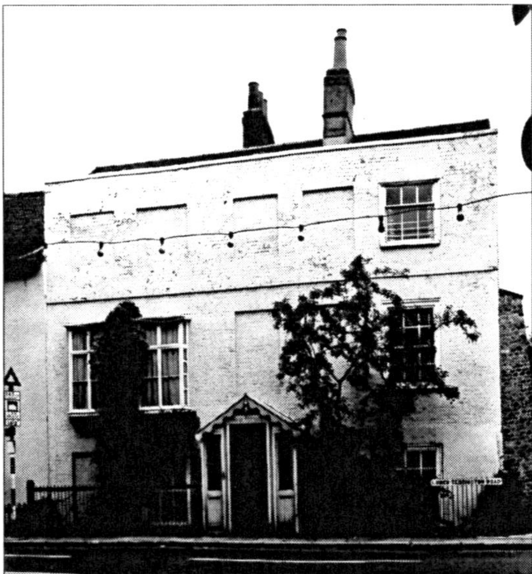

above: Both properties lost their *Riverside* gardens when the Timber Yard arrived. left and below: The relatively windowless and featureless street facades show in these 1970's views.

Number 2, *River Cottage*

Number 4, *Wolsey's Cottage*

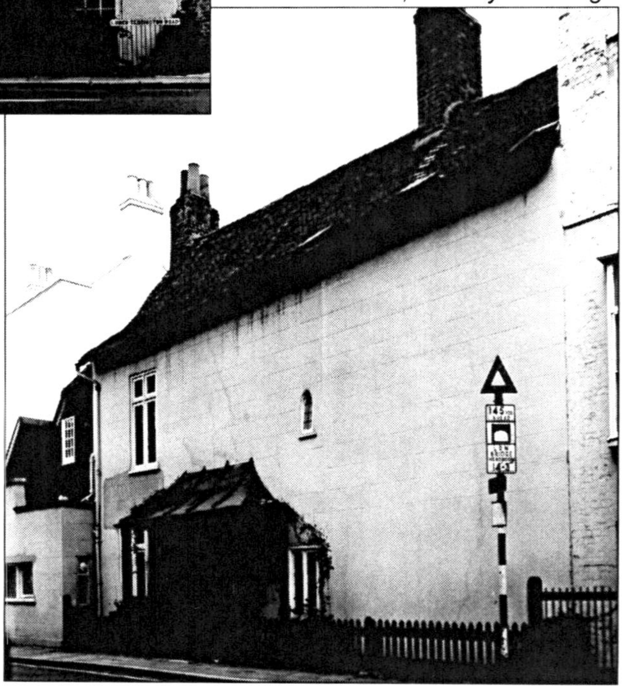

Wolsey's Cottage and River Cottage

Ayliffe Locations M & N (page 16) - now 4 and 2 Lower Teddington Road

These two properties, while now bearing a postal address in Lower Teddington Road, are probably more logically thought of as being the "top" end of the High Street and indeed, when built, were on the very edge of town going north towards Teddington. Many of the buildings in this area of the village date from the Middle Ages, in the case of *Wolsey's Cottage* from around the middle of the 1500's and *River Cottage* from early to mid 1700's.

An intriguing speculation in an English Heritage-produced brief study undertaken in 2000 was that both properties could have been part of a larger Medieval development consisting of five houses and stretching southward to Number 16 High Street. On this basis, the suggestion is that *Wolsey's Cottage* would have been the northern pair in the row of five and, on the assumption that the reconstruction of *River Cottage* in the eighteenth century retained the original point of entry, the front door of *River Cottage* would have acted as a centrepiece to the row's facade.

River Cottage has been greatly altered over time. It is listed by English Heritage and described as follows:

English Heritage Grade II Listing (January 1974):
Early-mid C18 house. Three storeys. Parapeted painted brick front, 5 bays wide (2:3) and one room deep. Brick band at second floor level. Window openings have flat, gauged brick heads. Several windows are blind (since reinstated); 2 left-hand first floor windows have mid C19 projecting oriel bays, remaining windows have almost flush, architraved sash boxes. The back wall is stuccoed on a timber frame. The interior includes a staircase with moulded handrail and turned balusters and a fully panelled room on the first floor on the south side.

The building was converted into offices in 1974 but was re-converted into a 5-bedroom private house in 2011.

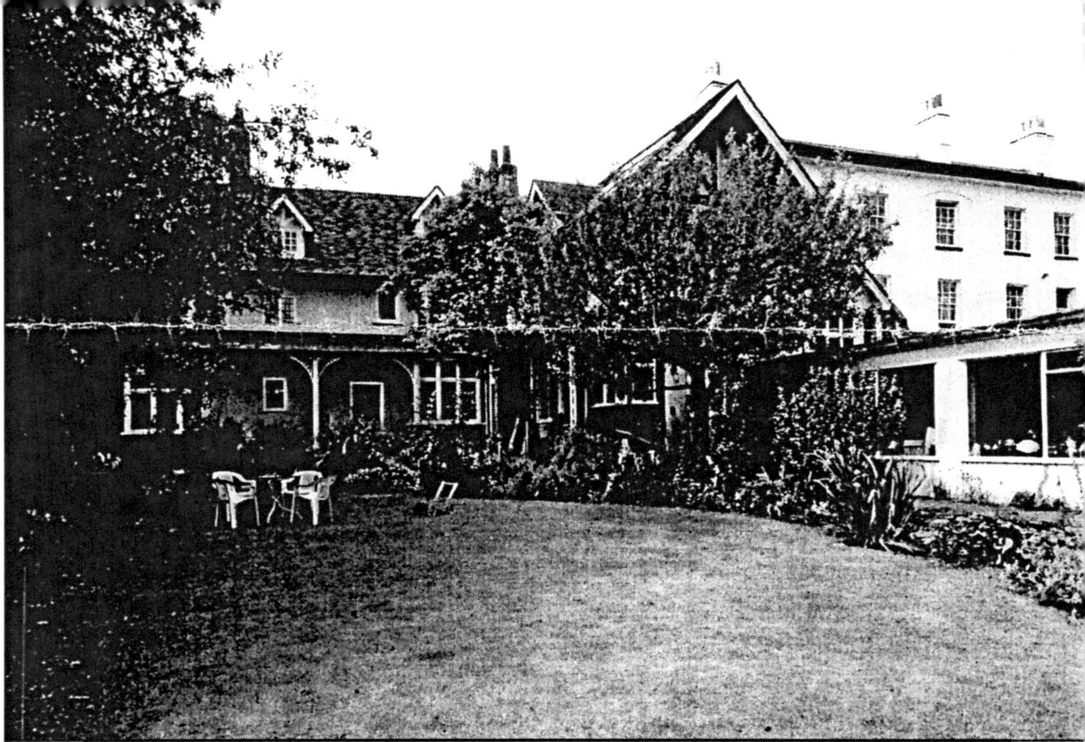

above: The east front of Wolsey's Cottage faces its garden. Note the former Montessori Nursery building on the right.
below: The magnificent seventeenth century chimney piece and panelling

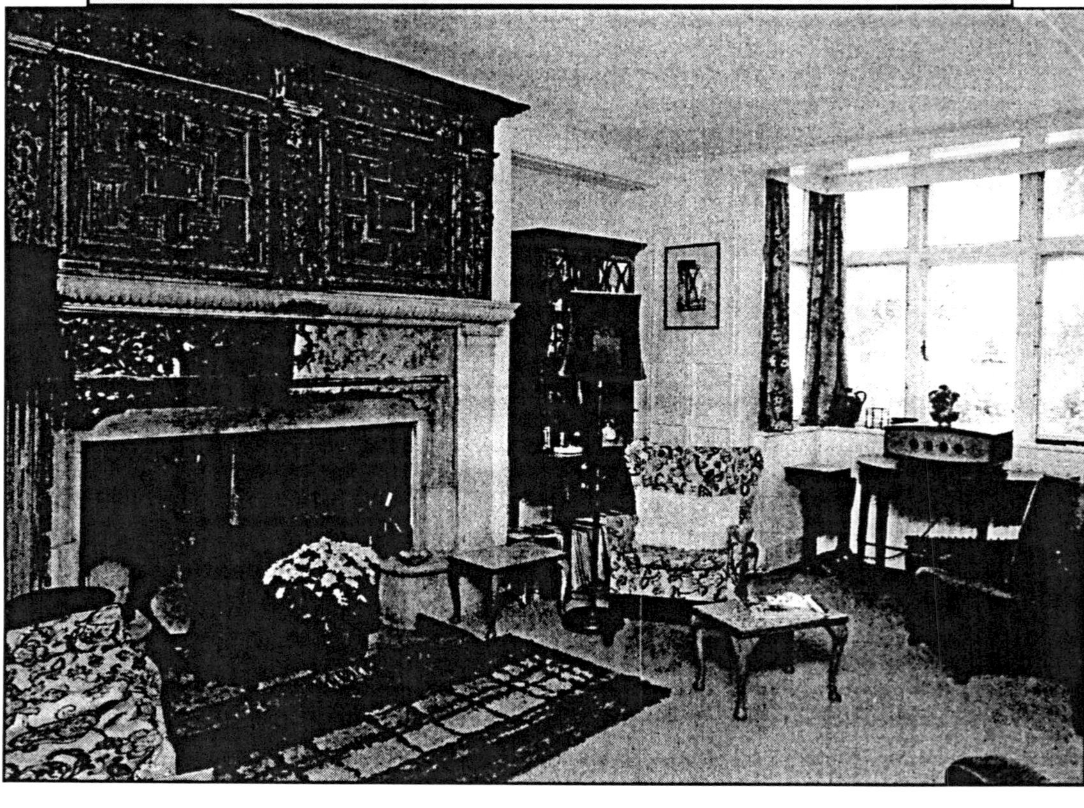

Number 4 owes its name to the legend that Cardinal Wolsey stayed here with his mistress during the construction of Hampton Court Palace - an extreme version of the tale also includes a tunnel linking the two properties. A portrait of Wolsey painted on a wooden panel and removed from the cottage in the late nineteenth century adds fuel to the rumour. Ironically the panel has since turned up hanging at the Palace itself but is apparently devoid of any historic or artistic merit, being rather unkindly described by the Surveyor of the Queen's Pictures as "a very depressing little picture and merely a derivation of the standard likeness". But while the experts rob the village of one of its more enduring and endearing fantasies, they agree on the merits of its seventeenth century chimney-piece and contemporary panelling. As the English Heritage Grade II listing entry says:

English Heritage Grade II Listing (June 1983):
Late C16 house. Two storeys but former north crossing has been reduced in height. A re-set window of circa 1600 first floor north end with moulded frame, mullion and transom. Inside, the ground floor south room has original panelling and fireplace with fine carved stone chimney-piece and oak overmantel.

Both properties have their backs turned to Lower Teddington Road and face their gardens which used to run down to the river. This explains the somewhat bland street-side appearance of *Wolsey's Cottage* and the number of hitherto blind windows in *River Cottage.* The fashion for Regency Gothick in the first half of the nineteenth century accounts for the stucco scored to resemble ashlar and the pointed window into the closet on the first floor - both visible on the road-facing wall of *Wolsey's Cottage.*

The sequence of detailed map sections at the top of Page 52 shows the former orchards disappearing under the Gridley Miskin timber yards (now the site of Marina Place) - when James Gridley himself was the occupant of *Wolsey's Cottage* with his office in the north wing of the property overlooking his empire. A major remodelling of this house - inside and out - was undertaken in the 1920's which created the current appearance of the eastern facade. A further - and locally very well-known - extension was the addition in 1964 of a nursery school room on the side of the garden, reached through the door at the north end. This housed the Montessori Nursery which flourished there for many years. This was run by a member of the Udales, a family who were associated with both properties. Eric Udale first moved into *River Cottage* in 1922 before transferring into the newly remodelled *Wolsey's Cottage* seven years later. When he moved away, his son Michael and his wife continued to live there - maintaining a family association with the property that eventually lasted over seventy years.

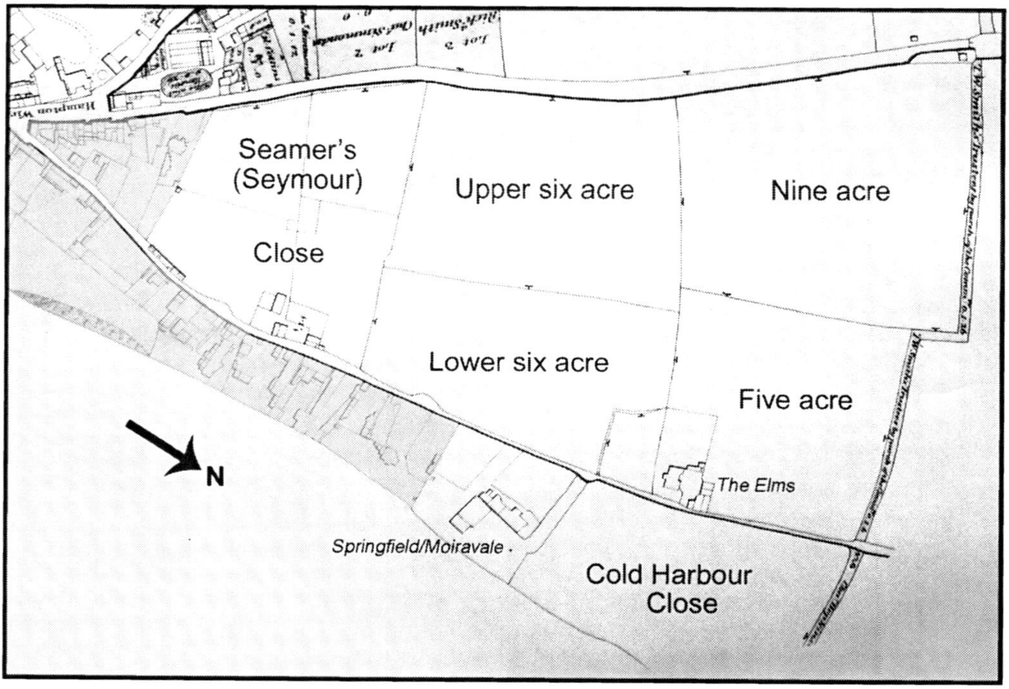

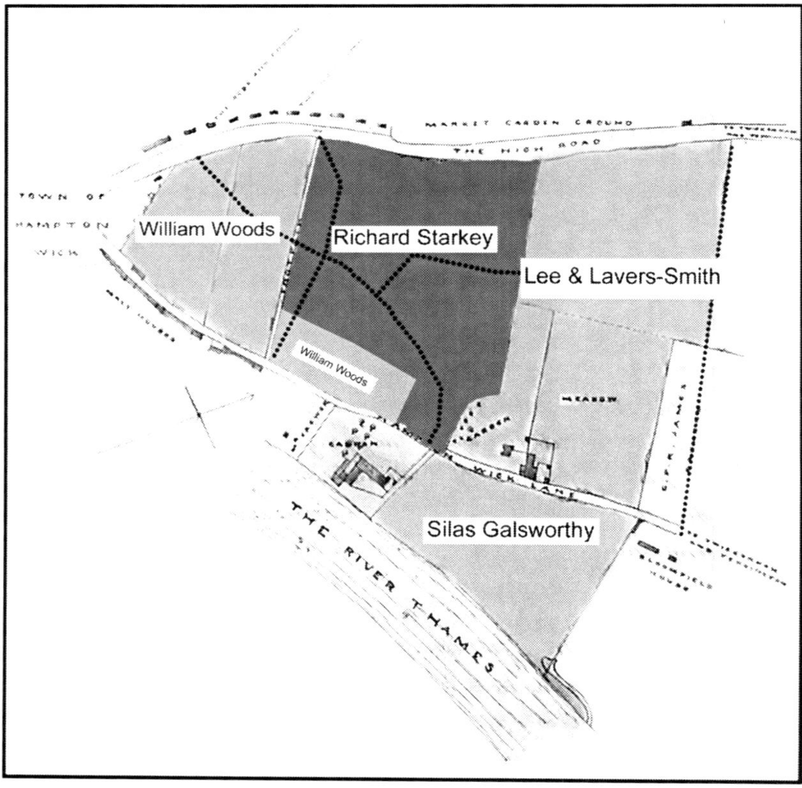

Top: The Elms Park Estate in 1850 when it was purchased by John and Henry Guy. It had two mansions and six fields totalling around 40 acres.

Left: The land was split between four developers who laid out a network of access roads

Developing The Elms Park Estate

The earlier sections of this book have shown how Lower Teddington Road - one of the original roads in Hampton Wick - was developed. All the houses mentioned in Ayliffe's memories of the 1840's have been identified and explored. By then, all available land had been absorbed, and further development required existing owners to release land for building. The key site was The Elms Park Estate which had been bought in 1850 by John Guy, a wealthy local solicitor, along with his brother Henry.

The estate (see map opposite) comprised two major properties - *The Elms* and *Springfield/Moiravale* - and six fields totalling around 40 acres. Cold Harbour Close was 8 acres of meadowland running alongside the river north of *Springfield* and was leased along with that property. The four fields of arable land - named Nine, Five, Upper Six and Lower Six Acres - were originally let along with *The Elms* as a 26-acre residential farm unit. The five acres of meadowland variously (and apparently simultaneously!) known as Seamer's, Sellman's and Seymour Close were divided with fence and rail into four units which were sublet by different local residents (e.g. Richard Fortnum at *Walnut Tree House*).

Guy and his brother divided the land into a series of lots which they sold off. Three property developers - William Woods, Silas Galsworthy and Richard Starkey - were responsible for much of the initial building programme, laying out the road system and gradually filling the plots with a range of properties to suit all budgets. They were followed in the 1890's by the partnership of Henry Lee and Charles Lavers-Smith.

The First World War placed a firm check on the demand for, and supply of, new housing. Although the inter-war period saw a resumption in activity, the reopening of hostilities in 1939 heralded events that would dictate the future pattern of development of The Elms Park Estate. *The Elms* mansion itself was destroyed by bombing and the Middlesex County Council purchased both its now-vacant plot and all remaining available land in what had been the Nine and Five Acres to provide sites for two new schools. So from 1950 onwards, further development was once again dependent on a pattern of redevelopment of, or infilling between, existing properties.

The next few pages will recount chronologically the story of development of The Elms Park Estate from 1850 to the present day, and along the way meeting some of its more colourful developers and residents.

The 1850's

The first developments took place on the west side of Lower Teddington Road, immediately opposite the range of malthouses and was carried out by William Woods around 1852. He created two detached houses and two pairs of semi-detached properties. These correspond with the original Numbers 11 Lower Teddington Road (demolished in 1989), 15/17 Lower Teddington Road and 14 Seymour Road (both demolished in 1965) and the surviving 23/25 Lower Teddington Road. The style of architecture of those properties from this period that are still in existence (almost certainly shared by those that have been demolished) is typical of the late, Regency complete with its shallow double-pitched roofs hidden behind parapets placed over a prominent cornice and with a pronounced string course below the first floor multi-paned windows. That the design should be so relatively dated (they were actually built at the beginning of the mid-Victorian period) may reflect Woods' caution and - whether as a justification for, or result of, this - the properties remained empty for several years before receiving their first tenants.

Number 11 Lower Teddington Road was known as *Rose Cottage* - although it had 13 rooms. One of its earliest residents was Dr. Theodore

The Developers: 1 William Woods

William Woods was born in Hampstead in 1785. In various registers and census returns his occupation over his lifetime was progressively described as carpenter (1814), builder (1851), landed proprietor (1861) and gentleman (1866) which neatly summarises his career.

He and his wife Ann had two children, a son born in 1814 and daughter born three years later. Little is known of his early or middle life but by the time of the 1851 census, when he was a listed as a "visitor" at his daughter's house in Lambeth, both he and she were widowed. Woods was then living in Ivy Cottage on Swan Lane (now Lower Teddington Road) and was about to purchase part of the neighbouring Seamer's Close and start a building programme involving several properties.

Whilst this work was underway William Woods - already in his late 60's - had embarked on the probably the biggest project of his life. In the early 1850's, he had bought the most of the land that formed the Surbiton Park estate. Built in the mid-18th century, the estate house itself stood opposite the present-day Surbiton High School. The grounds fanned out from the house, stretching down towards the river. On this land Woods laid out several streets and built no fewer than 300 houses for the well-heeled, including some fine pairs of semi-detached houses as well as some substantial mansions. To maximise the attractiveness of this estate, he also built what became known as Queen's Parade to provide his clients with a graceful *Riverside* promenade leading towards Kingston Bridge.

Gunther who arrived from Germany in the 1860's and became a naturalised British Citizen. He was a well-established figure in the community since, as well as running a GP surgery in his house, he acted as local medical officer of health from 1864, his initial appointment being prompted by an outbreak of cholera in the village. On his retirement in 1908, his son Hermann Arthur Gunther took over both roles and continued the GP practice until he too retired in 1948 - a remarkable period of 84 years after the original practice had been established. The building was then converted into three apartments.

The second of Woods' two detached houses was located next to Number 11. Although access was gained from Lower Teddington Road, the building was deliberately set well back on its plot such that when Seymour Road was laid out in the next decade the house could also be reached from this new road. The building therefore ended up with the name of *Seymour Lodge* and a street address of 14 Seymour Road. Both facts also apply to the replacement building constructed in 1965 as 15 flats. Its pedestrian gate in Seymour Road has steps down to the pavement which had been lowered to pass under the railway bridge. There is a level access to the garage block from the rear. This originally ran between Numbers 13 and 15 but, for the 1965 redevelopment, the gap was made between Numbers 17 and 19 which in turn required the demolition of the original 1850's building next described.

Originally intending this facility to be exclusive to the Surbiton Park residents, Woods then brokered a deal with Kingston Council under which he would donate to the public his part of the promenade in return for the Council completing the rest of the stretch into the centre of Kingston. The finished project was opened by Queen Victoria in August 1856.

With such major activities to occupy him, it would have been understandable if Woods had discontinued and sold on his development plans in Hampton Wick especially as he had by this time moved out of the village and was living with his daughter in one of his own properties in Surbiton Park. Nevertheless Woods persisted with his Hampton Wick plans, laying out Seymour and Station Roads and completing a further 16 houses most of which were unsurprisingly very similar in design to the Surbiton Park properties.

William Woods was a very hands-on character and frequently at odds with the newly-formed Local Board. In 1865, discovering that the sanitary arrangements for the new houses in Station Road were inadequate, he started to dig out the road to create a new, much larger cess-pool. The work was severely delayed and the Local Board were poised to serve a Court Order on Woods - a course of action that was only cancelled by Woods' death in January 1866 at the age of 81. The only beneficiary of his will was his daughter - and sole business partner - to whom he left £9,000. By the time of her death seven years later, her effects were worth £800. It seems a relatively scant reward for their lifetime efforts.

Numbers 15 and 17 Lower Teddington Road were known as *1 and 2 Lansdowne Villas*. This noble-sounding name was used in several immediately local contexts - *Lansdowne House*, *Lansdowne Terrace* and even Lansdowne Road - but all efforts to establish an historical connection with the Marquesses of Lansdowne or their estates near Bath proved futile. The real - rather more prosaic - origin of the name is simply that William Woods' daughter was, at the time Numbers 15 and 17 were being built, living in 11 Lansdowne Road, Lambeth. *Lansdowne Villas* can be seen at the extreme left of the photograph on page 66 and were replaced by a pair of maisonettes in the 1960's.

Arguably two of the most elegant of the early Victorian properties in Hampton Wick (and currently in excellent condition), Numbers 23 (*Lucerne House*) and 25 Lower Teddington Road (*Gomer House*), were the pick of Woods' 1850's crop of houses.

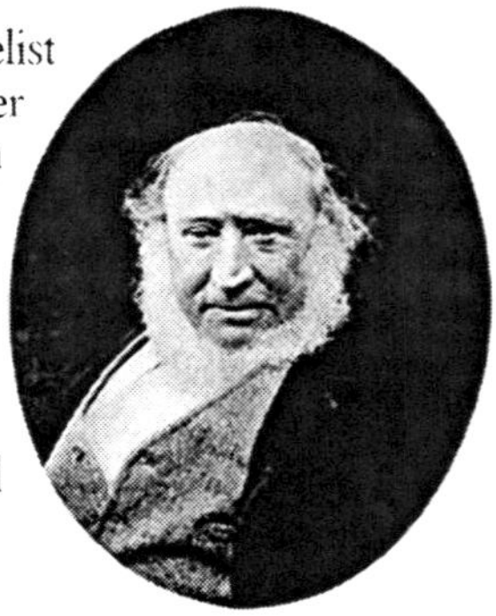

The first occupant of Number 25 was the novelist RD Blackmore (right) who named *Gomer House* after a favourite dog. Soon after moving into Hampton Wick in 1858, he inherited a significant sum of money, enabling him to give up school-mastering (which he loathed) and buy land near the Station in Teddington on which he built (another) *Gomer House* and established a market garden. His most famous novel Lorna Doone was written there and published in 1865.

The Developers: 2 Silas Galsworthy

Silas Galsworthy was born in Plymstock in 1819. His father and uncle (grandfather of the Forsyte Saga novelist John Galsworthy) were speculative builders operating in Upper Stamford Street, London, so it was not surprising to find Silas himself living there and being recorded in the 1861 Census as "Proprietor of Houses & Builder employing 12 men and 1 boy". In the later years of his life Silas turned his attention to developing property in Hampton Wick and at the time of his death from a heart attack in 1869 at the age of 51, he was living at *The Maples* which he had just built for himself on Upper Teddington Road.

The 1860's

Developments were now taking place in many areas of The Elms Park Estate:

1. By 1860 Silas Galsworthy had acquired the Cold Harbour Close and was already at work on building a series of large-scale mansions with extensive gardens down to the river
2. In 1860/61 three houses were built along the line of what would become Seymour Road
3. By the mid-1860's, William Woods (working in tandem with Henry Guy) had laid out the line of Seymour and Station Roads and started filling in the area at the southern end where he had been building during the previous decade.
4. At the same time Woods also built a terrace of five large-scale semi-detached villa blocks along the west side of Lower Teddington Road.

Cold Harbour Close

Little is known about the appearance of the riverside mansions built on Cold Harbour Close since all have long since been demolished. From the evidence of architects' plans submitted when permission was being sought for alterations, it was clear they were built on a grand scale. That such large properties should have a relatively short life-span is probably explained by the size and attractiveness of their site - either a wealthy would-be resident could afford to acquire a property, demolish and replace it with a single dwelling more to their own taste or a property developer could build several units on a single plot. As examples of this:

- *Denbigh House* (34 Lower Teddington Road), originally built in 1860, was replaced by the present structure in 1936.
- The Broom Park estate was built on the site of just three of Galsworthy's 1860's mansions.

First houses on Seymour Road

Westbourne Villa (2 Seymour Road) was built around 1861. Almost the first resident was Richard Elsam who was born in Queenhithe near St Paul's Cathedral in 1838. He practised as an architect and surveyor and was short-listed for the post of Surveyor and Inspector of Nuisances to the Hampton Wick Local Board on its formation in 1863. Although unsuccessful in this initial application, he was later given the appointment. In that capacity, he was the architect of the imposing Local Board Offices building at Number 47 High Street (next to *The Foresters*) which opened in 1884. He also revamped the Infants and Girls School in the same year on the newly-created School Road.

Elsam's career as an architect appeared to end abruptly in 1891 when he was declared bankrupt. He moved from Seymour Road and next appears in the 1901 census as Accountant and Auditor to the Hampton Court Gas Company.

His successor in Number 2 was Herbert Hankin Sherriff who renamed the house *Rossendale*. He was an insurance clerk and his son Robert Cedric followed in his father's occupation after having attended Kingston Grammar School. RC (as he was known) served in the First World War and was severely wounded at Passchendaele, later receiving the Military Cross. He started writing plays as a way of raising money for Kingston Rowing Club and his seventh play, "Journey's End" (1929), a bleak study of life in the trenches during the First World War, ran for two years at the Savoy Theatre and established Sherriff's international reputation. When subsequent success in the West End eluded him, Sherriff went to Hollywood where he became a highly successful writer of screenplays including "Goodbye Mr. Chips" and "The Dam Busters". Sheriff maintained close links with Kingston Grammar School for the rest of his life being a particularly generous supporter of the boat club which bears his name and which still benefits from a share of his royalties.

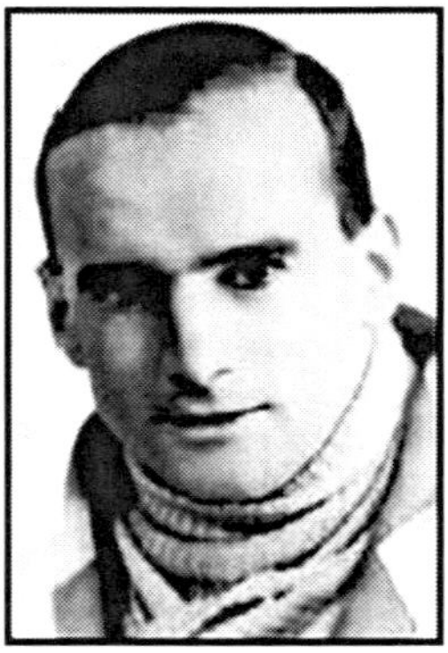

Northwick House, on the opposite side of Seymour Road, was built in around 1864 on land owned by the London and South West Railway. Following completion of the line in 1866, the land was released. The house faced Seymour Road but access was from the High Street (this stretch was then called Upper Teddington Road). When, in 1878, the landowner sold off the south west edge of the plot to create Northwick Terrace, this access was retained and still exists.

Number 25 Seymour Road (*Fairlea*) was built around 1863. Little is known of early residents but, from 1934 - 1984 *Fairlea*, became the Vicarage for St John the Baptist Church.

William Woods expands his portfolio

His first developments of the new decade took place to the north of *Lucerne* and *Gomer House* (Numbers 23/25 Lower Teddington Road) where Woods laid out two plots up to the corner of his new road (later called Station Road) and a further three along the new road. All properties were detached but varied in size from nine rooms each on the Lower Teddington Road plots with one sixteen-room and two eleven-room houses on Station Road.

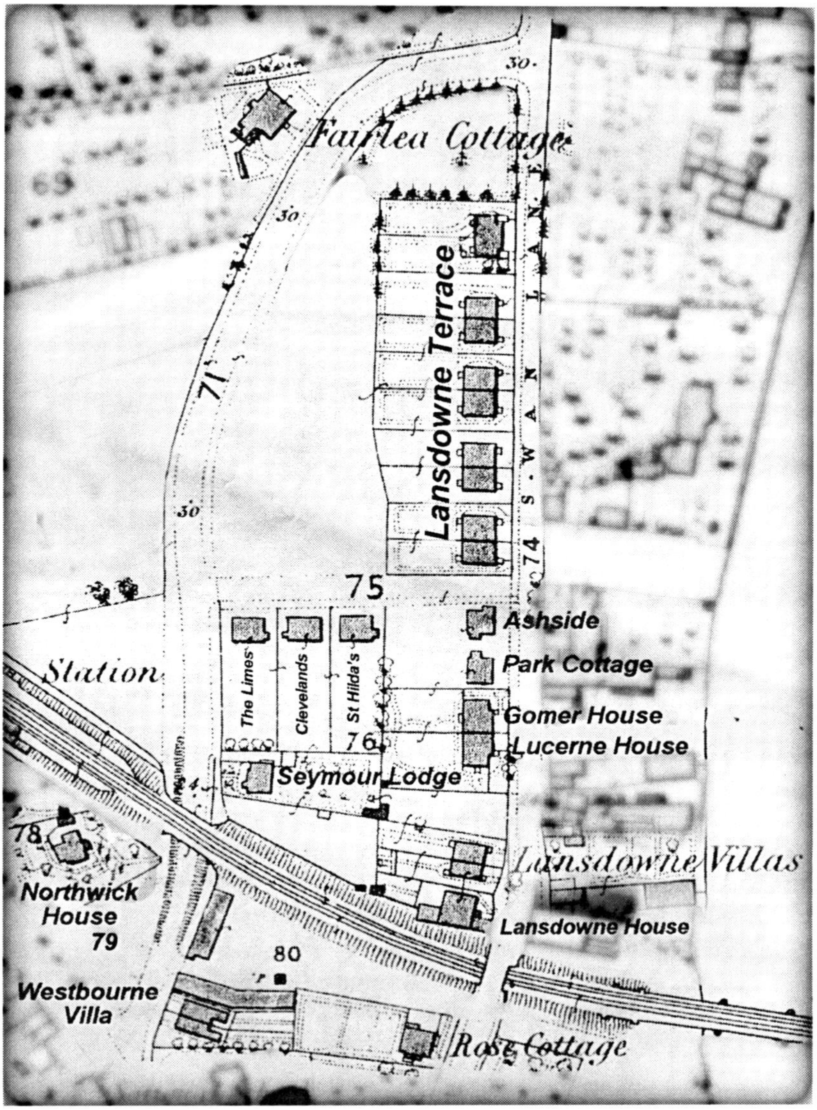

above: Developments in The Elms Park Estate up to 1865. Twenty five properties had been constructed - all bar the three in Seymour Road having been built by William Woods.

Park Cottage (Number 27) and *Ashside* (Number 29) were built to the same two-storey plus attic and semi-basement design but, whereas the former is fully stuccoed, Number 29 is exposed brick.

All three properties that Woods built in Station Road have now been demolished, Number 10 in 1937, and Numbers 12 & 14 in 1972. From the one available photograph, it seems that Numbers 10 and 12 Station Road were similar in design to *Park Cottage* and *Ashside* but with an additional storey. Number 14 Station Road with its 16 rooms would have been a more substantial design.

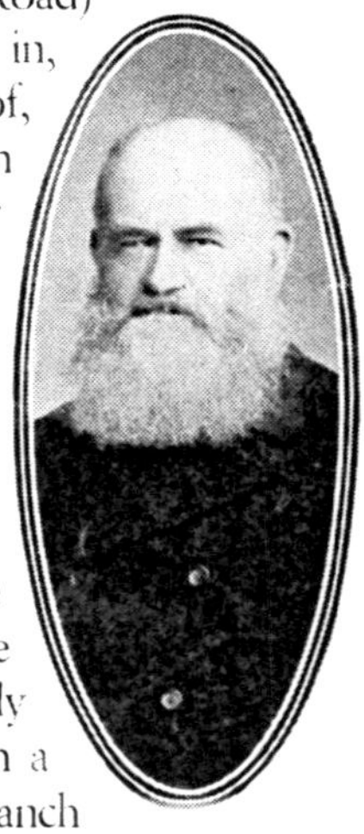

The first occupant of *St Hilda's* (Number 14 Station Road) was Denham Robert Coates Robinson (right). He lived in, and was a prominent member in the community of, Hampton Wick for almost 50 years. He was born in Chelsea in 1835. His father was a Lieutenant Commander in the Royal Navy, serving it seems more for honour rather than reward since Denham himself attended Counter-Hill Academy in Deptford, a school for children of impoverished Royal Naval officers. He became a clerk in the War Office in Whitehall, where he spent his whole working life. When first married, he and his wife lived at Spring Grove (Heston) close to the L&SWR station of the same name (now Isleworth station) - which would have provided him with an easy journey to work. As the family grew, the Robinsons looked for larger premises but with a similar commute. The imminent arrival of the L&SWR branch line into Hampton Wick made the newly-built 14 Station Road ideal, and they moved in just before the birth of their third child. Their remaining five children were all to be born here. After 41 years, the Robinson's "downsized" from their 16-room house at 14 Station Road into *Seymour Lodge*, an 8-room house - also built by William Woods - at 14 Seymour Road.

At the same time as he was building the fill-in houses, William Woods constructed a development of ten semi-detached Italianate villa-style houses. All shared similar eight-room three-storey plus semi-basement layouts but differed in the external finish - ranging from full-stucco (Numbers 31 to 43) to brick-only (Numbers 49/51) - and with varying levels of ornamentation around the windows. It appears that Woods was attempting to appeal to a range of both budgets and tastes.

Woods himself died just as *Lansdowne Terrace* was being completed. However his daughter continued the developments until all the land that her father had bought back in 1854 had been filled. Numbers 19 and 21 Lower

Richard William Starkey and his hallmarks

Starkey was born in 1846 at Dursley (just north of Bristol), where his father was a Tea Dealer and Grocer. Richard's mother and wife both hailed from Swansea and Richard himself lived there for a period - a Welsh connection of which it seems he was fiercely proud and which influenced his later choice of road and house names. Whilst in Swansea, Starkey went into partnership as a Brick Manufacturer but the business was dissolved in 1876 and the partners both independently filed for bankruptcy. Starkey was discharged in 1879, around the time he came to Hampton Wick. He and his wife Margaret initially lived in Lower Teddington Road whilst building his own house in Seymour Road where the last two of the couple's nine children were born.

He had bought the rights to develop both the Upper and Lower Six Acre fields of The Elms Park Estate (except for their immediate boundaries with the Upper and Lower Teddington Roads). He laid out his master plan for the area and in July 1883 the Local Board approved his proposal for "a new road leading out of the Seymour-road" which he subsequently named Glamorgan Road. Under the plan he built nine houses in Seymour Road and eight in Glamorgan Road before the end of the decade.

In the early 1890's Starkey built a further three properties on the corner of Seymour Road and Lower Teddington Road but then appears to have shifted his focus elsewhere for a few years as there is no further evidence of his work locally until, in 1902, his wife obtained permission to build five properties on the east side of Seymour Road (Numbers 16 −22) and Number 7 Station Road. All the drawings were signed R W Starkey.

The Starkeys retired in 1916 when Richard was aged 70. They left *Penmaen* and went to live in Torquay. Richard died five years later and Margaret in 1940 aged 90.

In the period 1879 −1890, Richard Starkey built over twenty houses in "his" part of The Elms Park Estate. Whilst he employed several different designs - which he would probably have drawn himself with the aid of pattern books - he incorporated four common features which hallmarked all his creations of the period:

1. The windows have stone lintels finished with the same bevelled edge and chamfered central notch
2. The top course of all chimney stacks uses a characteristic dog-tooth pattern which acts as a support to the surmounting crown. (The dog-tooth device was also often repeated below the capping on the front boundary wall)
3. Barge boards, often with a characteristic trefoil pattern in the foot, many having an identical cross-strut and finial design.
4. A wooden porch (probably purchased from a catalogue as a standard kit of parts)

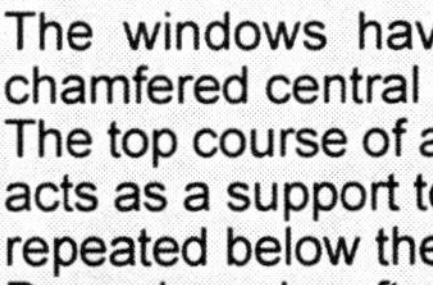

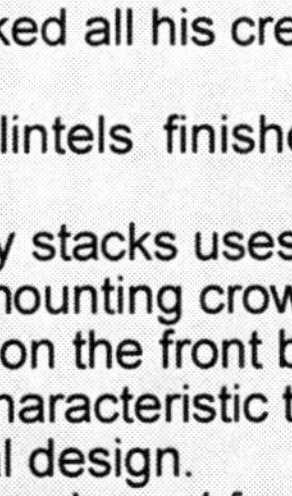

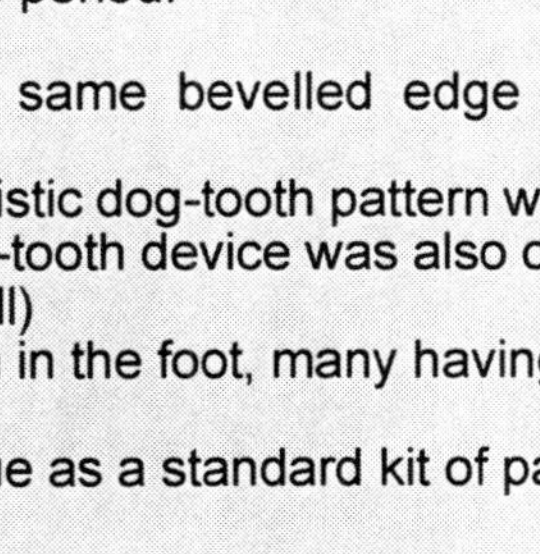

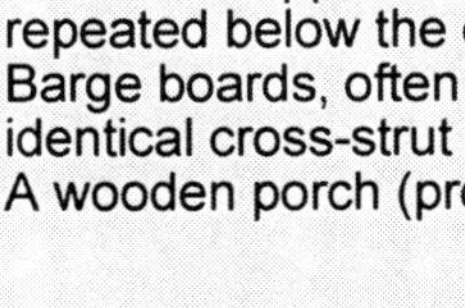

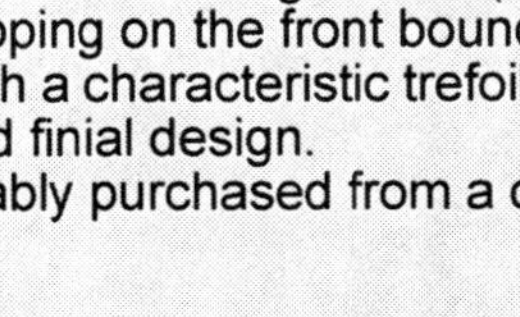

Teddington Road (*1 & 2 Laburnham Villas*) are a pair of semi-detached eight-roomed houses ranged on three storeys and a semi-basement. Unlike his previous paired houses on this stretch, Woods built *Laburnham Villas* in a halls-adjoining configuration. The sides, quoins and lower storey are all covered in stucco which has the effect of framing the exposed brick on the first storey. Although set reasonably well back from the road, the building itself was accommodated on a narrow plot with little gap between itself and Numbers 17 & 19 which later led to the neighbouring properties being demolished to provide access for off-road parking on the land behind. Finally, and built in 1869 - three years after the completion of *Lansdowne Terrace* - 13 Lower Teddington Road was the last of Wood's fill-in properties and the last - as *Lansdowne House* - to use the Woods' familiar house name. The land had been bought from Wood's daughter by the London & South West Railway Company in 1864 but, once the bridge and embankment works had been completed, L&SWR sold off the surplus, on which the Woods now built their final property in Hampton Wick.

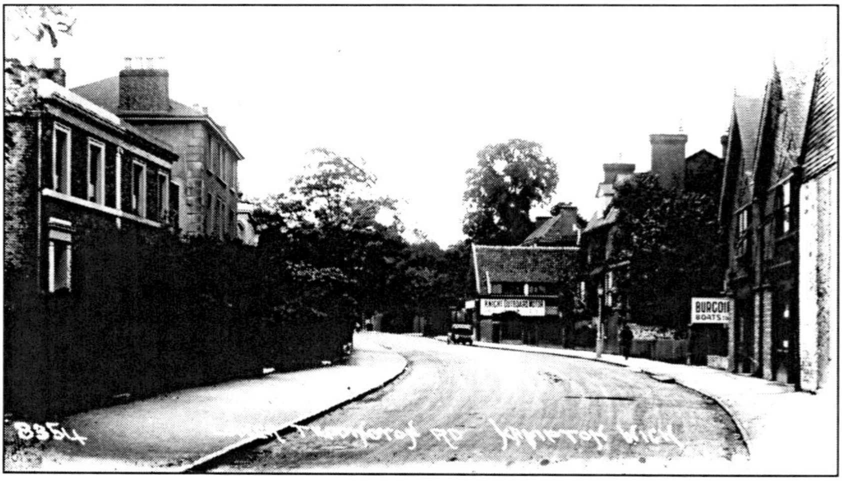

above: Lower Teddington Road in the 1920's with William Woods' Lansdowne Villas on the extreme left and Laburnham Villas beyond

The 1870's

Field 79 (see bottom left of the map on page 63) was one of the two adjacent fields originally bought from Benjamin Birchley by L&SWR in 1862. It was included in the auction of surplus land held by the Railway Company in May 1866. This corner of Seamer's Close was for a long time the site of a traditional fair held during the week after Easter. The triangular-shaped plot bordered on both Upper Teddington Road and Seymour Road and was completely built over during the 1870's. Three properties fronted onto Seymour Road: Number 1 (*Rose Cottage*) was a very simple narrow-fronted four room house with rear extension and double-pitched roof. Numbers 3 & 5 Seymour Road - then known as *1 and 2 Seymour Cottages* - were a pair of semi-detached houses each with four rooms and a rear extension, the building being covered with a pyramid-hipped roof. These latter properties were built by James Scotcher who ran a grocer's shop and painter/decorator business at 55 High Street. His son Frederick Charles Scotcher owned and lived in *2 Seymour Cottages* the other cottage being let. When Scotcher Junior died in 1906, his widow let the property to Ernest Whenman, a local builder and undertaker who added a shop on the side of the original cottage. The signwriting advertising his business is still visible on the end wall.

Meanwhile, round the corner in Station Road three similar configuration but larger-scale properties were built immediately behind the Station. Number 1 Station Road (called *Harley Villa*) was a six-roomed detached house with rear extension and pyramid-hipped roof whilst Numbers 3&5 were a pair of semi-detached houses each with six rooms, a rear extension and a double-pitched roof. The latter building has a stone between the adjoining first storey windows proudly bearing the legend: "Palmerston Villas 1873". The property was built by William Henry Pleasants who was third footman (within a retinue of 24 servants) to Lord Palmerston, Prime Minister of the United Kingdom from 1859 - 1865. Following the death of Palmerston, Pleasants became a warden at Hampton Court Palace and moved to Park Road, Hampton Wick before building the Station Road villas and naming them in honour of his former employer. William Pleasants lived in 2 Palmerston Villas for 48 years until his death in 1921. In 1905 his younger brother Jezreel bought 1 Station Road which he renamed Dalham Villa after the Suffolk village where the two brothers had been born.

As related elsewhere (see page 65) Richard Starkey arrived in Hampton Wick in 1879 and was soon to embark on a major programme of building (mainly speculative), which lasted for the next thirty years. His first project had been to build *Penmaen* (32 Seymour Road) which was to be his own house for the next 35 years. The house was named after a small village on the Gower Peninsular ten miles west of his adopted home town of Swansea. Unsurprisingly this was an impressive show house, containing eleven rooms ranged on three storeys and, whilst arguably too big for its curtilage, would nevertheless have enabled Starkey to display his skills as an architect and builder to his prospective clients.

The 1880's

As recorded in the map opposite, this decade saw the completion of developments on the west side of Seymour Road (Numbers 7 -23), an infilling of land leading up to the railway bridge on the east side (Numbers 4 -12) and a further substantial property (Number 28) next to *Penmaen*. At the same time, Glamorgan Road was laid out and four properties completed.

The triangular plot on which the word "Station" has been printed in the map on page 63 was one of the parcels of land bought by L&SWR (in this case from William Woods) and then released when surplus land was auctioned off in 1866. A development of three similar semi-detached properties was constructed each having seven rooms ranged on two floors, rear extension and an attic with dormer window. They featured a two-storey bay window and were built using distinctive polychrome brickwork. All three units were bought as pairs with the owners living in one half and letting the other.

The land marked as Field 80 on the map on page 63 was used by the Railway Company to accommodate sheds and a yard during the construction of the bridge and station. In the sale catalogue for the 1866 auction, it was described as being "Close to the station, and High Street, having a frontage of 120 feet, … well adapted for the erection of a Terrace of Shops". The purchaser was Frank Gaydon, a Kingston Marketplace jeweller, who erected one six-room detached house and two pairs of six-room semi-detached properties in 1883. All featured rear extensions and double-pitched roofs and prominently display their house-names on plaques above the front door.

In November 1883, Richard Starkey obtained detailed planning permission from the Hampton Wick Local Board to build on the west side of Seymour Road. Two styles of house were created: starting on the corner of Station Road, he built a series of five similar double-fronted 12-room houses with two-storey bays surmounted by castellations; beyond these were four single-fronted 9-room houses with rear extensions and single-storey bays (two with the same castellations as their larger neighbours). Amazingly, these properties were reported to have been completed by January 1884.

As mentioned elsewhere, Starkey had already reached agreement in July 1883 with the Hampton Wick Local Board for his plan to create a new road (to be called Glamorgan Road, another reference to his Swansea connections). This set off west between Numbers 15 and 17 Seymour Road before turning north west and running through to Normansfield Avenue. Since he only owned the land up to the boundary of the Upper Six Acre field (see map on page 56). the full line of the road would have had to be agreed with the owner of the adjoining Nine Acre field.

Starkey then proceeded to build eight properties on Glamorgan Road. They shared a similar three-bay nine-room layout with two-storey bay windows and hipped roof on one side and a small single-storey bay window with simple pitch roof on the other. The main roof was hipped with a short central ridge.

The only other development in the 1880's was on the plot next to *Penmaen.* On it was built *The Croft* Number 28 Seymour Road by Edward Albert Wright, who owned a significant number of properties throughout Hampton Wick. *The Croft* is a substantial 16-room house (which includes seven bedrooms), and appears to be the only property in this part of The Elms Park Estate which was not developed by Richard Starkey. By also being the largest in the area, it might be seen as an attempt by Wright to assert his own status as a property developer.

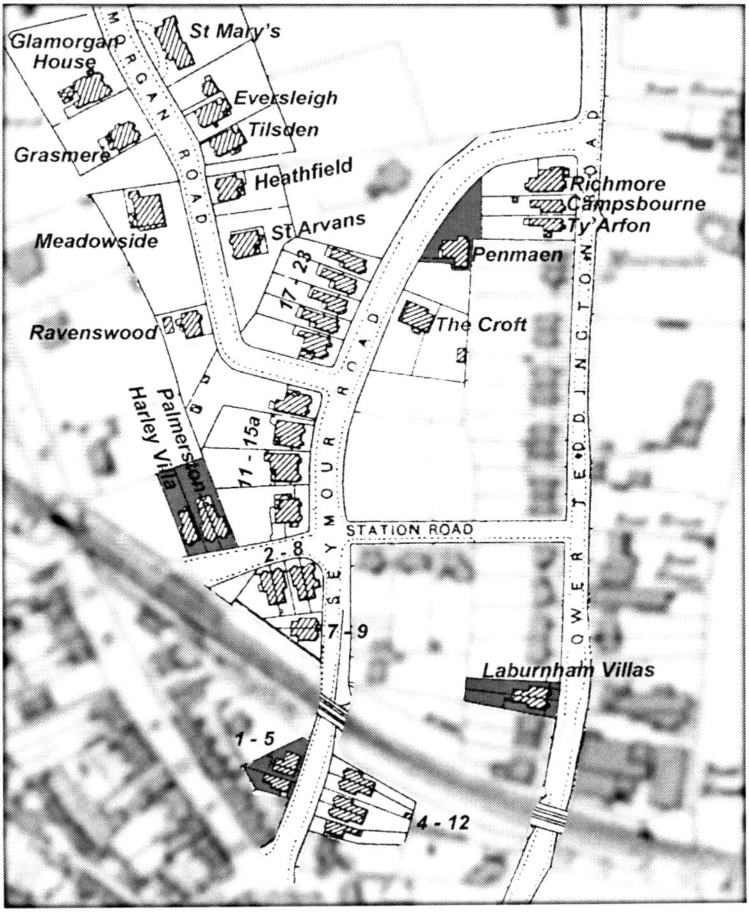

above: Developments in The Elms Park Estate in 1870 (shown against a grey background) and 1880 (with clear background)

The 1890's

Until now, the development of The Elms Park Estate had been concentrated in the fields to the south and east of the mansion house. However, the fields to the north and west now became the prime site of the developments that led to the extension of Glamorgan Road.

Back in 1855 when John Guy bought and split the original estate, he packaged *The Elms* mansion and its farm buildings together with the Nine Acre and Five Acre fields as a single lot which he then sold in the early 1860's to James Weston Clayton. Clayton had been living in one of Silas Galworthy's *Riverside* mansions and would probably have viewed this move into the 15-acre "home farm" on the opposite side of the road as a step up the property ladder. However, he had just been appointed Managing Director of Day and Martin's Boot Polish Manufactory near St Paul's Cathedral and, before he had time to settle in to *The Elms*, he was required to move in to the Factory Manager's house in High Holborn.

The next owner was Charles Sparrow, a retired City of London goldsmith who ran the property as a farm for the next 25 years. Around 1890, he sold the house and gardens to Frederick Jacobs (see page 116) whilst selling the rest of the land separately for housing development to Henry Lee and Charles Lavers-Smith (who were brothers-in-law, the former being a builder).

The developers immediately set about capitalising on their investment by building and renting out three detached houses (Numbers 13, 15 and 17) and two pairs of substantial semi-detached houses (Numbers 14/16 and 31/33) on Glamorgan Road. Enoch Kempson also acquired a plot on which he built Numbers 19/21 Glamorgan Road. However, a proposal in 1893 by Kempson to build a further five pairs of these substantial semi-detached houses on the opposite side of Glamorgan Road never materialised.

Contemporary sketch-maps (included in the deeds of 28 Glamorgan Road), show that the developers also planned a second road - to be somewhat self-importantly known as Lee Road - to branch off Seymour Road and run broadly parallel to Lower Teddington Road, midway between it and Glamorgan Road. It was following the existing field boundaries and would have given access to ten additional building plots. In the event, the road was never built. Following the deaths of Lee and Lavers-Smith in 1909 and 1916 respectively, the remaining land west of the planned road was bought by the canny owners of *Eversleigh*, *St Mary's* and *Wood Dalling* (10, 12 and 14 Glamorgan Road respectively) - a purchase which would later have a significant impact on developments in this area both between the two wars and in more recent times.

Meanwhile, on the extreme north-eastern side of this area, St Helier's (Number 69 Lower Teddington Road) had been built in 1890. The house was later renamed *Raeburn House* but was demolished in 1968 to be supplanted by the present *Raeburn Close.*

Also in this decade, Richard Starkey built *Richmore* at the corner of Seymour and Lower Teddington Roads. This was a large house of similar proportions to Starkey's own next door. He also built two further single-fronted properties (*Campsbourne* and *Ty'Arfon*) Numbers 51 & 53 Lower Teddington Road) on this same plot. These were exact replicas of Numbers 17-23 Seymour Road.

Perhaps the most intriguing of all the properties built in this decade was also by far the largest - the 1896 fifteen-room *St Mary's* (Number 12 Glamorgan Road). The plot is at the northern extremity of Starkey's land, and the building has the dog-tooth brickwork on its chimneys and boundary wall that are a hallmark of his work. However, the owner was one William Horace Hope who was himself an architect and surveyor, so whether the building was Hope's own design or another of Starkey's creations is as yet unknown.

The 1900's

Richard Starkey returned to his Seymour Road land-bank to build a further set of five properties. The first (*Deepdale* Number 11 Station Road) was a detached house whose layout took advantage of its corner plot. The other four (Numbers 16 - 22 Seymour Road) were built as two very similar pairs of semi-detached houses though Numbers 16/18 additionally have prominent dormer windows showing the presence of a third storey. Comparing these houses with those opposite - which Starkey had built only about twenty years earlier - it is interesting to see how styles had changed from the mid-Victorian to the Edwardian periods - the slightly dour Gothic of the former gives way to a much lighter and airy appearance of the latter, complete with their newly fashionable French windows and balcony for the main bedrooms.

Meanwhile, Lee and Lavers-Smith were continuing to build in Glamorgan Road adding two further pairs of semi-detached houses at the north-western end (Numbers 23/25 and 27/29).

After a lapse of nearly fifty years, two new houses were built on the original Cold Harbour Close. As befitted their prestigious location, these were substantial properties: *Ee Juan* (Number 30 Lower Teddington Road, now *Warneford*) had 15 rooms and *Bindown* (Number 32 Lower Teddington Road now *Teddington Lodge*) had 12. Nevertheless, their proximity to each other on the boundary of the adjacent plots seems strangely inappropriate for properties of this stature.

Finally, a pair of very substantial semi-detached houses (Numbers 9/11 Station Road) were built in 1907 on land which had been owned by Denham Robinson (see page 64) who lived across the road at *St Hilda's.*

These then were the only houses built on The Elms Park Estate during the first two decades of the 20th century as the threat, actuality and aftermath of the First World War suppressed demand for new housing until the late 1920's.

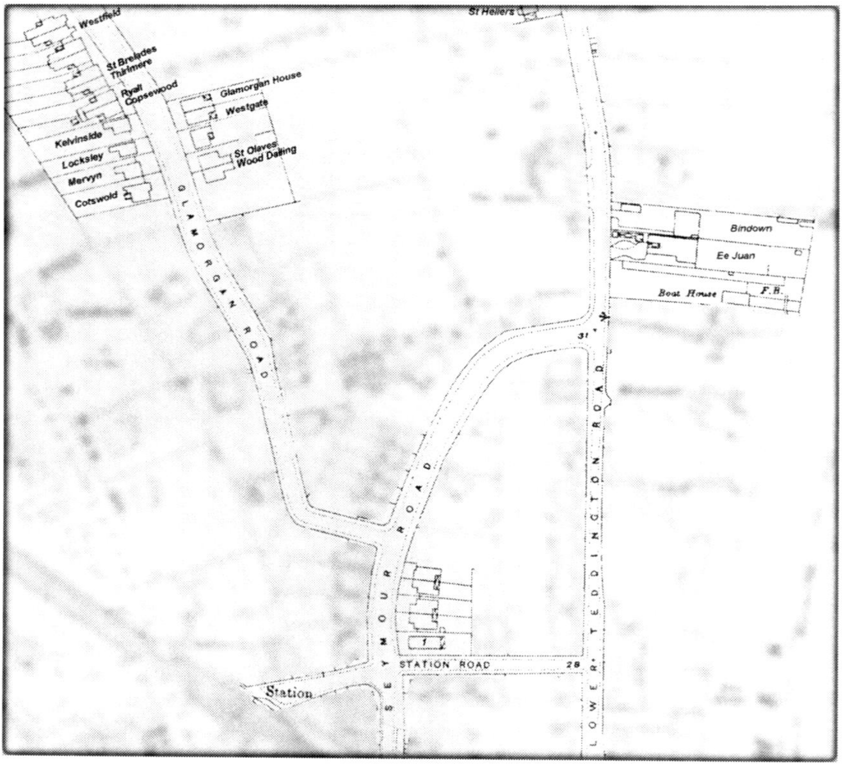

above: Developments in The Elms Park Estate at the beginning of the twentieth century leading up to outbreak of the First World War.

The 1920's

In 1920, the executors of Lee and Lavers-Smith sold a parcel of land at the north-east end of Glamorgan Road. The purchaser was The Elms Sand & Ballast Co. whose offices were at 31 High Street, Hampton Wick. By 1926 the company had apparently extracted all useable material from the site and they sold it - complete with its open quarry hole - to Henry Bambury, a builder who in July 1927 submitted a successful planning application for four pairs of semi-detached houses (which became Numbers 24 - 38 Glamorgan Road). Bambury himself moved into the last-built (Number 38) and lived there for over fifty years. The plots of the four properties occupied about one-third of the total area of Bambury's 1927 purchase and, at the time the 1934 Ordnance Survey was issued, the rest was clearly shown as still being a quarry site.

Meanwhile, in the first of many infill developments that would take place from this date on, Numbers 24/26 Seymour Road were constructed in 1924 as a pair of semi-detached houses located in what had been the garden of *The Croft.* This section of Seymour Road was renumbered to accommodate the new properties.

The 1930's

The decade started nervously following the Stock Market falls but by mid-decade the demand for new housing was once more back in full swing.

The process of infilling was well underway, the first example of the new decade being at Number 30 Seymour Road in what had been the garden of Starkey's show-house *Penmaen.* Perhaps in deference to the architect of the donor property, the new house was very much in the style of Starkey's own Victorian creations - including prominent barge boards, a two-storey bays and a wooden porch - but the inclusion of the first built-in garage in The Elms Park Estate showed how housing requirements were evolving.

The orchard that once belonged to *The Elms* was now developed to provide sites for three properties: a pair of semi-detached houses and a detached residence all sharing several common - and fashionable - 1930's architectural features and again all three having built-in garages.

Across Lower Teddington Road from these three properties, *Oak Villa* was demolished and replaced with a substantial five-bay two-storey house called *The Moorings*. To fit onto its narrow plot, the property was turned sideways with its narrower end towards the river and with the principal rooms opening onto a river-facing terrace and balcony.

Just downstream, another redevelopment was taking place as the original *Denbigh Lodge* (Number 34 Lower Teddington Road) was replaced by a new house bearing the same name.

Infill was taking place in Station Road too as Number 5a/b was built in the garden of *Abermaed* (11 Seymour Road). The new property, originally planned as a single house, was remodelled as a set of apartments - the first of many to be created in this area.

The biggest single project took place towards the end of the 1930's with the creation of Monmouth Avenue. As seen earlier, the owners of Numbers 12 and 14 Glamorgan Road had purchased additional land behind their properties from the executors of Lee and Lavers-Smith. Twenty years later, the first part of their investment was being realised.

Monmouth Avenue was a clever exercise in optimising use of the available space. From the outset, it was conceived as a cul-de-sac emanating off Glamorgan Road beside Wood Dalling (Number 12) and ending after 100 yards in a generous-sized turning circle. The overall building site was laid out as a flower with a stalk, with six "petal-shaped" wedged plots radiating off the flower head and a further five plots arranged along the stalk. The orientation of the whole was such that it fitted within the garden at the side and rear of Wood Dalling together with the empty plot behind the rear gardens of Numbers 16 - 22 Glamorgan Road.

The developer was Robert Wake & Co, a builder from Kingston who himself occupied the first property to be completed in 1938. All the properties were to be bungalows - the first in this area of Hampton Wick - though whether this was to meet a specific demand or whether to avoid objections to planning permission is not clear. It seems that the original intention had been to complete all eleven properties in one phase, but the second world war interrupted the project and in the event only five were completed by 1939.

One project that *did* get completed just before the outbreak of the war was the demolition and replacement of Number 10 Seymour Road by a three-storey block containing 10 flats, in a council housing development undertaken by Twickenham Borough.

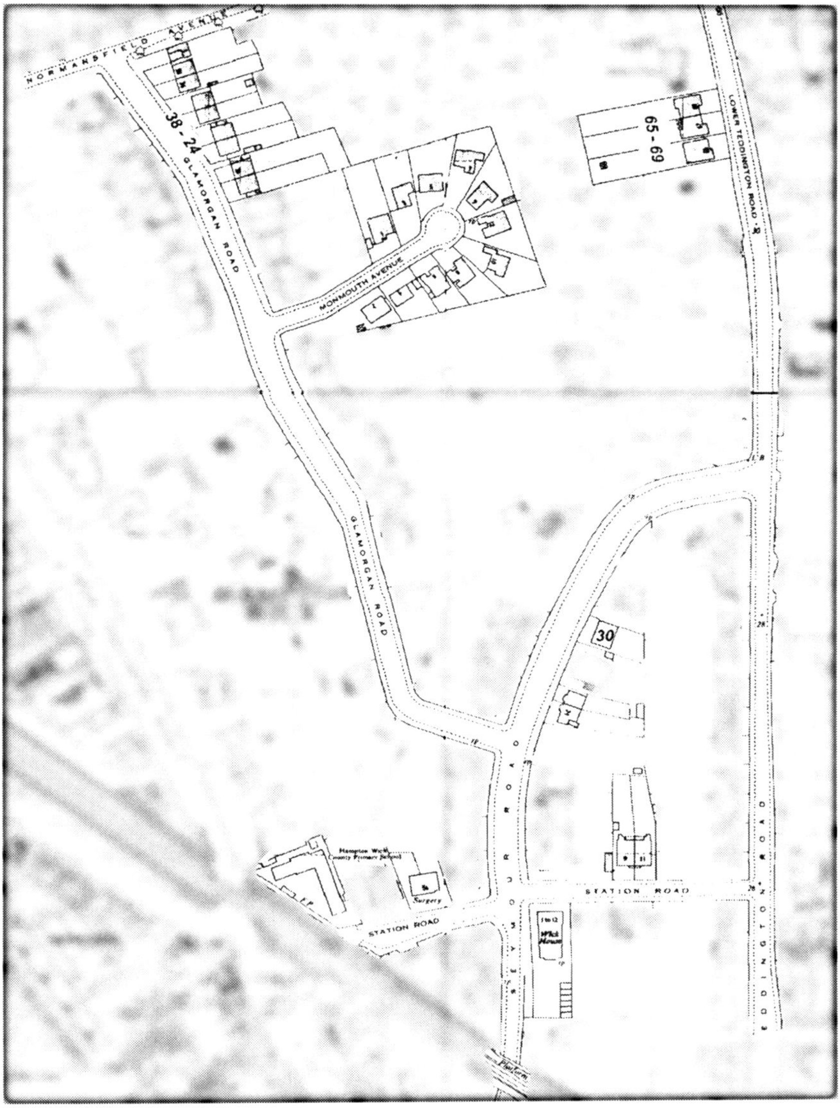

above: Developments in The Elms Park Estate between the wars were mainly focused on the north-eastern end of Glamorgan Road.

The 1940's and 1950's

There was no new building undertaken in The Elms Park Estate area during the second world war, but neither was there a great deal of damage or destruction of buildings either. Given the proximity of the Hawker Aircraft Factory (the Hurricane fighter was designed and built in Kingston), the National Physics Laboratory (where the 'bouncing bomb' and several other key programmes were developed) and the presence of two and a half thousand troops camped in Bushy Park during the later stages of the conflict, Hampton Wick was certainly close to some prime targets. It might therefore be expected to have suffered serious damage (as happened to neighbouring Teddington). With one notable exception, the fact that it got away so relatively lightly was either due to luck or the consummate skill of the Luftwaffe bomb aimers.

The exception was the loss of *The Elms* mansion, destroyed by incendiary bombing in 1943 with a consequence for the area that was to be far-reaching. It seems that the site of the mansion and much of the rest of the open space remaining to the north and north west was purchased by Middlesex County Council. It is believed that the disused quarry was probably used as landfill for rubble from the Teddington bomb destruction. The entire area was then set aside for future County Council use. It became wooded and overgrown, and parts were a favourite stopping place for gypsies and travellers.

One project that was unaffected by these events was Monmouth Avenue and building resumed, the remaining six plots being filled between 1949 and 1959.

The immediate post-war period saw a marked increase in the number of houses in The Elms Park Estate that were converted for multiple occupation and later into self-contained flats. One such candidate for conversion was *Moiravale* (Number 26 Lower Teddington Road) and plans were submitted for approval (see page 23). However the developer, Harold Venables, also had ambitions to make fuller use of the rest of site and converted the stable/garage block into accommodation called *The Courtyard* (1950) and built *River Garth* (1951) on a plot carved out of the northern part of the garden. The final piece of his jigsaw - a block of three flats in the south-east corner - was not put in place until 1960 with the building of *Thames Reach*.

Seymour Court was built in 1957 on the one remaining plot that Richard Starkey had left unoccupied, opposite the end of Glamorgan Road. The development was a two-storey block containing four flats. An similarly-configured building *Glamorgan Court* was created in the side garden of 3 Glamorgan Road in 1959. The next decade would see these developments joined by several other purpose-built blocks of flats.

The 1960's to 1980's

This was a period of intense building activity including several large schemes which have had a major impact on the character of the area that was originally The Elms Park Estate. Headlines of the period include the building of two schools and two Care Homes, the creation of the Broom Park estate (with a total of 147 properties, of which 54 are within the Hampton Wick parish boundary) and a 16-unit development of flats in Glamorgan Road.

Middlesex County Council had reserved large areas both on the north west of Lower Teddington Road and across the parish boundary on Broom Road in Teddington for their future needs. Their forward planning came to fruition with the completion of three schools within four years: *Teddington Secondary School* (1962) on the old sewerage farm in Broom Road together with *Hampton Wick Infants and Nursery School* (1964) and *St John the Baptist Junior School* (1965) on the former The Elms Park Estate. Until now, Normansfield Avenue had been nothing more than a leafy lane, very little upgraded from the footpath that had followed this route for centuries. The Council widened and tarred the road, which now provided an important access to the new schools. Their arrival not only changed the vibrancy and traffic patterns of the area, but also provided a much-needed increase in local school facilities and capacity. It seems amazing that the cramped buildings they left behind on the High Street and Station Road could have accommodated so many pupils but there are still many residents of Hampton Wick who have happy memories of their school-days in the old premises.

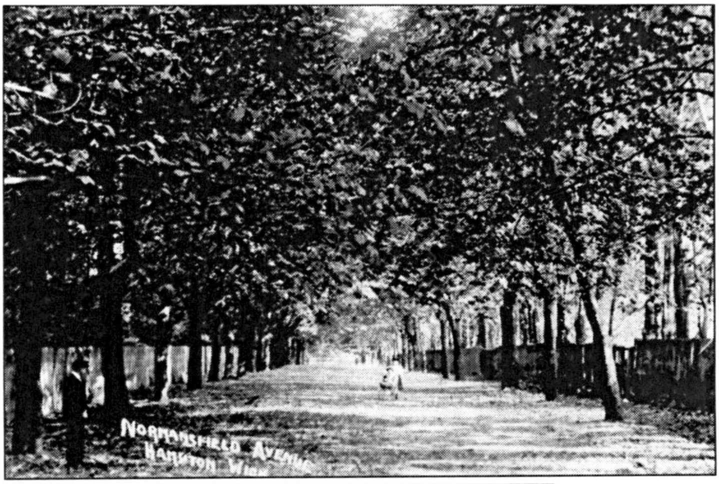

above: Normansfield Avenue c 1910

The creation of Broom Park in the early 1970's, opposite the Infants School on Lower Teddington Road, was the largest single building project in Hampton Wick since Park Court was erected in the mid 1930's. Whereas the latter comprised 71 flats, Broom Park involved building 108 houses together with a high rise block containing 39 flats. The whole site was created by combining the grounds of just three properties: *Riverbank* and St *Helen's* (36 and 38 Lower Teddington Road) together with Chesfield, the largest of the three. All the properties had originally been built around 1860 by Silas Galsworthy (see page 8) although Chesfield was extensively rebuilt in the 1881.

Meanwhile, two other new buildings were similarly to change the profile of Glamorgan Road. Two of Starkey's 1880's properties - Numbers 5 *Meadowside* and 9 *Glamorgan House* - were about to be redeveloped. Both properties were located on large plots and not surprisingly, therefore, the two properties together had been the subject of previous redevelopment proposals. Charles Batten, who moved into *Glamorgan House* in 1928 conceived an impressive four-storey Art Deco complex to contain 48 (later reduced to 40) flats. The plans were approved by Hampton Wick UDC in 1936, but the project was never built - at least, not in Glamorgan Road: the project eventually materialised as Park Court! Subsequent proposals concerned the two properties separately. *Glamorgan House* was demolished in 1967 following the death of its last resident who had lived there for 36 years. It was replaced by *Lindley Court*, a development containing 16 flats each with their own garage. They had a typical 1960's design with multiple interlocking blocks of brick, glass and wood cladding and single pitched roofs. This provides an interesting contrast with what might have been (see below).

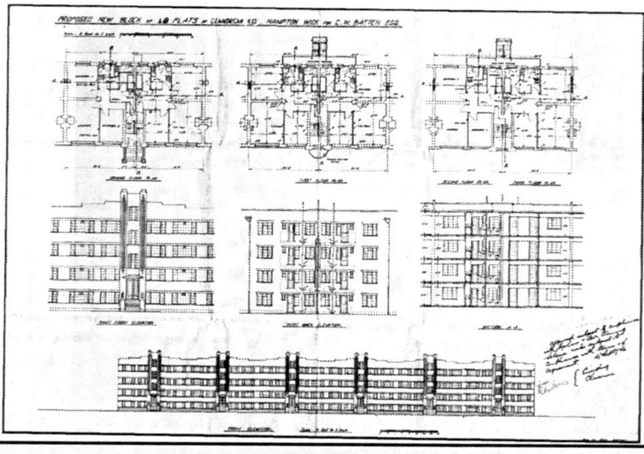

above: A 1930's proposal for a block of 48 flats on Glamorgan Road, never built here but eventually materialised as Park Court.

Meanwhile, New Ideal Homesteads of Epsom, who since the 1930's had been one of London's most prolific developers, had recently created 12 new properties in Beverley Road (off Upper Teddington Road). The area backed on to the land occupied by *Meadowside*. In February 1959 New Ideal submitted a plan for the redevelopment of *Meadowside* and its curtilage as a complex of 18 flats of identical "Abbey" type design to those in Beverley Road. Although immediately approved by the Council, the developer changed his mind and returned in May 1959 with a fresh plan for three semi-detached and two detached houses. This was again approved by the Council in June 1959. This plan was never implemented. A year later a revised, lesser scheme - for two houses and a bungalow - and which used just the garden leaving *Meadowside* itself intact was submitted and yet again approved by the Council in July 1960. This finally resulted in the building of a "Lynton", a "Newton" and a "Queenbury" - three stock designs from the New Ideal Homesteads catalogue. These were designated by the Post Office as being Numbers 3a, 3b and 3c Glamorgan Road even though it was Number 5 that had donated the land. More ambitious plans, and a new developer, were now in place for *Meadowside* though this time the Council was proving stiff opposition and it was not until the 1970's that it was finally demolished (or sabotaged?) and replaced by a development of 24 flats. These were built as sheltered accommodation and known as *Robert Black House* which opened in 1978.

Until now, the only large-scale provision of care for the elderly was at the Council-run home at *Moiravale*. However, *Robert Black House* itself was predated by three years by *Orione House* a care home run by The Sons of Divine Providence

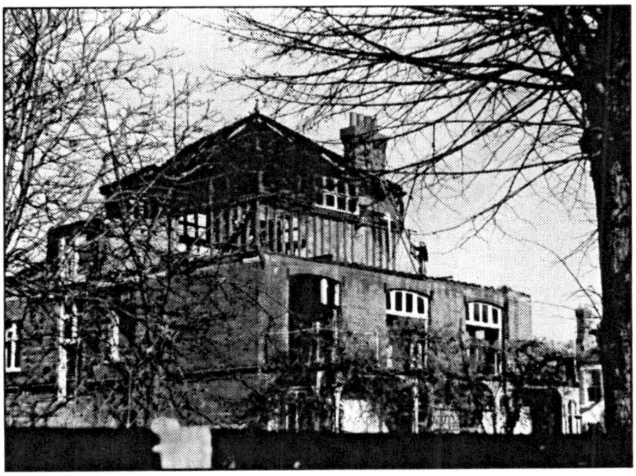

above: *Meadowside* was devastated by a mysterious fire which made its demolition an inevitability. Sabotage was suspected but never proven.

(see page 108) This had been built on the land formerly occupied by Numbers 12 and 14 Station Road, two of William Woods mansions of the 1860's.

Other redevelopments of the period included Raeburn Close, an 8-unit maisonette-style development that replaced Raeburn House at 71 Lower Teddington Road and Winterton Court a ten-unit block of flats at 43/45 Lower Teddington Road which replaced 7 & 8 *Lansdowne Terrace.*

The most significant " infill" was at 36 Lower Teddington Road. This was an extensive house built in 1962 by Sir Donald Gosling (see page 121) on the site of the former Cambridge House, another of the 1860 portfolio of mansions created by Silas Galsworthy. The original property was built for Thomas Barker who lived there with his three sisters. When the youngest sister died in her 80's sometime around 1904, the house remained empty and then disappeared off the map altogether - literally - since the building is not shown at all on the 1915 OS edition. Its very large - and desirable - plot remained empty until Sir Donald's arrival over fifty years later. What happened in between currently remains a mystery.

1990's to Present Day

In the last thirty years, The Elms Park Estate has witnessed the creation of three new roads, the building of three infill properties and the redevelopment of a further five existing properties.

Baygrove Mews was established in the back garden of Number 2 Upper Teddington Road. Access is provided via a driveway in Glamorgan Road, running beside *Glamorgan Court.* Built in 1996, the development consists of three 4-bedroom mews houses. The architect pays passing tribute to Richard Starkey's nearby properties by using prominent bargeboards with a trefoil pattern on the two gable ends and adopting a design for the central porch that is similar to Starkey's characteristic design.

Lexington Place, completed in 2005, owes its existence to that astute land purchase previously noted that had taken place around 1920. Otto Secretan, a shipbroker who lived in *Eversleigh*, 10 Glamorgan Road had purchased extra land at the rear of his property which he added to his existing garden. Now, his successors were able to obtain planning permission to develop this very extensive plot to provide three townhouses and eight flats all accessed via a new road running off Seymour Road beside *Fairlea.* In addition, the side garden of

Eversleigh was included in the scheme, allowing a further six-bedroom house to be built - Number 10a Glamorgan Road. In a protracted negotiation, the council sought to ensure that the developer retained as many of the mature trees on the site as was possible.

Two years later, a very similar development was being planned by the successors of Ralph Burdett, Otto Secretan's one-time neighbour and owner of *St Mary's*, 12 Glamorgan Road. Like Secretan, Burdett had also added his 1920's purchase to his existing back garden and, by 2007, the total plot was now considered sufficient to support two three-storey five-bedroom houses and one one-bedroom bungalow. This development, now known as *Aspen Close*, is accessed from Glamorgan Road via a drive that runs between Numbers 12 and 10a.

The first of the three infill projects of this period started in 1979, when a developer successfully applied for planning permission to erect a four storey link block, starting at first floor level, between Nos. 37 and 39 Lower Teddington Road to provide an additional three one-bedroom flats and provision of an access drive and four parking spaces. The project was completed in 1981.

In 1987, permission was granted to build a two-storey house on the corner of Monmouth Avenue and Glamorgan Road, formerly part of the garden of 2 Monmouth Avenue

Almost twenty years later, permission was given for a new two-storey three-bedroom house in the garden of *Abermaed*, Number 2 Glamorgan Road.

Certainly the most recent and arguably the most ingenious of the infill projects in this period involved a wedge-shaped plot, located between Number 2 Station Road and a row of three lock-up garages abutting the railway embankment. In 2001, the developer sought permission to erect a detached building either as a single dwelling house or for use as three flats. Permission was refused and a subsequent appeal was dismissed, both times on the grounds that a separate building would look incongruous. In an admirable riposte to this objection, the developer returned with plans for a semi-detached building which was an exact replica of its now-terraced neighbour at Number 2. Permission was granted.

Redevelopments took place at 12 Glamorgan Road (1992) where the former coach house of *St Mary's* was converted into a house and at 4a Glamorgan Road (2006) where a bungalow was converted into a three-bedroom two-storey house. A more major redevelopment took place at the former *Moiravale*, 26 Lower Teddington Road and was completed in 2006. The new development, named *Thameside Place*, involved remodelling the original house with its early 19th. century origins and building a new structure in the ground to provide a total of 13 high-class properties for people aged over 55.

The redevelopment of the site containing a bungalow at 4a Glamorgan Road brought to light some interesting planning principles. The original 2005 application to demolish the existing 1962 three-bedroom bungalow and replace it with a two-storey three-bedroom house was refused on the grounds that "by reason of the absence of evidence to demonstrate that the existing building is incapable of improvement or conversion ... the lack of any substantial housing gain ... would represent a non-sustainable development making inefficient use of urban land". The applicants then submitted a scheme for the "construction of additional floor and new roof to existing bungalow and new front facade" which was deemed acceptable.

More recently still, the old primary school buildings in the corner of Station Road were finally redeveloped after a protracted planning process. The site is roughly triangular in shape with a small frontage onto Station Road. After the primary school moved to Normansfield Avenue, the old buildings were used as warehousing and offices. An application in 2000 to build ten flats housed in two buildings was refused (and a subsequent appeal dismissed) on the grounds that the proposal would result in the loss of an employment site. A fresh application in 2007 overcame this objection by reserving the ground floor of the four-storey building for commercial use. However the council still refused permission based mainly on the size and height of the building but the application was upheld at appeal and the present building was completed in 2011.

Wick Lodge, 22 Lower Teddington Road reused the site and the name of the previous bungalow property built in the 1920's.

The latest two redevelopments are, at the time of writing, being completed. Number 12 Glamorgan Road is currently being converted into a pair of five- and four-bedroom family houses.

Meanwhile, Number 2 Seymour Road was being offered for sale in March 2012 as a 16-bedroom house for £850,000. The small-print confessed that what was actually being sold was an eleven-room property "with consent to demolish existing building & construct a new building comprising of four x 1 bedroom flats, three x 2 bedroom flats with scope for an additional flat (and) six possible micro-studio units with separate access".

In fact, the property being replaced is one of those with which this account of the development of The Elms Park Estate started - *Westbourne Villa*, built in 1862, was the first house to be built on what was to become Seymour Road.

Having thus come full circle on the history of the development of the whole area of Hampton Wick east of the High Street, it is now appropriate to take to the streets themselves and view the richness and variety of the houses that currently line the pavements.

PART TWO: EXPLORING THE PRESENT - walking guides

There is so much interest and enjoyment to be had by walking the streets of Hampton Wick with eyes open, curiosity aroused and time to see and enjoy the surroundings. Satisfying that curiosity is the purpose of the remainder of this book.

It is probable that most people would think of a street as being primarily a thoroughfare - a place of passage from one location to another. Their principal focus is on getting swiftly and safely to their destination and the immediate surroundings are of little consequence. However a street is also a public space, bordered by frontages of the (mainly) private properties - frequently built on both sides of the street. If these properties are of interest then the street becomes more like a corridor in a museum or gallery - a place where you are more inclined to saunter along, pausing to examine and enjoy one exhibit before moving on to the next. We are fortunate that our streets so amply repay time invested in such an approach.

The second half of this book is therefore specifically designed to help those wishing to go out and see what has been bequeathed to us by the former residents, architects, developers, financers and legislators who helped to create today's Hampton Wick. The material is arranged as a series of five walks (see over), each beginning with a brief overview of the street and its history together with a detailed street plan. The walk starts at house number 1 and describes in words and pictures exactly what is to be seen on each side of the road. At any point along the walk, the left hand page refers to the (odd-numbered) building(s) on the walker's left and vice versa. The walker's attention is drawn to English Heritage Listed Buildings and to Buildings of Townscape Merit as designated by the London Borough of Richmond upon Thames. Where appropriate the walker will also be referred to relevant material in the first part of the book.

	Area	Page	Duration
1	Lower Teddington Road	85	60 minutes
2	Station Road	125	15 minutes
3	Seymour Road	133	40 minutes
4	Glamorgan Road	144	30 minutes
5	Monmouth Avenue	158	10 minutes

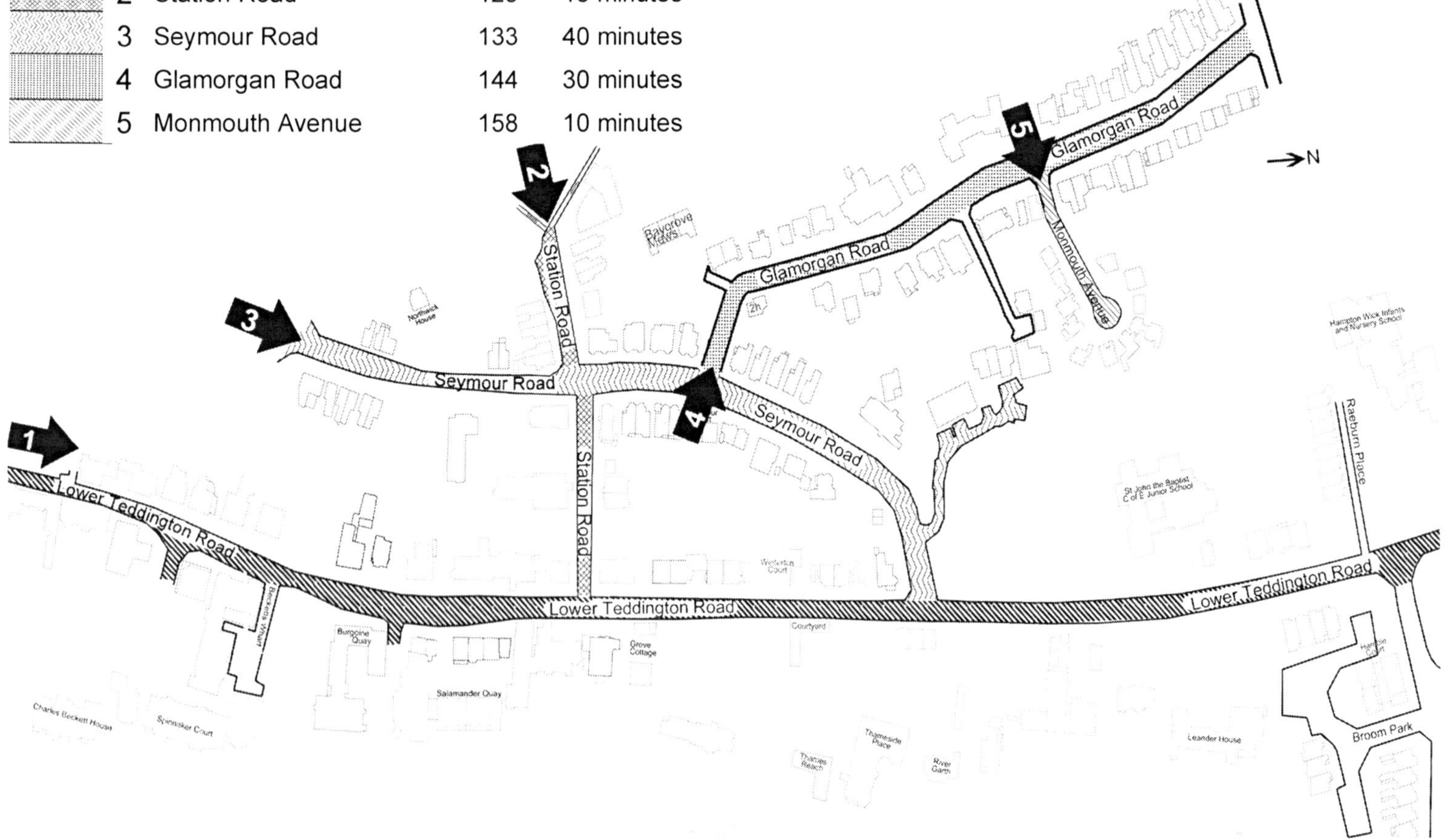

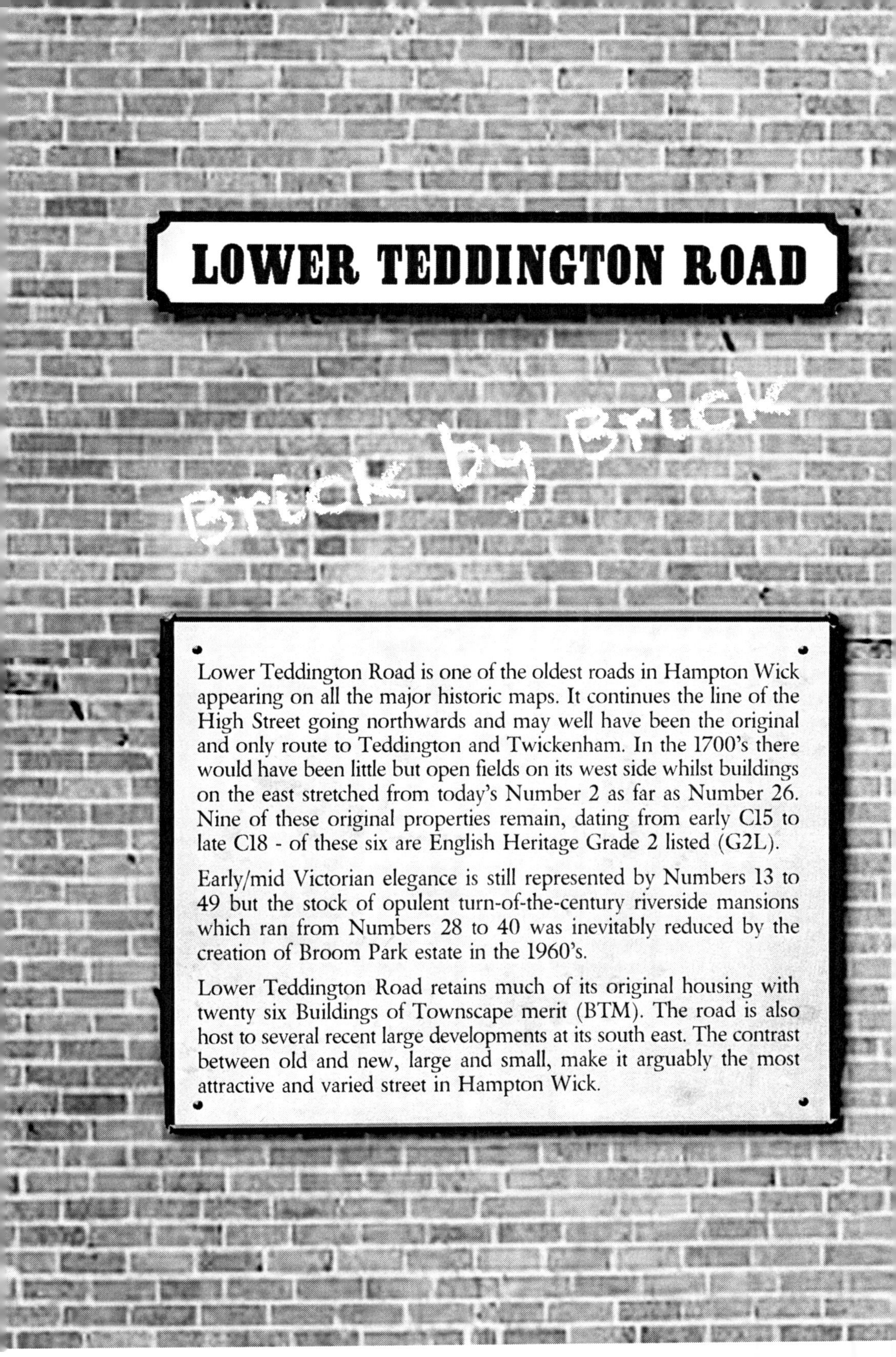
LOWER TEDDINGTON ROAD
Brick by Brick
Lower Teddington Road is one of the oldest roads in Hampton Wick appearing on all the major historic maps. It continues the line of the High Street going northwards and may well have been the original and only route to Teddington and Twickenham. In the 1700's there would have been little but open fields on its west side whilst buildings on the east stretched from today's Number 2 as far as Number 26. Nine of these original properties remain, dating from early C15 to late C18 - of these six are English Heritage Grade 2 listed (G2L).
Early/mid Victorian elegance is still represented by Numbers 13 to 49 but the stock of opulent turn-of-the-century riverside mansions which ran from Numbers 28 to 40 was inevitably reduced by the creation of Broom Park estate in the 1960's.
Lower Teddington Road retains much of its original housing with twenty six Buildings of Townscape merit (BTM). The road is also host to several recent large developments at its south east. The contrast between old and new, large and small, make it arguably the most attractive and varied street in Hampton Wick.

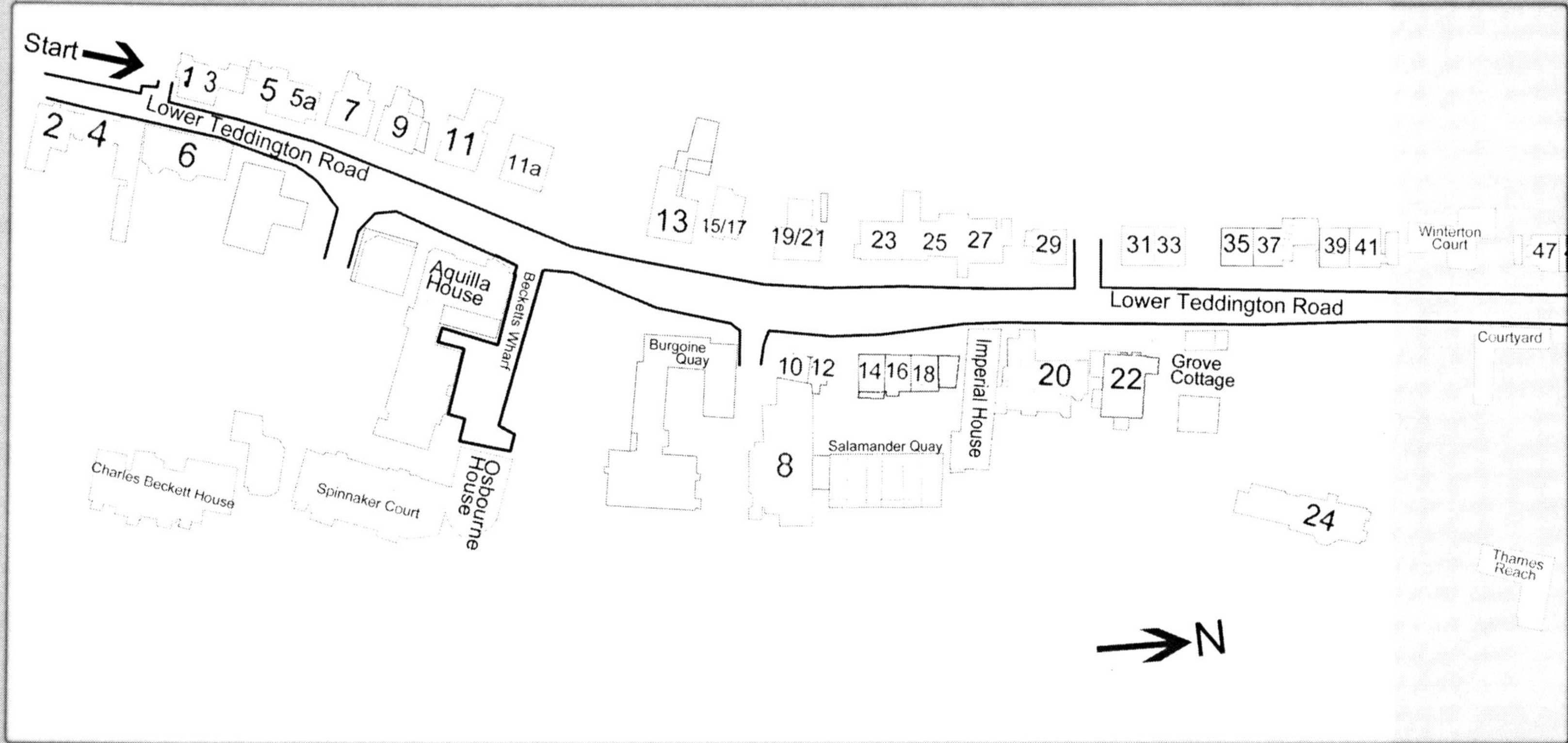
Start
Lower Teddington Road
1 3
5 5a
7
9
11
11a
2 4
6
13
15/17
19/21
23
25
27
29
31 33
35 37
39 41
Winterton Court
47
Lower Teddington Road
Courtyard
Aquilla House
Becketts Wharf
Osbourne House
Burgoine Quay
10 12
14 16 18
Imperial House
20
22
Grove Cottage
8
Salamander Quay
Charles Beckett House
Spinnaker Court
24
Thames Reach
N

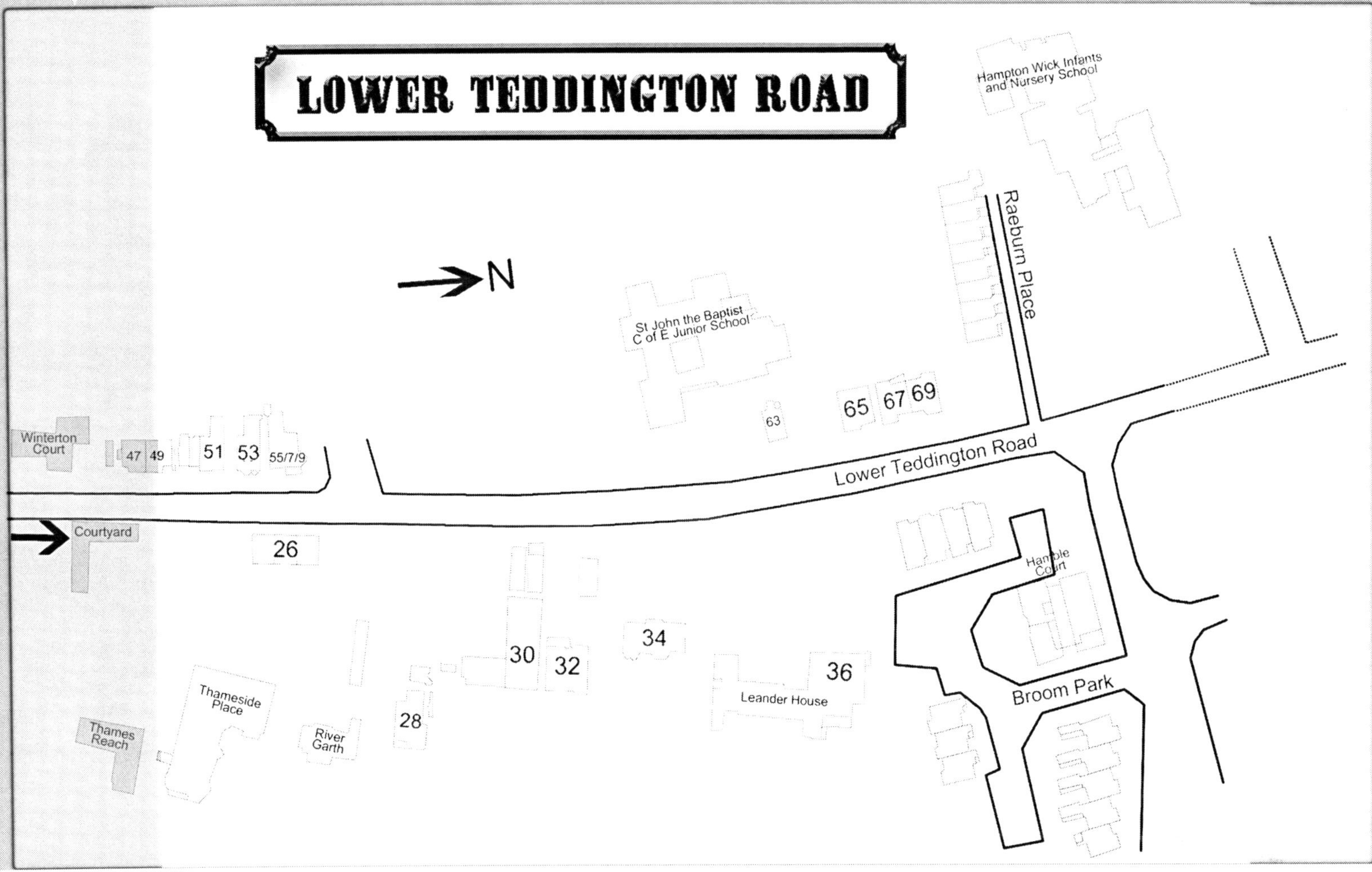
LOWER TEDDINGTON ROAD
N
Hampton Wick Infants and Nursery School
Raeburn Place
St John the Baptist C of E Junior School
65
67
69
63
Winterton Court
47
49
51
53
55/7/9
Lower Teddington Road
Courtyard
26
Hample Court
30
32
34
36
Leander House
Broom Park
Thameside Place
Thames Reach
River Garth
28

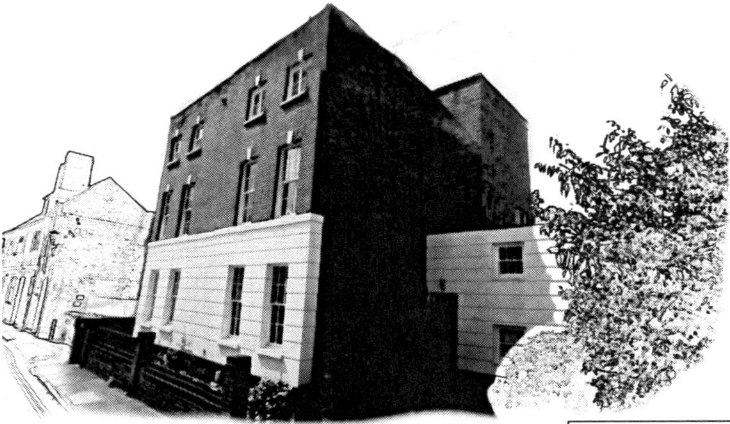

Building of Townscape Merit

above: *Home Lea* and *Home Villa*,

1 and 3 Lower Teddington Road

Built around 1800 by Edward Chitts. Ryley Barnes ran a school in Number 3 during the 1830's. Theophilus Smith lived there in the 1870's and was also a schoolmaster though probably at the Endowed School on the High Street. Rosina Bates used both properties as a Lodging House in the 1880's. William Turner, son of the High Street bootmaker, lived in Number 3 from 1914..

The unusual photograph below was taken in early 1904 when a section of the High Street starting opposite The Foresters and running up almost to Seymour Road has just been demolished and the tram tracks are about to be laid. The demolition allowed a rare glimpse of the back of Numbers 1 and 3 Lower Teddington Road. The roof had always been a design problem with this building. Here it is shown with conventional low-pitched twin hipped roofs but it constantly leaked and was eventually removed and replaced with a flat roof.

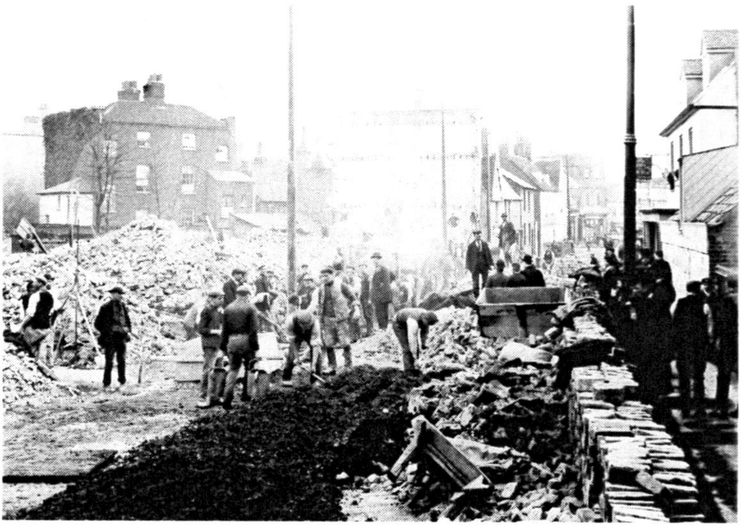

Photo:
WFJ Hodgson
Kingston Camera
Club 1906

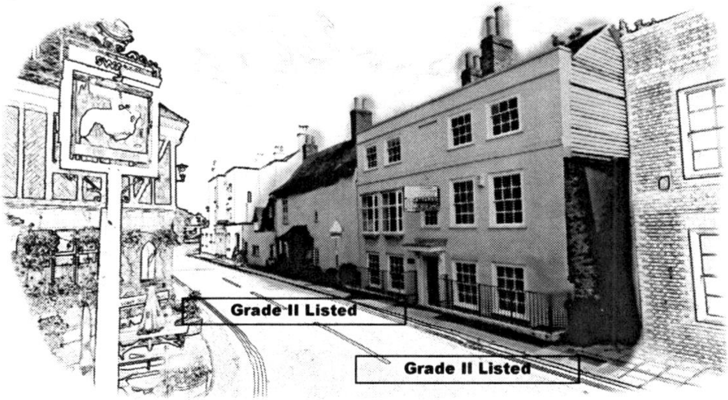

above: *River Cottage* and *Wolsey's Cottage*
2 and 4 Lower Teddington Road

Both timber-framed; *Wolsey's Cottage* is mid to late C16 and *River Cottage* is early-mid C18. English Heritage have suggested that both premises may originally been part of the same larger property (see page 53). The cottages were built to face the river explaining the lack of windows on Wolsey Cottage. Early photos also show most windows on *River Cottage* blocked out to reduce window tax imposed by William III in 1696.

below: *Rivermead*, 6 Lower Teddington Road

Early C19. Again, the roadside facade is actually the back view of the property which originally had orchards running down to the river (see page 45). The gardens were extensive and ran almost as far north as the present railway line.

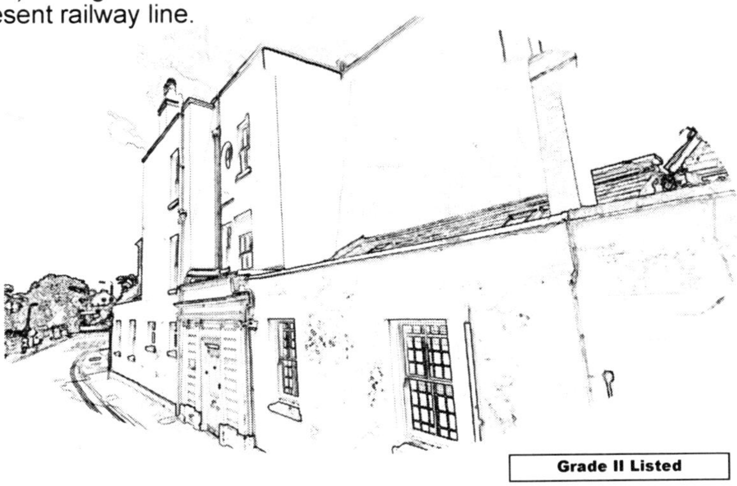

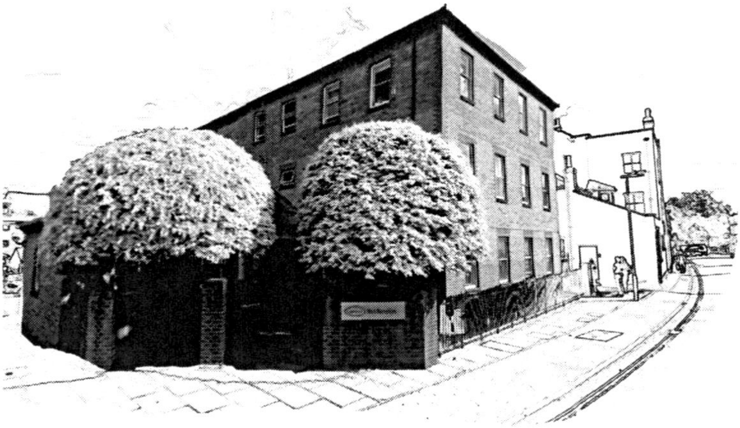

above: *Hamon House,* 6a Lower Teddington Road

Built 1985. Once the UK headquarters of Hamon Films (despite their name, they were not a media company - they made components for cooling towers). The building is now used as a Reception and extra office accommodation for Added Value, a brand development and marketing insight consultancy and part of the WPP group currently based in *Riverside*.

below: 1 Becketts Place

Built around 1990. Recently vacated by Gazprom, Russia's natural-gas export monopoly.

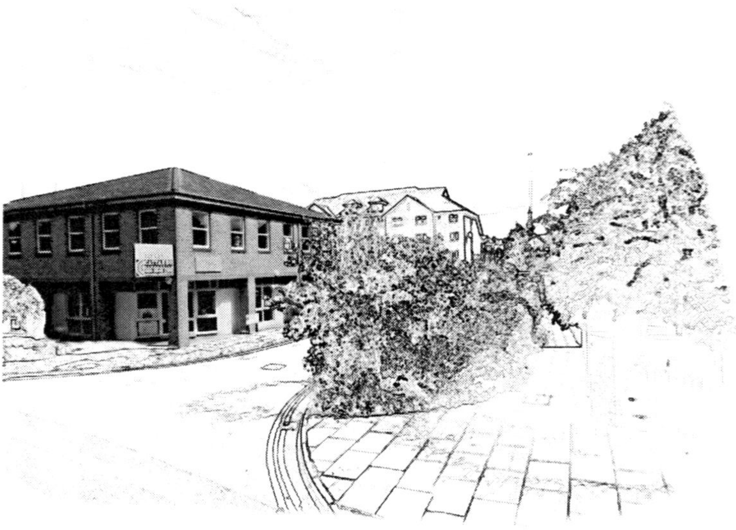

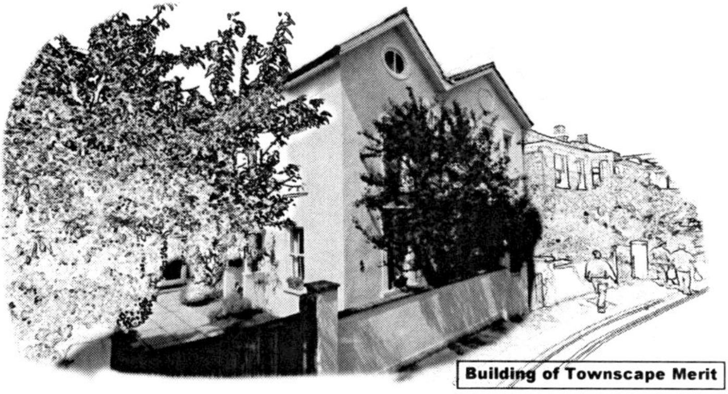

above: *Woodlands*, 5 and 5a Lower Teddington Road
Built around 1870, originally as one property, it was run as a boarding house from 1896 to 1909. It was divided into two from 1925.

below: *Edgcumbe* and *Trevarra*,
7 and 9 Lower Teddington Road
Built in the early to mid 1880's, the original house-names share an apparent Cornish origin though why remains a mystery since the properties had different owners from the outset. Number 7 is nowadays divided into five flats.

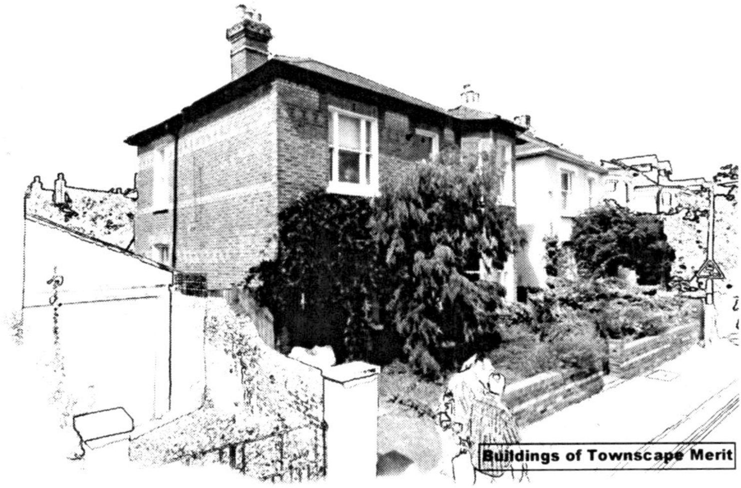

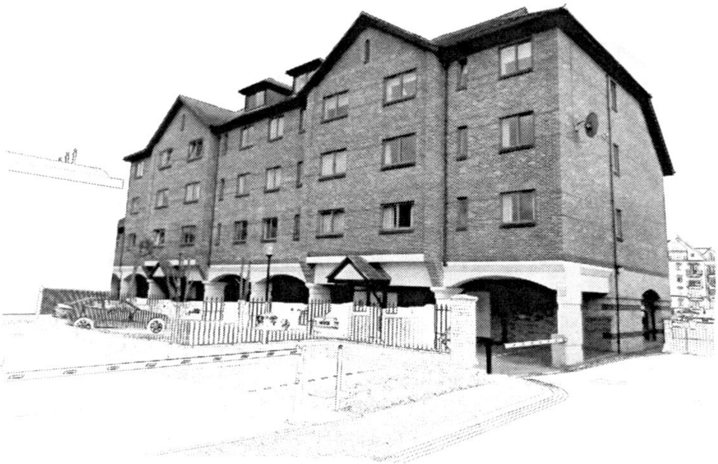

above: Spinnaker Court, 1a Becketts Place

Built in 1990 by Alfred McAlpine, the development includes a range of riverside offices on the ground floor and 20 flats on the upper storeys, each with a balcony overlooking the river (below).

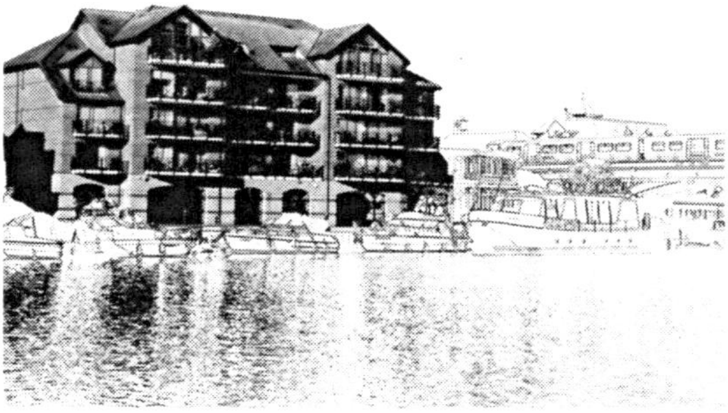

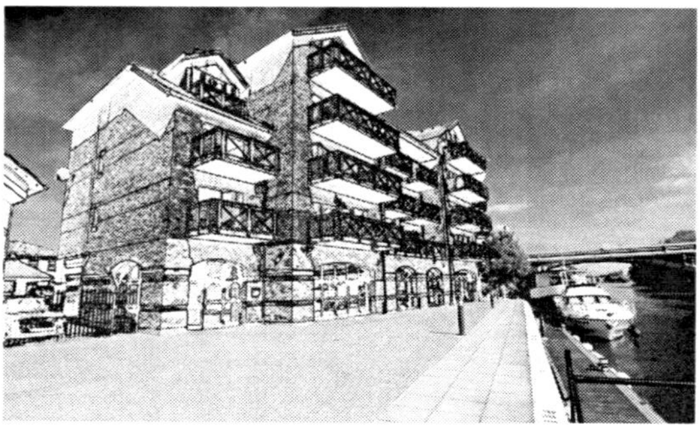

The River Walk

(bottom left and right)

Both developments in Becketts Place were designed to take advantage of the river views. However, as a result of conditions inserted into various Planning Permissions issued by Richmond Council over the years for this stretch of The Thames, this is no longer a residents-only private view - there is now a complete public riverside path stretching from *Riverside* at the northern end to Old Bridge Street at the south. It may be accessed from Beckett Place itself either through the gate between Charles Beckett House (CBH) at Spinnaker Court or, if locked, via a passage passing between CBH and Beckett Place building.

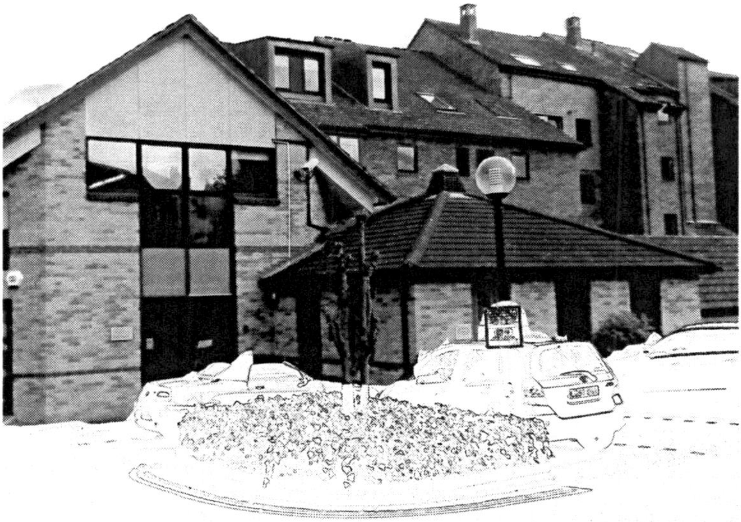

above: **Charles Beckett House and Becketts Place**
Built in 1984 by Higgs & Hill on the original *Rivermead* garden (see page 45), there are 22 flats all facing the river (below). The adjacent building (aka The Boat House) is used as a meeting and training space and was built as part of the Spinnaker Court project.

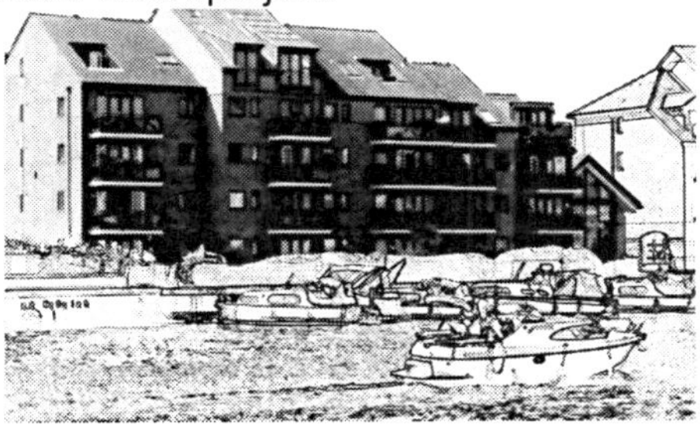

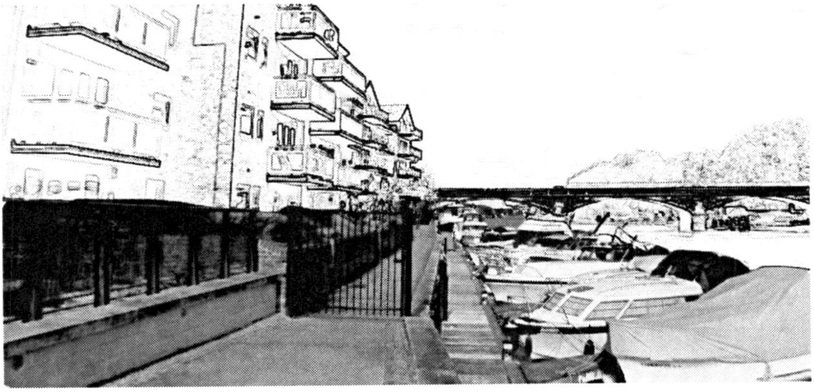

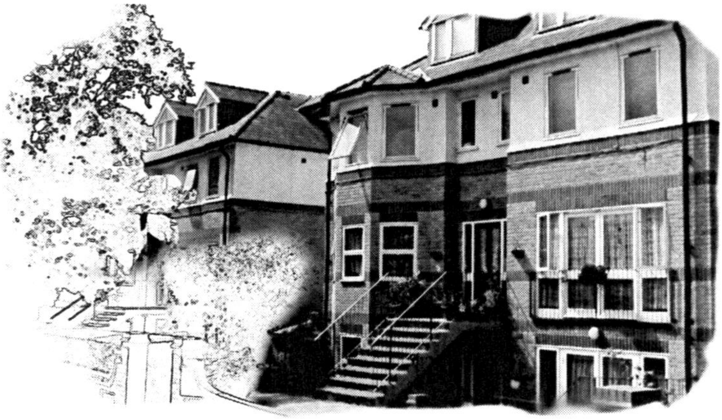

above: **11 and 11a Lower Teddington Road**

Built in 1990 and run by London & Quadrant Group, the properties contain 8 and 11 flats respectively. Excavations during building yielded Roman pottery in the back garden but all traces of a Roman villa had long since vanished.

below: This 1863 map shows the site of the original Number 11, called *Rose Cottage*. Despite the cosy image conjured up by its name, the building had 13 rooms, being another of William Woods' Italianate villas, similar to the houses just the other side of the railway bridge and built at the same time (around 1858). For 80 years, *Rose Cottage* was the home and surgery of Dr. Theodore Gunther and later his son Dr. Hermann Gunther. The building was converted into 3 apartments in 1949 and demolished in 1989.

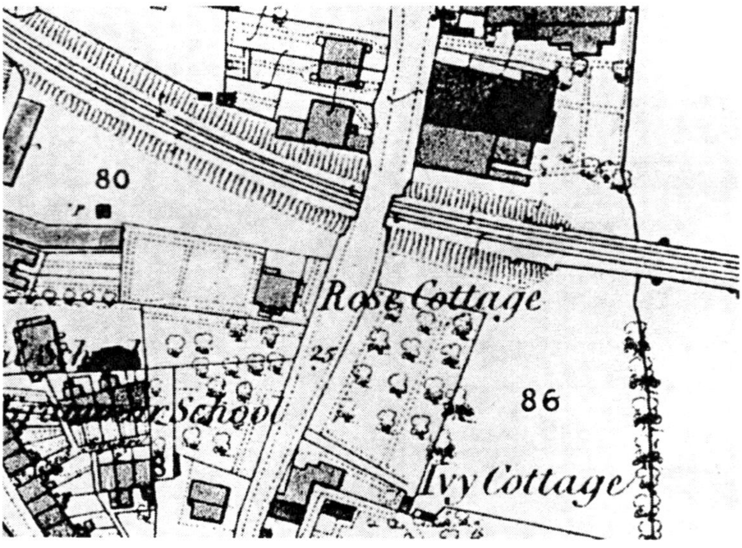

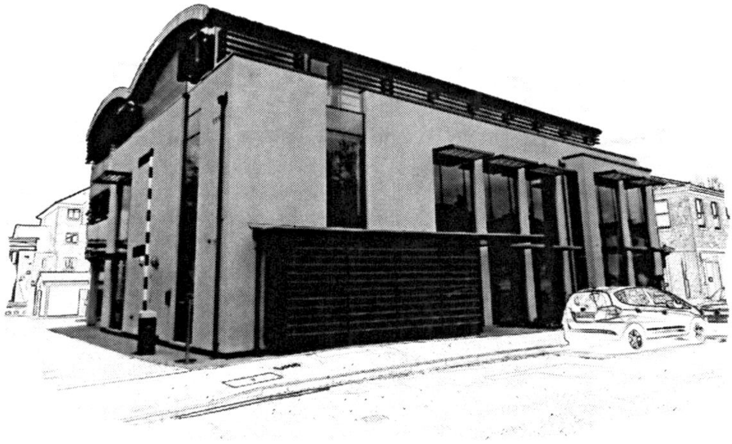

above: *Aquilla House*, 1 and 2 Becketts Wharf
Completed in 2011, this development comprises B1 class offices and 26 flats (including 15 for affordable housing). The offices are currently occupied by Smart Training as their headquarters.

below: *Osbourne House*, 3 Becketts Wharf
Despite its 1930's Art Deco appearance, this is a comparatively recent building. The drum-shaped river facade (inset) is worth seeing - walk down past *Aquilla House* and round the side of *Osbourne House*. Afterwards, walk downstream along the river bank (past the houseboats) to get the best views of *Riverside* (next page) then return to Lower Teddington Road, passing Burgoine House on your left.

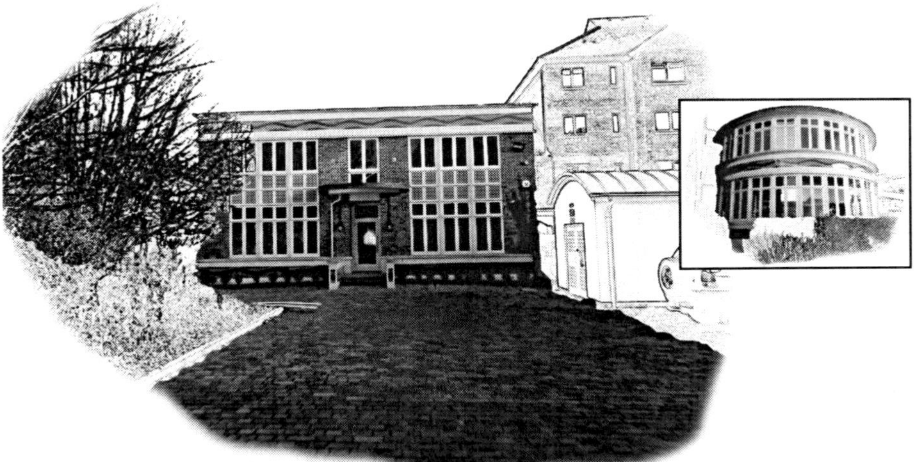

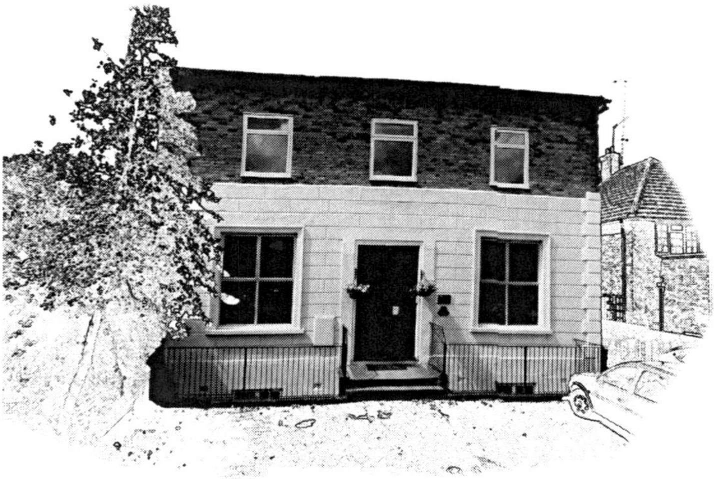

above: *St Mary's*, 13 Lower Teddington Road
Built around 1880, some thirty years later than the other properties on this stretch. It looks curiously out of proportion, the ground floor suggesting the house was planned to be larger than it has finally turned out. The property was converted into a nursing home with 8 beds in 1963 and in 1984 became the head office of the English Delegation of the Sons of Divine Providence. (see box on Page 108). A Day Centre for the Elderly is located in the grounds behind.

1863: The Coming of the Railway

When Kingston upon Thames was finally connected to the rail network, it was by means of a branch line from Twickenham through St Margarets and Teddington. From there, the line arrived at Hampton Wick on an embankment to raise it to the level needed to cross the River Thames. Soon after leaving the station, the railway crosses Lower Teddington Road and almost immediately reaches the first arch of the Kingston Railway Bridge. The bridge was first discussed in 1860 and completed in 1863. With the railway needing to forge a way through the existing residential layout, it is remarkable that the provision of embankments and the crossings of the road and river was achieved with very little disruption: just three properties were acquired and demolished and even these were modest workers' cottages; the total compensation paid for them was less than £0.5m in today's equivalent currency.

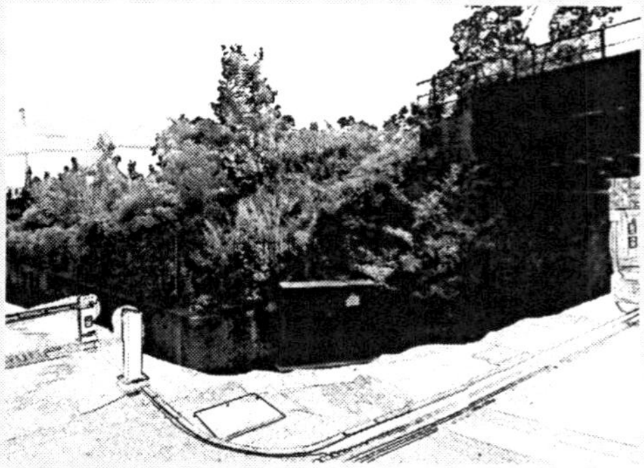

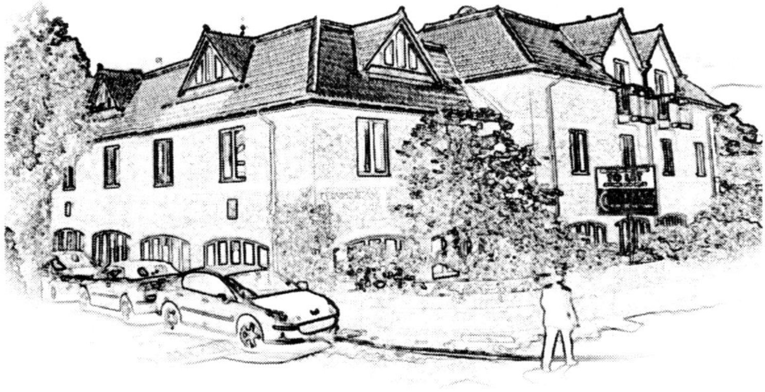

above: 8a Burgoine Quay

Built on the site of three old malthouses (see next page) this office block was opened in 1990. It currently houses several organisations including Brand Learning marketing consultants, Hospitality and Leisure Manpower, an international research, training and consulting group and the offices of the property developers themselves.

below:

Immediately before, the site had been occupied by the Thames Works factory of AVA Ltd. And, before that, by the old Hampton Wick mortuary.

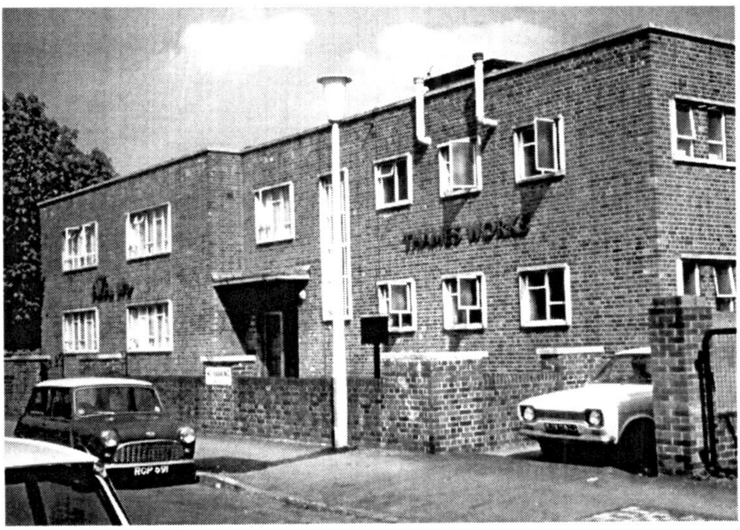

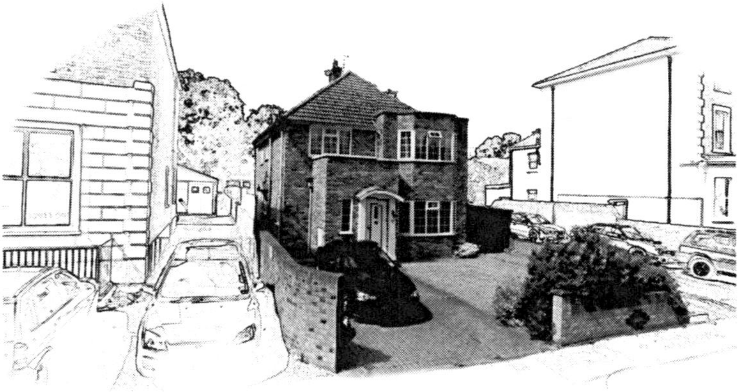

above: **17 and 19 Lower Teddington Road**

These maisonettes were built in 1965, replacing a pair of semi-detached properties known as Lansdowne Villas (see below) similar in proportion to Number 13. Sarah Miller lived in the original property from 1880 and, after her husband died, ran a school for girls up until the outbreak of the First World War.

below: **Lower Teddington Road in the 1920's**

On the immediate right are the facades of the three malthouses (see page 105) that were on the site now occupied by Burgoine House. Posters on the door suggest that Burgoine's were using them as retail premises. The entrance to the boatyard is just beyond. The car is parked outside Number 18 (now Imperial House) which was being used as a marine workshop. Note the loose surface on the road. The building on the immediate left is *Lansdowne Villas* (see above).

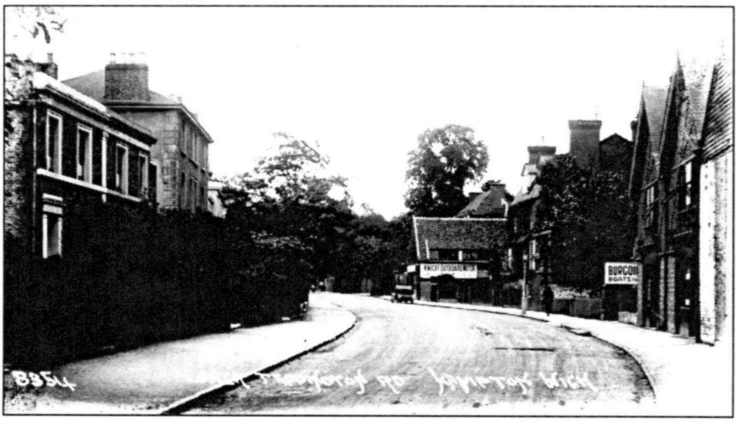

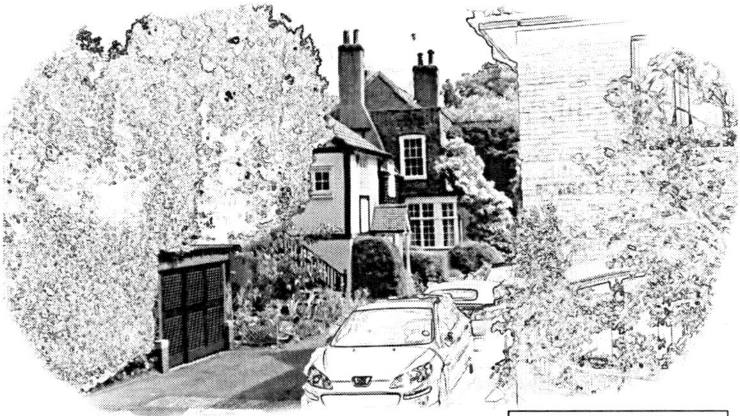

Grade II Listed

above: *Riverside*/Burgoine House,
8 Lower Teddington Road

The original house (now part of a complex of houses and office) dates from the early 1800's and was the home of the maltster who operated the three malthouses that stood on the site now occupied by Burgoine House. In 1870 *Riverside* became Burgoine's Boatyard where for forty years the Burgoine brothers built steamers, launches and sailing craft. The business then concentrated on boat hire and pleasure cruises. Later the family diversified into property development and the whole of the east side of Lower Teddington Road from Number 6 to Number 18 shows the results of their immediately local projects.

Walk down the driveway to the river to appreciate the beauty of the house and its river view (below). Note the gable end of the malthouse which overlooks the houseboat moorings which were once home to the punts, skiffs and pleasure steamers of the original boatyard business (see page 38).

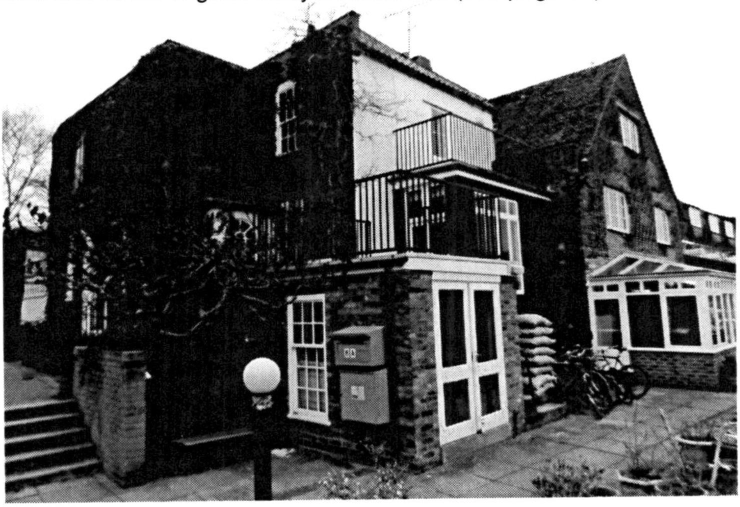

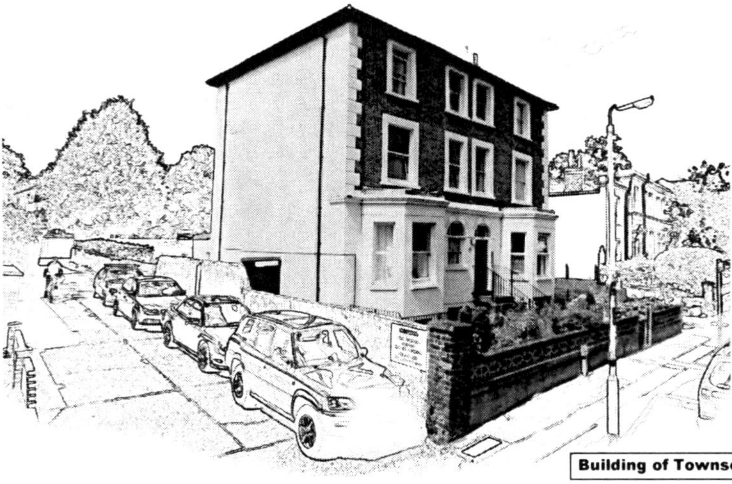

above: *St Stephens*, 19/21 Lower Teddington Road
This villa block - originally known as *Laburnham Villas* was part of William Wood's first phase of building after he acquired Seymour Close in 1850 (see page 58). Quoins (cornerstones) were a device used by architects and builders to give the impression of strength and firmness to the outline of a building. In this case they contrast markedly against the brick facade.

Malthouse Cottages, 10 and 12 Lower Teddington Road; *Salamander Quay* and *Old Castle Wharf* (opposite, top to bottom)

1. These two cottages were used for workers in the nearby malthouses and were rebuilt around 1890. Walk down the drive on their left to get a better view of:

2. *Salamander Quay* - a block of twelve flats and maisonettes arranged on three levels. These were created in the late 1970's by remodelling the original 1925 *Riverside* Flats development which had in turn been built on the land previously used by Burgoine's boat building yard (see page 40).

3. *Old Castle Wharf* was the name used for many years to describe the labyrinth of accommodation and small artists/film studios at the river end of The Old Malthouse.

A small passage running up the side of this latter building leads back to Lower Teddington Road.

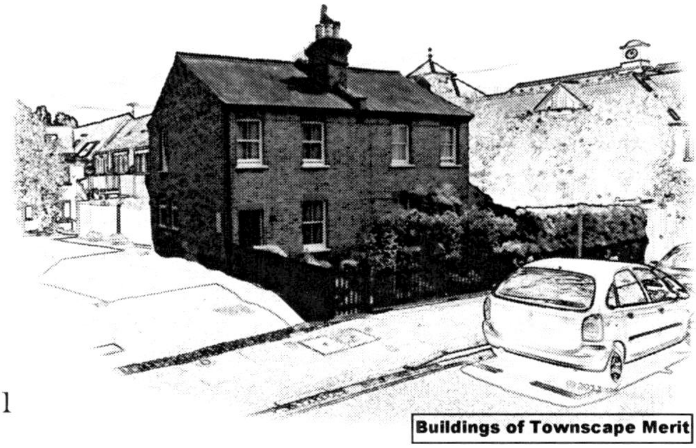

1

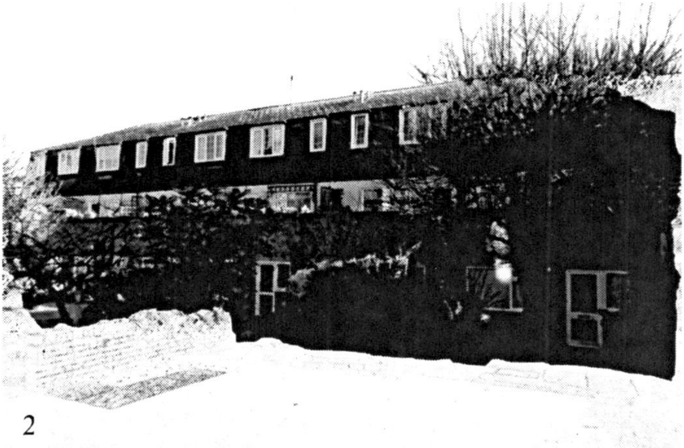

2

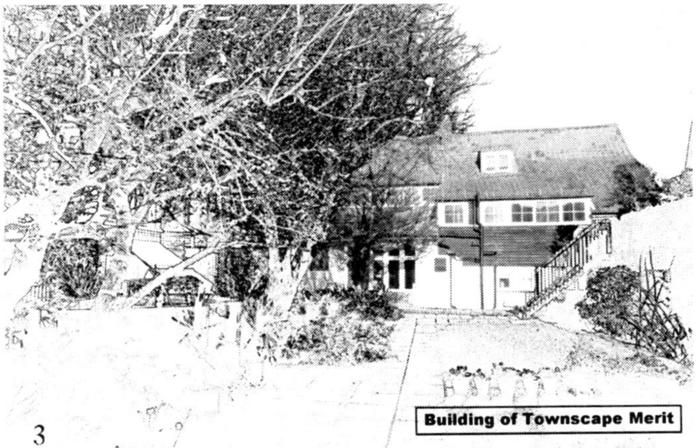

3

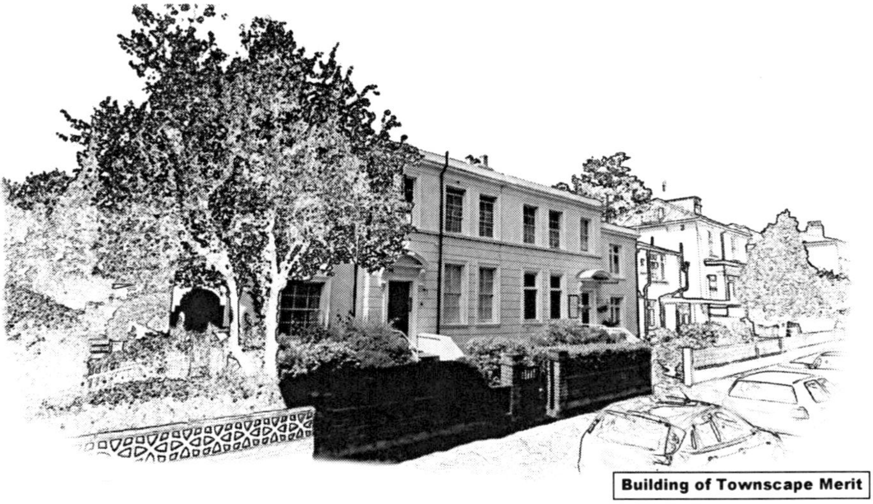

above and below: 23 and 25 Lower Teddington Road and a famous resident
For details see opposite

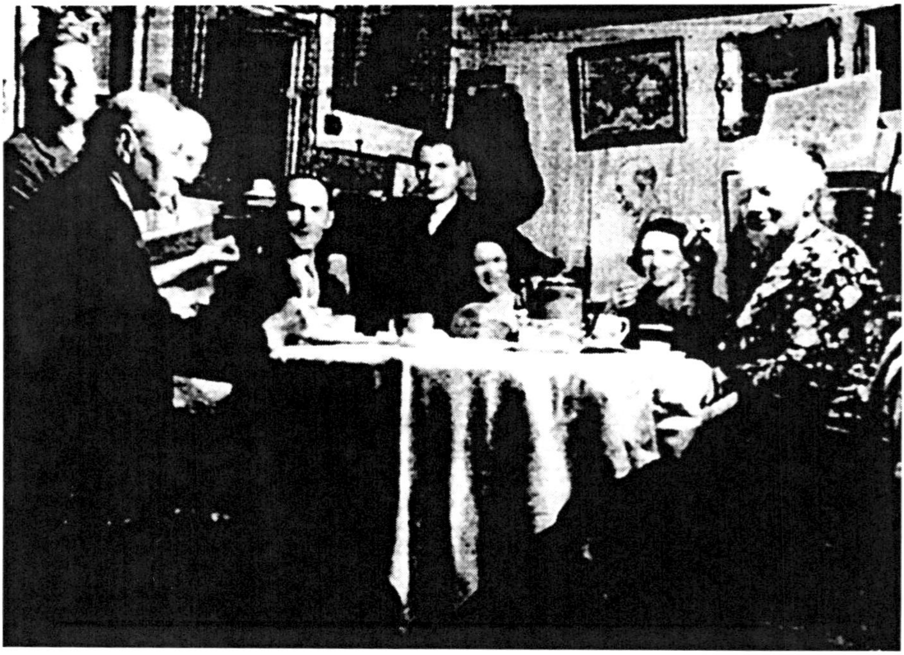

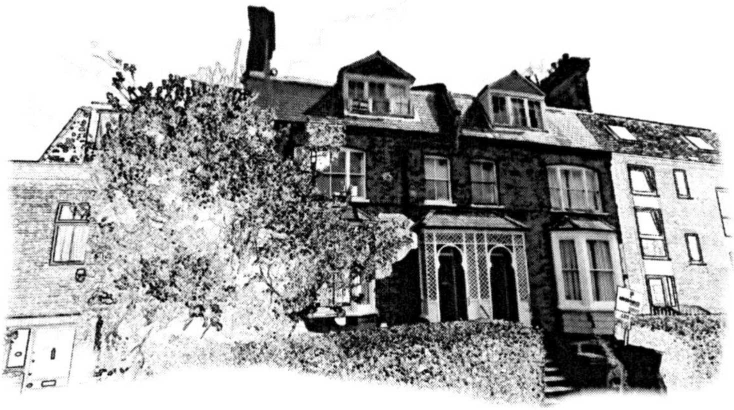

above right to left: Number 14 Lower Teddington Road, *Thames Bank* (16), *Woodlands* (18) and *The Pantiles*
The substantial semi-detached properties in the centre of this group were built around 1876 on the site of a malster's house and yard. *Thames Bank* is divided into six flats and *Woodlands* into two. Number 14 was added to the south end in 1977 and contains three flats. *The Pantiles* was an earlier (1937) extension at the northern end to which a second storey mansard roof extension was added in 1962.

Opposite top: *Lucerne House* and *Gomer House* (now *St Cecilia's* and the *Chapel of Our Lady of Westminster*) 23 and 25 Lower Teddington Road
This pair of semi-detached houses were built in 1852 by William Woods (see page 58). The first occupant of Number 25 was the novelist RD Blackmore (see page 60) who named it *Gomer House* after a favourite dog. His most famous novel Lorna Doone was published in 1865.

Opposite bottom: Another talented resident of *Gomer House* was the artist Lucy Millett who lived there from 1927 until her death in 1950. She taught at the Lambeth School (the first women to do so) and also ran her own "Hampton Wick School of Art" at her studio at *Old Castle Wharf* just across the road. The charming 1935 photograph opposite shows her presiding at a mandatory tea interval during a class. Note the distinguished-looking model (sitting on left of picture and portrayed in the sketch at the end of the table) is included in the tea-party. Lucy also founded the Thames Valley Art Club which celebrated its centenary in 2006.

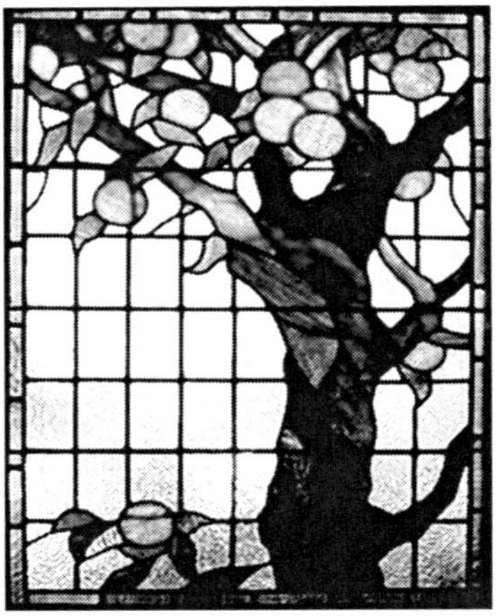

left: **Stained Glass Panel**

Created by artist William Spencer Bagdapoulos when living at *Lucerne House* (Number 23 Lower Teddington Road) from 1917 - 1929. The window is still in situ in the front door.

Born in 1889 of a Greek father and English mother on the Ionian Island of Zakynthos, Bagdapoulos' family came to the UK in 1908. After leaving Hampton Wick, Bagdapoulos travelled to the USA where he is probably best known.

below: **27 and 29 Lower Teddington Road (originally called *Park Cottage* and *Ashside*)**

These properties were built around 1864, at the same time as *Lansdowne Terrace* (Numbers 31 to 49) and also probably at the same time and to the same design as three houses built just round the corner in what was to become Station Road. Number 27 is now integrated with Number 25 and forms part of what is called House of Our Lady of Westminster.

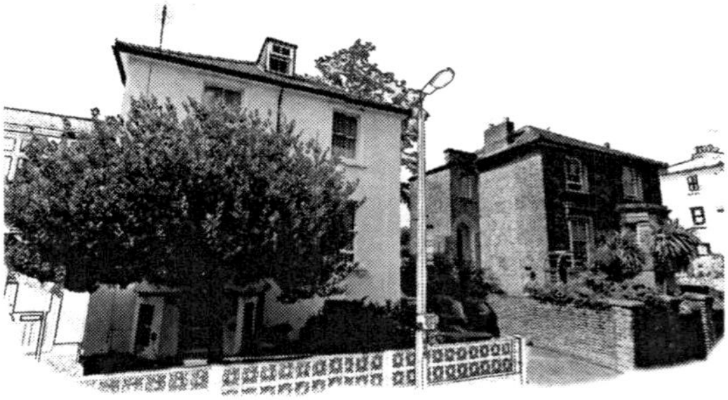

Buildings of Townscape Merit

Malting

One of the main industries in Hampton Wick in the eighteenth and nineteenth centuries was malting - the process of converting barley into malt for use in brewing beer. The village's location on the river made for easy transportation of both raw material and finished product as well as providing an assured supply of water needed for the process. The presence of several breweries in Kingston and Twickenham provided a local market for the maltsters of Hampton Wick.

The process took place in a malthouse, typically long, low buildings, no more than two storeys high, in a vernacular style. In the first half of the eighteenth century, Hampton Wick is known to have had at least seven malthouses, six of them on the river's edge on Lower Teddington Road and the seventh near *The Foresters* on the High Street.

The malting process involved soaking barley in a cistern (typically of 10,000 litres capacity) for a day or more to start the germination, then spreading the swollen grains out onto the growing floor, the depth dictated by the temperature, but sufficiently deep to encourage vegetative growth over the next fourteen days or so.

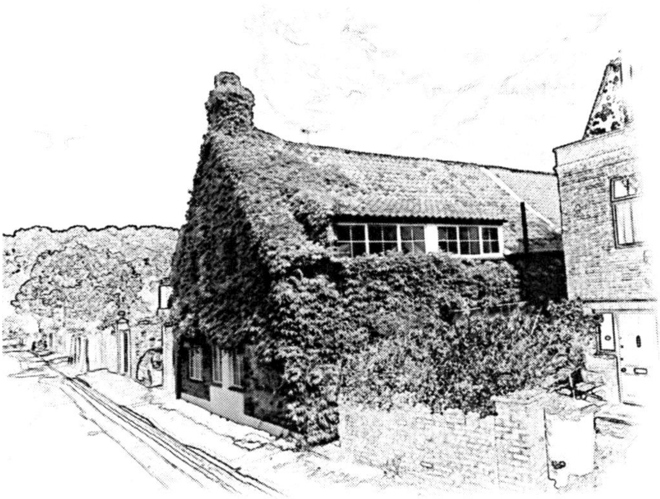

Building of Townscape Merit

above:

Imperial House/The Old Malthouse/Old Castle Wharf

Originally one of six malthouses on this stretch of the river, this building is now one of the only two that still exist. When malting operations ceased, the road end of the building was used for light engineering works, the middle was used for accommodation and the river end became artists' studios. In 1947 the small factory unit at the front was converted into offices (as shown in the photo below) with the supporting wooden pillars retained as features.

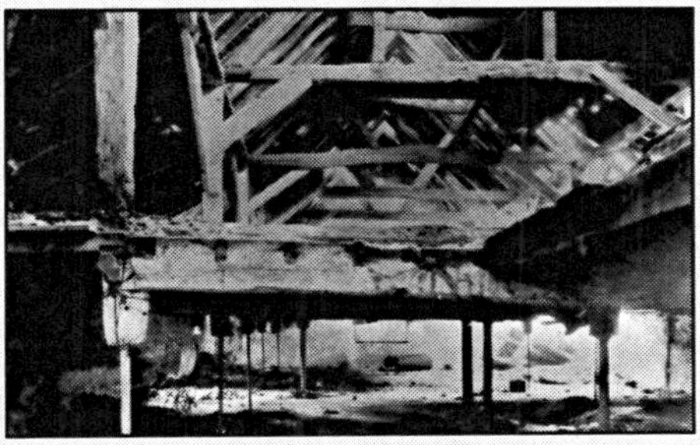

The maltster's art was in regulating the progress of the germination - through turning and gradually spreading more thinly - to achieve a balanced sugar level within all the grains but halting the process before the stem burst the husk. The final stage was to roast the grain in a kiln for two to four days.

The shape of malt-houses was dictated by the need for plenty of floor space (to allow the grain to be spread thinly) and for effective controllable ventilation - both characteristics being necessary to allow the maintenance of ideal temperatures for the various stages of germination especially in warmer weather.

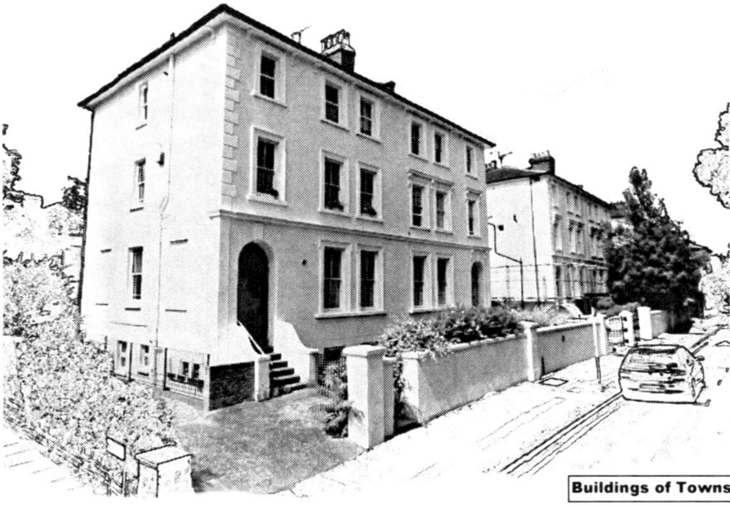

Buildings of Townscape Merit

above: 31 - 35 Lower Teddington Road (part of what was known as *Lansdowne Terrace*)

William Woods built this terrace of five near-identical semi-detached villa blocks around 1864. Each property was arranged on three floors plus a basement. and was originally occupied by a single family. By 1950 almost all had been divided into flats.

below: Lower Teddington Road around 1910

Apart from the unmetalled road and gas streetlights very little has changed in the hundred years since this postcard photograph was taken by Richard Young & Co. of Teddington.

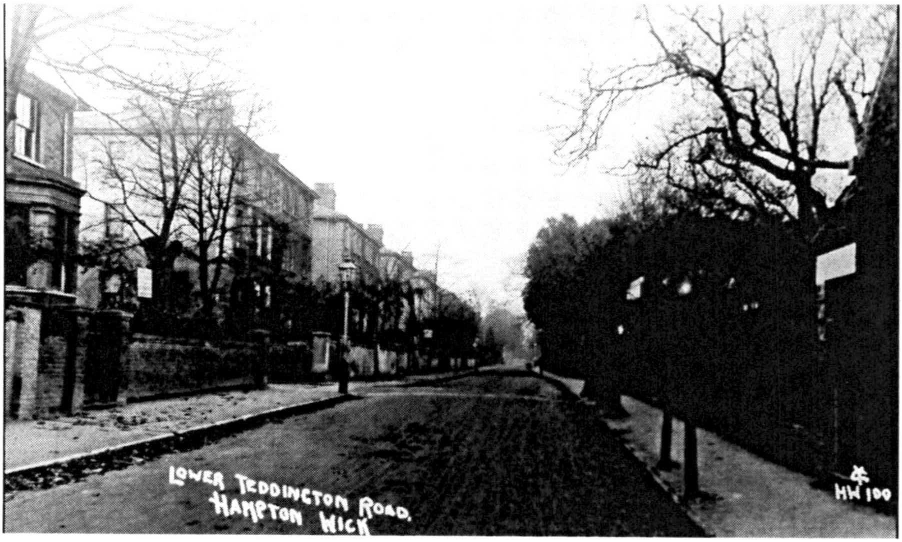

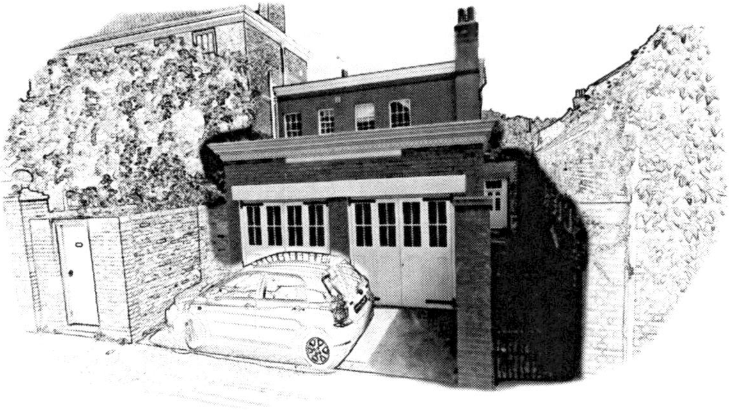

above: **20 Lower Teddington Road (now - again - part of *Walnut Tree House*)**

The footprint of *Walnut Tree House* was expanded significantly around 1880 (see page 35). In 1920 the then-owners divided the property into three parts, Numbers 20, 20A and 20B. The southern wing, which included this coach-house, had its own separate entrance and garden. Initially the coach-house itself with its north facing window was used as an artist's studio but was later converted into two garages. The whole house is now back in single ownership and these (now false) garage doors disguise the large games room that is now behind them.

below: The first occupier of the newly divided Number 20 in 1920 was Enoch Ward (1859 - 1922). He was noted as a social-realist artist, sketching the poor at work. He submitted thousands of sketches to magazines of the time, such as 'Pall-Mall' and 'Black-And-White'. *Silk Weavers at Spittalfields* seen here was typical of his work and was produced to illustrate an article in the inaugural edition of 'The Studio Magazine' in April 1893.

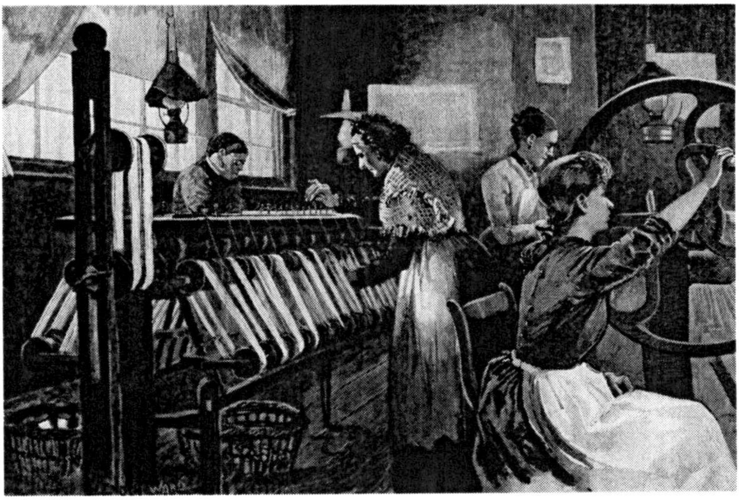

Sons of Divine Providence

Almost all properties on the west side of Lower Teddington Road from the railway bridge to Station Road and beyond belong to The Sons of Divine Providence. This religious congregation is part of the Order founded by Saint Luigi Orione in Tortona, Italy in the 1890's. The movement is devoted to providing homes and day centres for the elderly and people with learning disability. They operate more than 300 foundations in different parts of the world. Their Hampton Wick operation now comprises Number 13 to Number 35 Lower Teddington Road (with the exception of the maisonettes at Numbers 15/17).

The Sons of Divine Providence opened their first UK home in Streatham in 1952. A few years later they began their connection with Hampton Wick when Cecilia Cooper, who owned Number 23, *Lucerne House* - but who actually lived in a bungalow on Trowlock Island - gave the house to the Order. The following year the neighbouring Number 25, *Gomer House*, was purchased with funds raised by the Friends of Don Orione and the two properties were amalgamated and enlarged. By 1958 the Sons and some of the residents from Streatham moved into the new complex which was renamed Westminster House. The original house donated by Miss Cooper included a room which she had adapted into a chapel. Now significantly extended and known as Our Lady of Westminster, this continues to serve the community including offering a well-attended Polish mass.

In 1963 No. 13 Lower Teddington Road was purchased and converted into an eight-bedded nursing home to provide in-house nursing care for ill residents. It was opened in 1966 and named *St Mary's* Nursing Home. By the late sixties the Hampton Wick complex provided a residence for elderly gentlemen in Westminster House, a nursing home in *St Mary's*, a hostel on the upper floors in St Stephen's (No. 21) and offices on the ground floor in St. Stephen's.

The original home opened by the Order in Streatham became the subject of a compulsory purchase order and the compensation offered was used to purchase two large houses with extensive grounds in Station Road which were then demolished to provide the site of a home for forty residents (see page 131). The new home was opened on 12th October 1974 and was named *Orione House* in honour of the Order's founder.

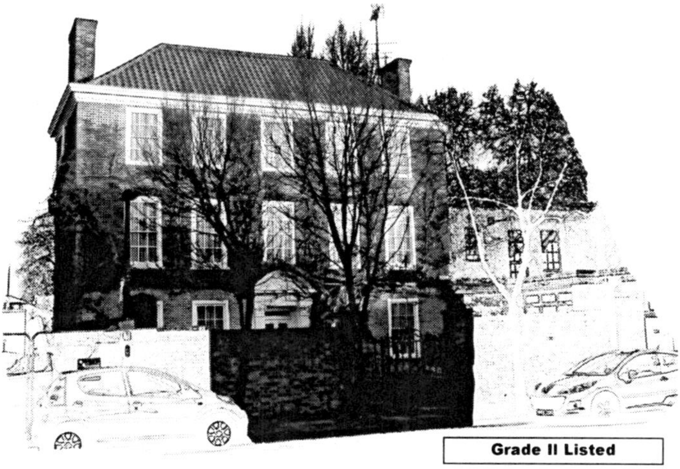

Grade II Listed

above: *Walnut Tree House*, 20a Lower Teddington Road

There is some agreeable irony in the fact that the oldest and newest buildings on this section of Lower Teddington Road should end up next to each other. *Walnut Tree House* was built in 1728 for a maltster (see page 105). It has been extensively enlarged over its history but the original three-storey brown brick facade topped by dentilled eaves and a hipped pantiled roof still graces this corner of Hampton Wick. *Wick Lodge* was completed in 2012 on what was originally the site of one of its neighbour's malthouses. The planning process which scrutinised the design required that it show due respect for its venerable neighbour. However, whilst the resulting road facade may seem timidly conservative, the river facade of glass and steel (inset, below left) boldly celebrates the importance of the site - as does the cinema, gym and pool in the basement.

below: *Wick Lodge*, 22 Lower Teddington Road

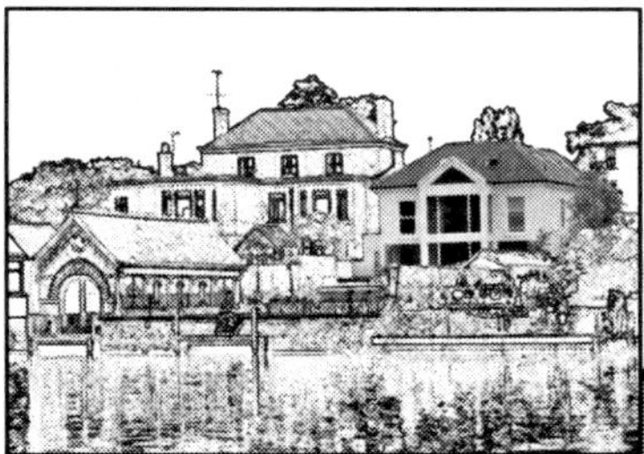

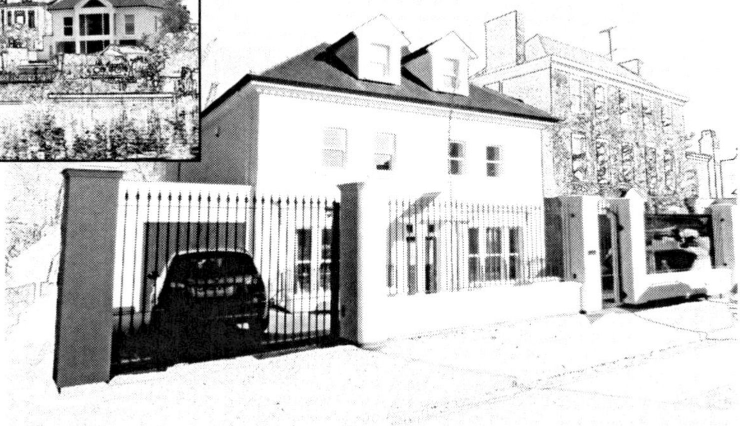

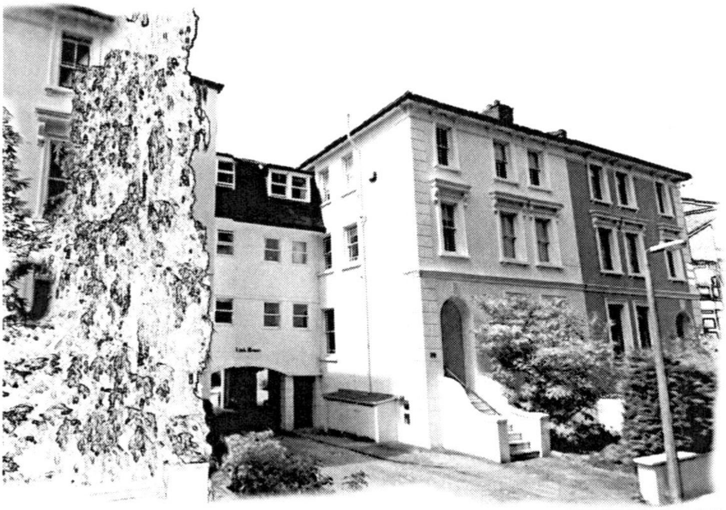

Building of Townscape Merit

Link House (above) and *Winterton Court* (below)
37/39 and 43/45 Lower Teddington Road

These developments show two different approaches to increasing the capacity of William Wood's original *Landsdowne Terrace* villas. The link between the two blocks (above) was built in 1980 to provide an additional three one-bedroomed flats. In 1972, a complete block of *Landsdowne Terrace* was demolished and replaced with a new building (below) to provide ten flats.

Since these two schemes were completed, properties in *Landsdowne Terrace* have been designated as Buildings of Townscape Merit, providing now some future protection for the integrity and external appearance of the remaining blocks.

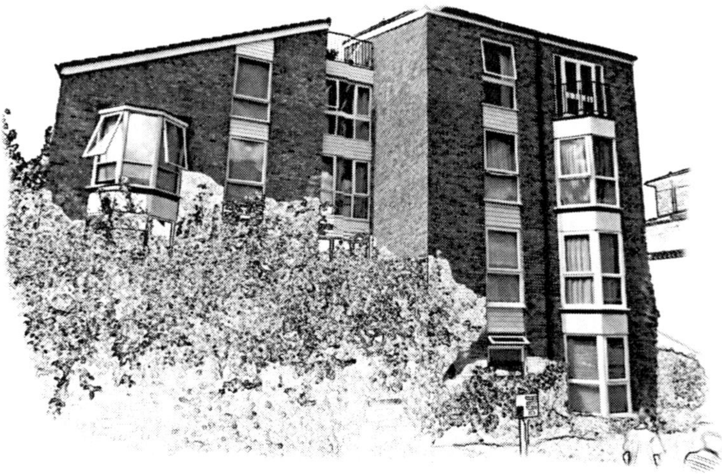

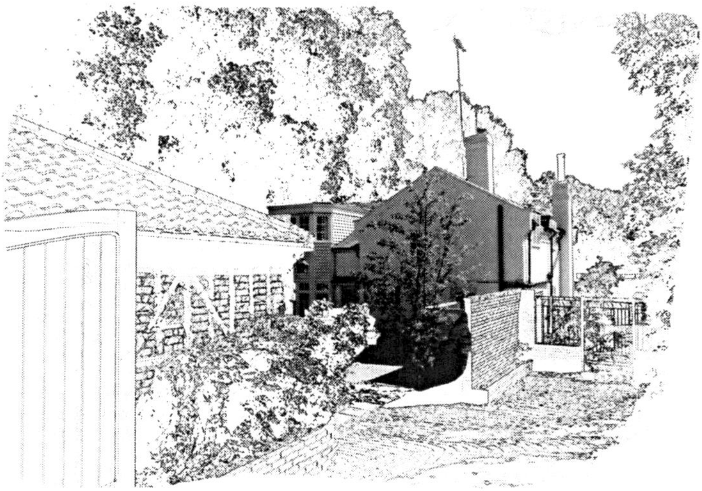

above: *Grove Cottage*, Lower Teddington Road

This property was created in 1950 out of the original coach-house and stables built for *The Grove* next door. A second storey was added to the extension on the north side in 1990. Beneath the southern boundary lies a 20,000 volt cable which comes under the river from a sub-station on the Kingston bank. Recent replacement of this cable cost several £ million.

below: *The Grove*, 24 Lower Teddington Road

Built in 1750 by the 2nd Earl of Halifax (see page 26), the main house retains much of its original appearance with its brown brick front seven bays wide under a slated mansard roof. The central porch was an early Victorian addition and the southern extension, originally built in the 1850's as a billiard room has been progressively enlarged over the last twenty years. The house remained a single property until it was divided into five apartments in 1950.

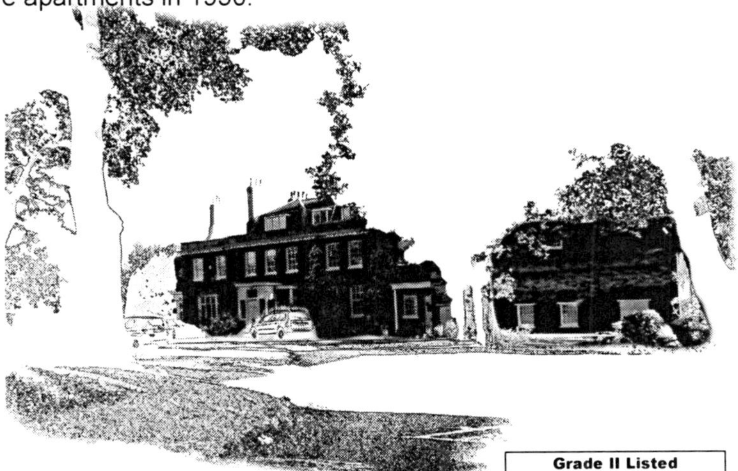

Grade II Listed

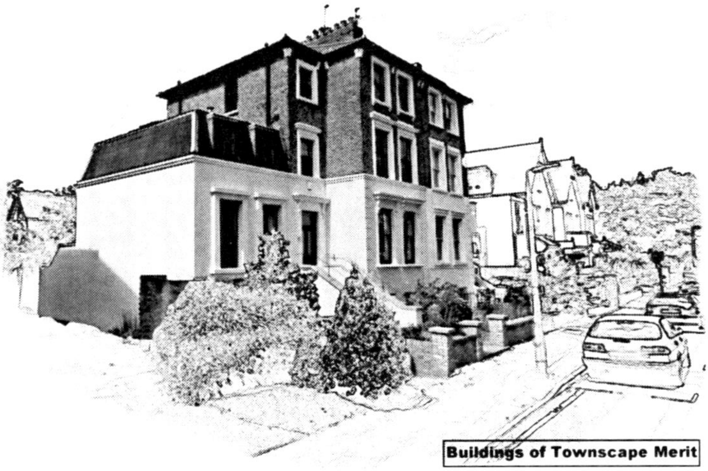

above: **47 and 49 Lower Teddington Road**
Number 47 shares with Number 41 the distinction of still being in single occupation (though both were briefly divided into two flats). The three-storey southern extension was built in 1990. Number 49 contains four flats.

opposite top: *The Courtyard*
opposite bottom: *Thames Reach*

Both properties lie within the original boundary of *Thameside Place/Moiravale* (see Page 23). *The Courtyard* was created in 1952 from the stables and garage block. One of the early residents was Thomas Hicks (aka Tommy Steele) who created a music room which was used as a recording studio by his successor, Justin Hayward of the Moody Blues who also added several extensions.

Thames Reach is a development of three flats competed in 1961.

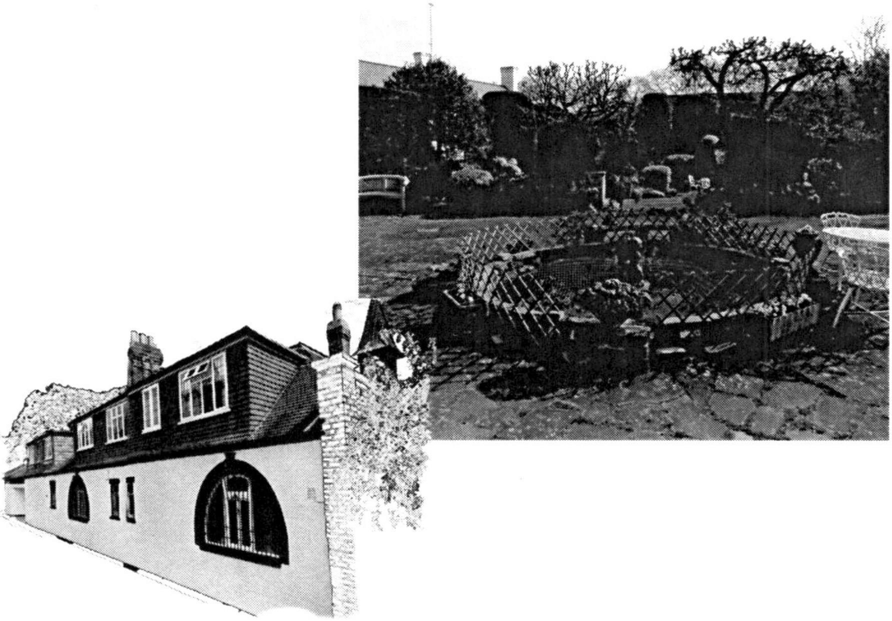

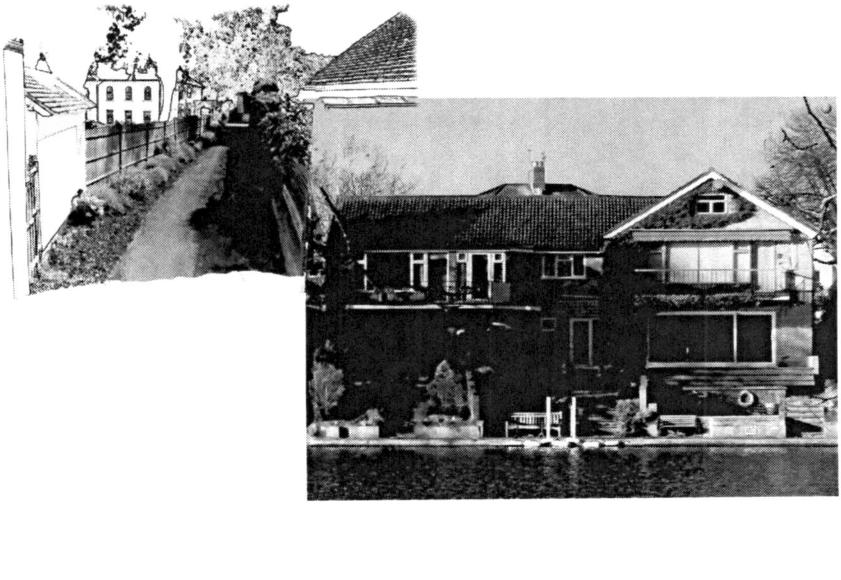

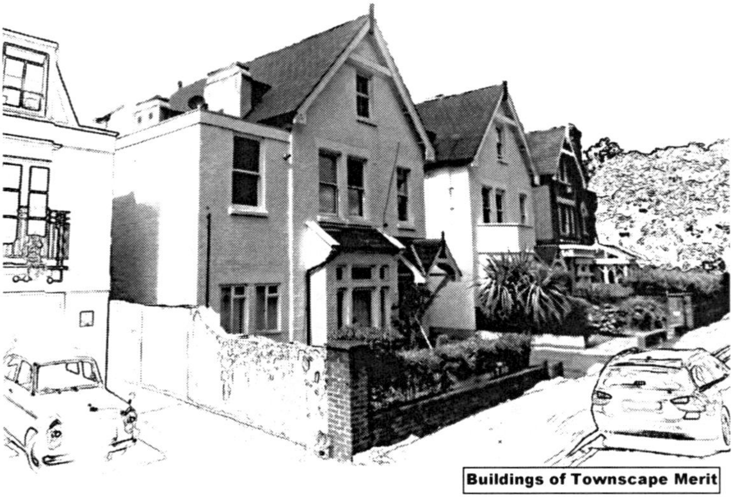

above: *Ty'rafon* & *Campsbourne*, 51 & 53 Lower Teddington Road
Built around 1890 by Richard Starkey as single-occupation houses, each property is now divided into four flats. *Ty'rafon* is Welsh for "River House".

below: 55, 57, 57a & 59 Lower Teddington Road
(and *Richmore* 34 Seymour Road)
Built at the same time as Numbers 51 and 53 (see above) also by Richard Starkey, *Richmore* was originally a single large dwelling accessed from Seymour Road. In the early 1980's the back half was separated off and split into four flats.

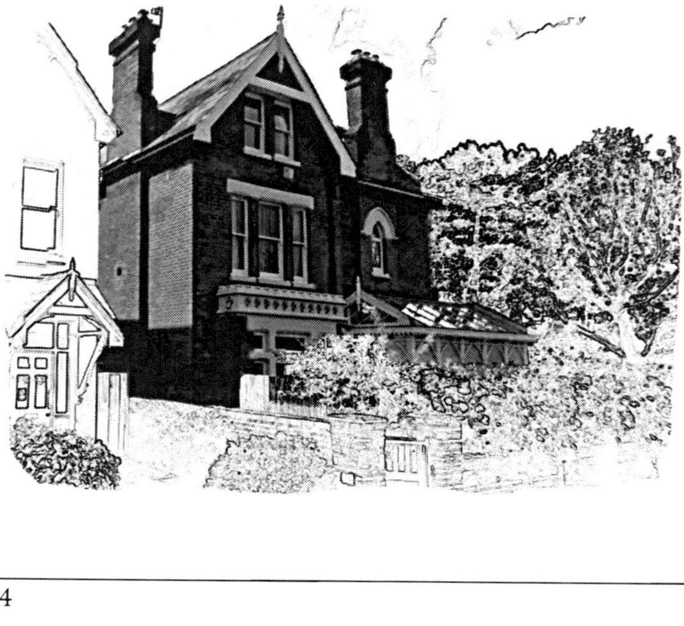

right: ***Moiravale/ Thameside Place***

26 Lower Teddington Road
Originally built around 1805 as a modest residential annexe to an existing starch factory (see Page 21), the total site now accommodates 13 residential units.

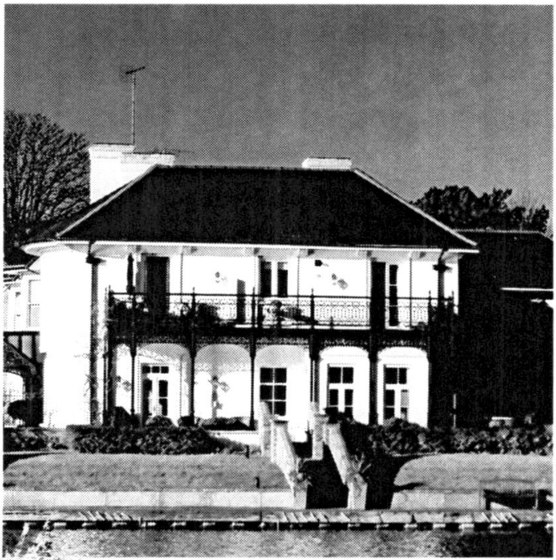

Building of Townscape Merit

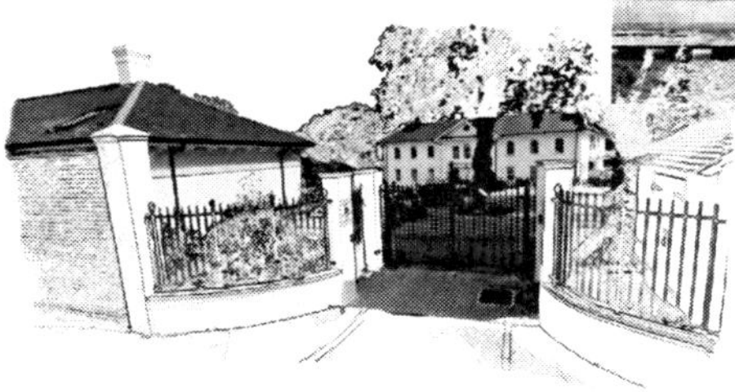

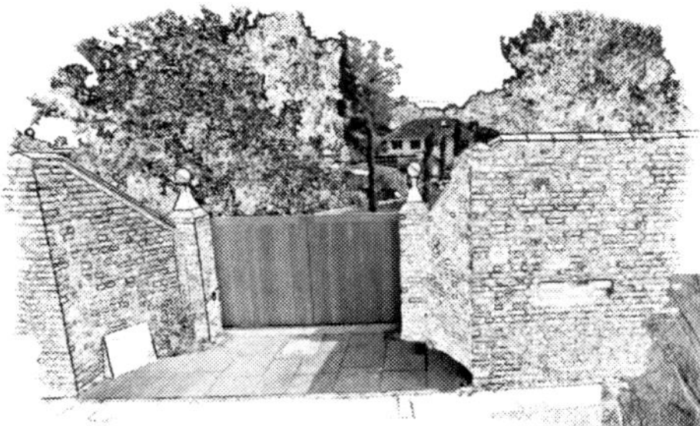

below: ***River Garth***

Built in 1952 on the kitchen garden and greenhouses of *Moiravale*. The plot is spade-shaped with a narrow road access but has a river frontage of similar size to its donor site Number 26.

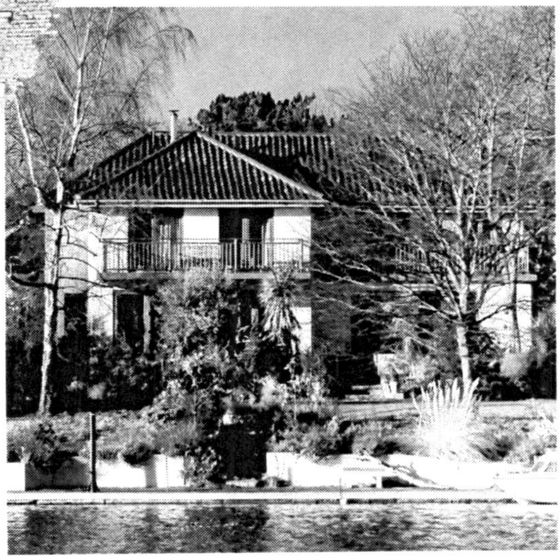

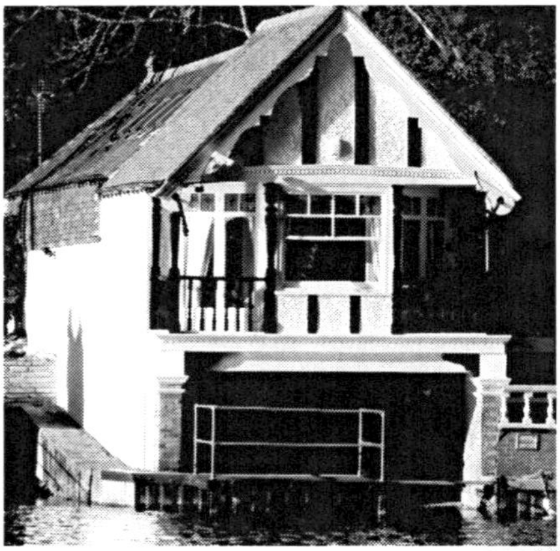

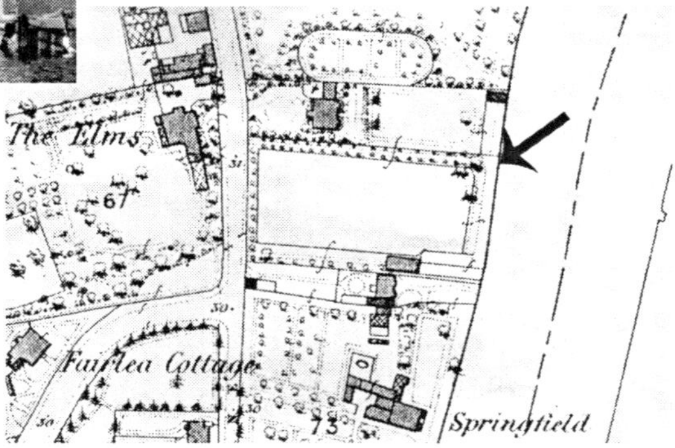

The Elms (destroyed in WWII)

The boathouse (above) is the only remnant of this once-substantial property. Although the house was not on the river's edge, it retained access down an avenue to its boathouse (arrowed). It rivaled its neighbour *Springfield* (now *Thameside Place*) in size and opulence. For over fifty years from 1890, *The Elms* was home to Frederick Jacob and his son who imported and sold lager beer (below) a little-known beverage at that time.

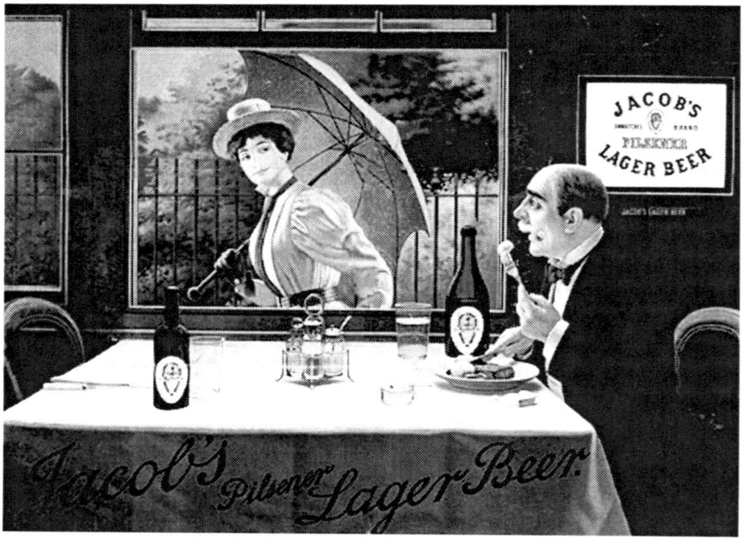

right: *The Moorings*
28 Lower Teddington Road
Built in 1937 on the site of a previous 1865 dwelling known as *Oak Villa.* The building is placed "sideways" to make the most of its narrow plot.

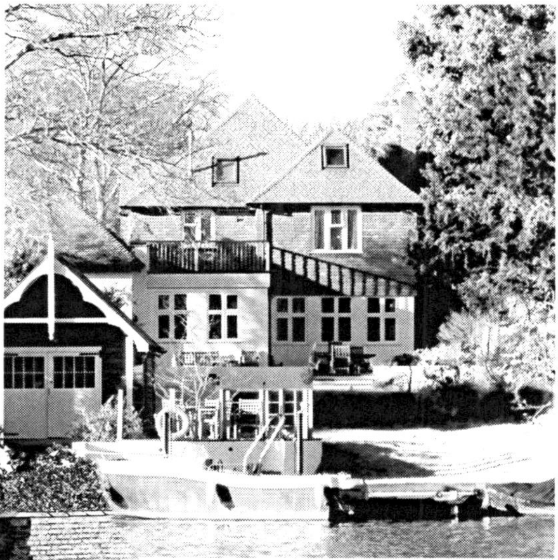

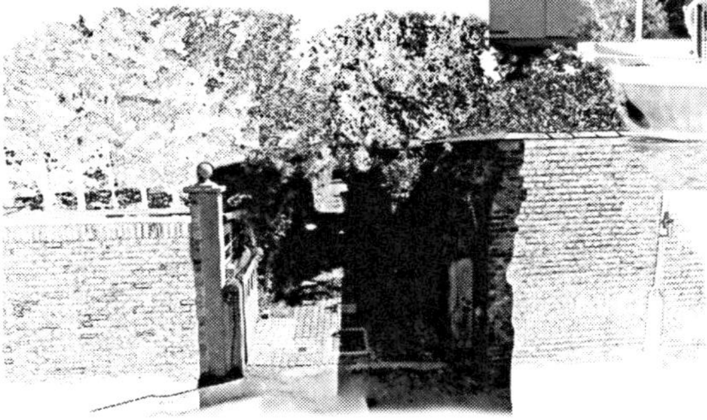

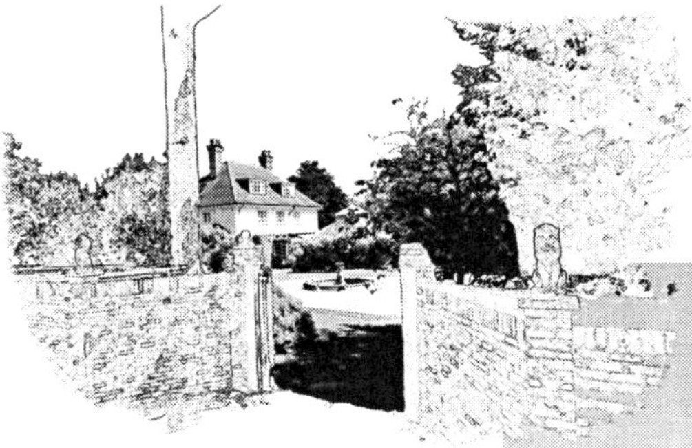

right: *Warneford*
30 Lower Teddington Road
Built in 1902, the building was originally known as *Ee Juan*. The orangery was added sometime between 1915 and 1934.

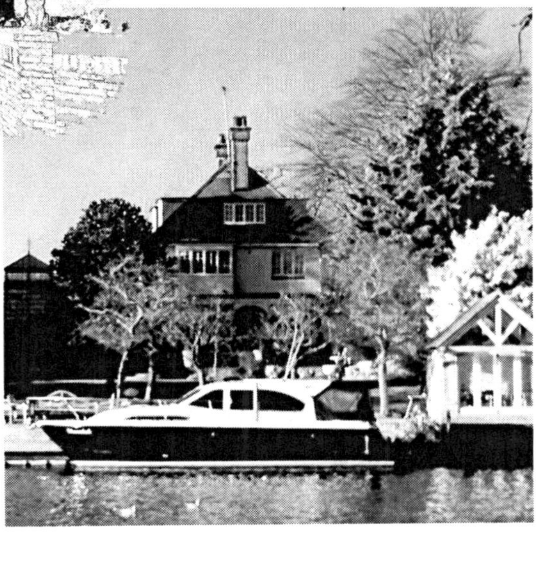

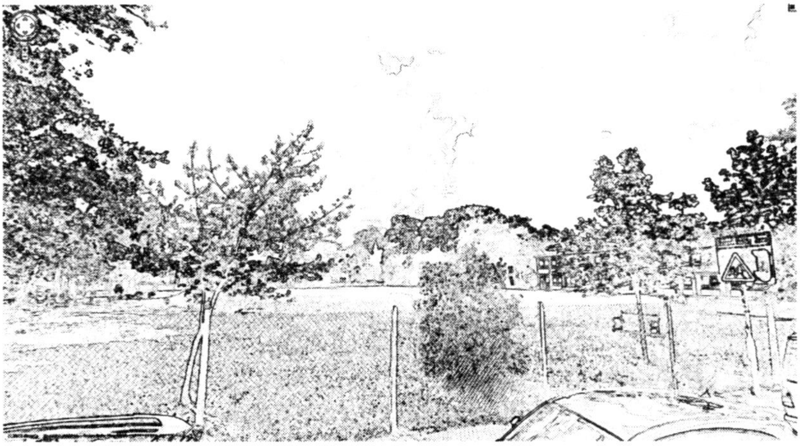

above: St John the Baptist School Playing Field

The site of *The Elms* with its extensive grounds presented the Middlesex County planners with an ideal space for a new school and playing fields to replace the cramped premises of the old school (below) which was located on the High Street opposite today's Post Office. The original Endowed School for boys had opened with 108 pupils in 1843. The building included a Public Library and Reading Room run by the teaching staff. The replacement school building opened in May 1965 with accommodation for 320 children.

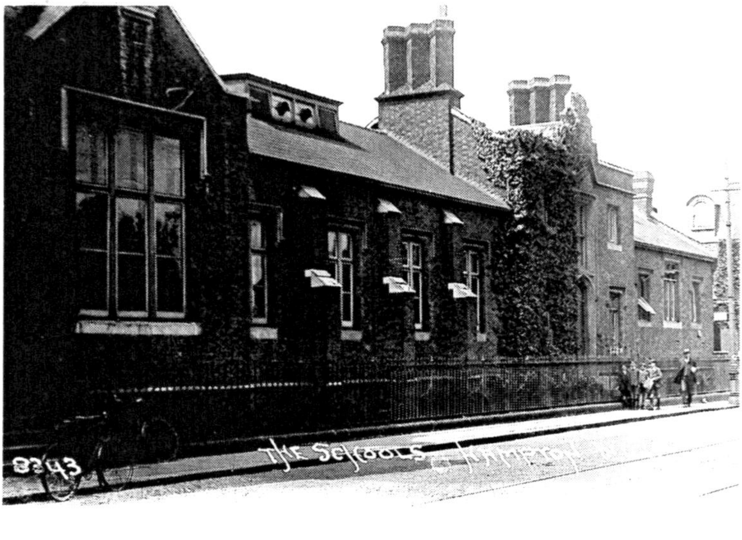

right: *Teddington Lodge*

32 Lower Teddington Road

Built in 1902, the original name was *Bindown*. The house was extended by four rooms to the north in 1906 creating the double-fronted twin pitch roof structure.

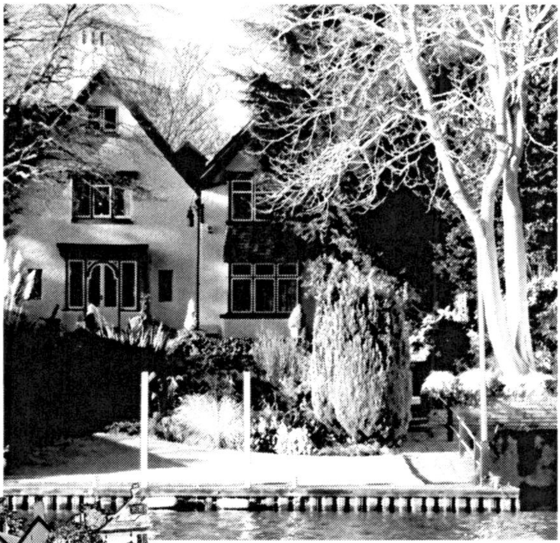

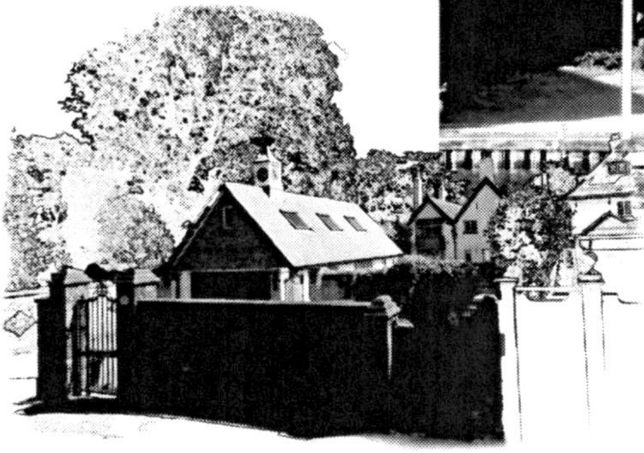

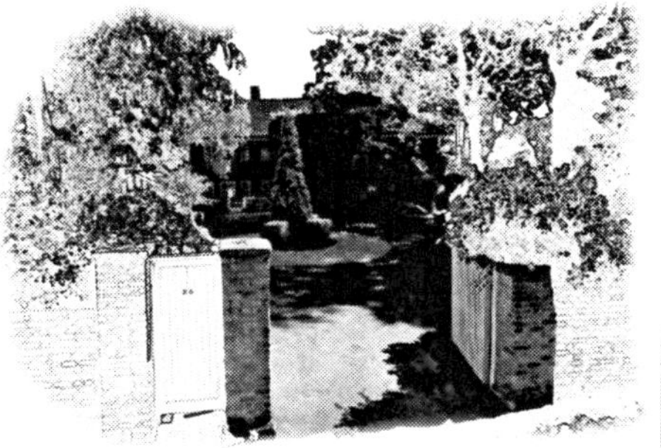

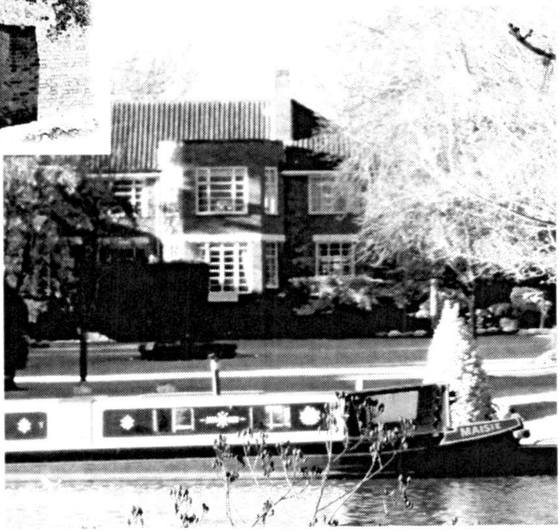

right: *Denbigh Lodge*

34 Lower Teddington Road

The original 12-room building (called *Denbigh House*) was built in 1858. It was demolished and replaced by the present property in 1937.

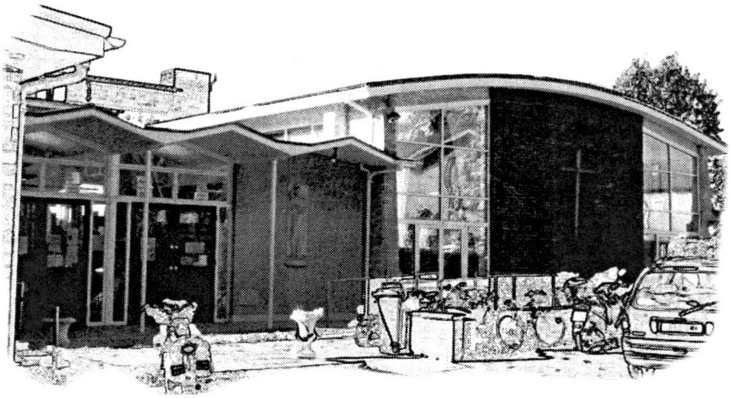

above: **Main entrance of Junior School**

"An attempt has been made in the layout of the building to combine a feeling of informality and spaciousness. The effect ... is that of one entity, the buildings, gardens and play areas merging into a whole. The child entering the school should not find its surroundings overpowering but find the scale comfortably related to its familiar surroundings at home."

J Barrington-Baker & Partners, Chartered Architects 1965

below: **Caretaker's House, 63 Lower Teddington Road**
Built 1963.

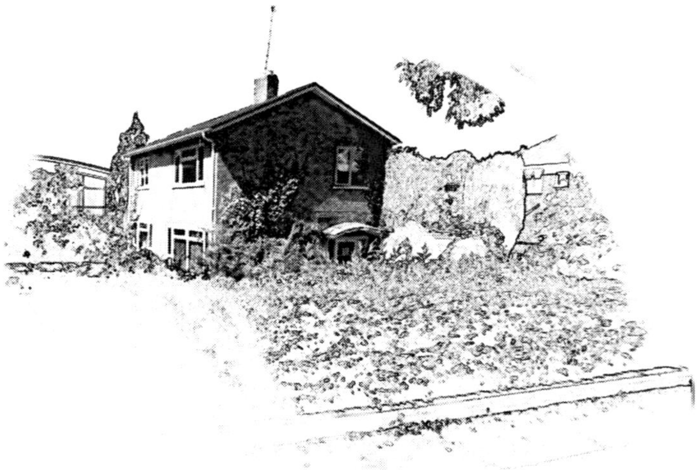

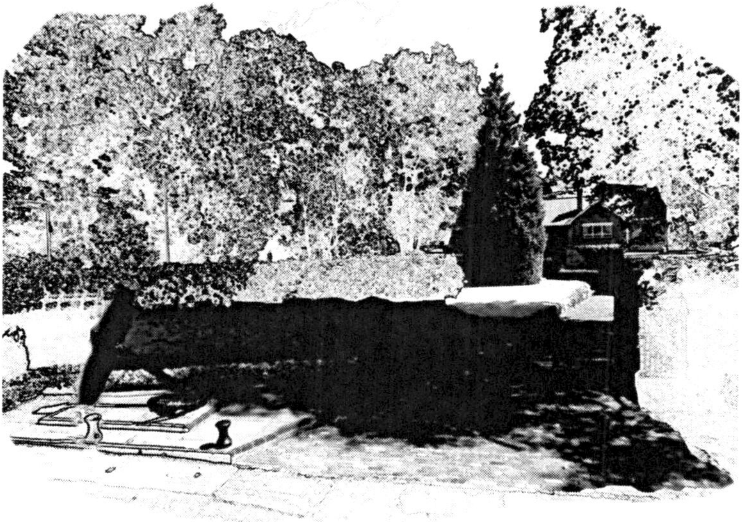

above: *Leander House*, 36 Lower Teddington Road

The property was built by Donald Gosling (now Rear Admiral Sir Donald Gosling KCVO) in 1963 in the garden of *Riverbank*. He named the house after HMS Leander on which he had served when he first joined the Royal Navy in 1944 at the age of 15. He famously made his fortune by buying wartime bomb-sites in city centres and turning them into car parks. His National Car Park empire sold for £800m in 1998. He spent £50m of this on a yacht (also called *Leander*). The Gosling Foundation charity has made many generous local contributions including funding the Golden Jubilee Fountain and the replanting of 2,000 trees in the lime avenues, both in Home Park.

below: An anchor from the 1866 *HMS Leander* flanks the main gate of the house.

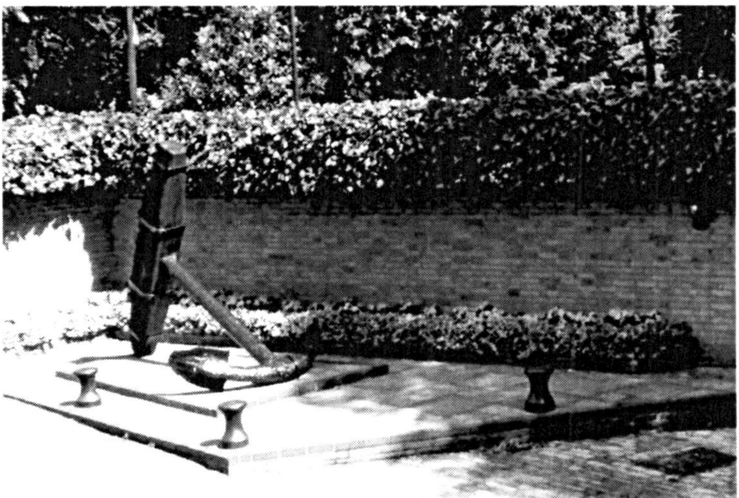

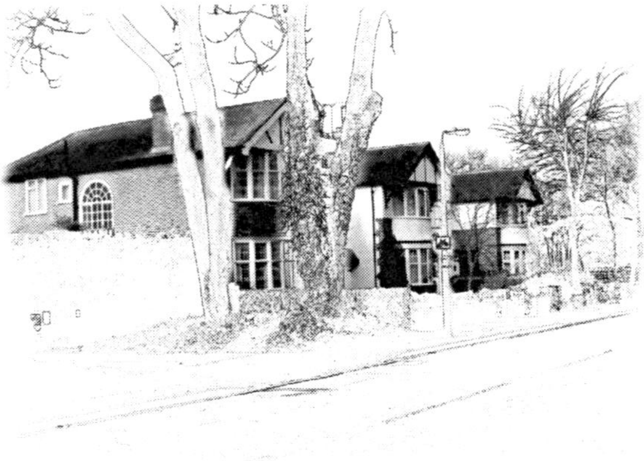

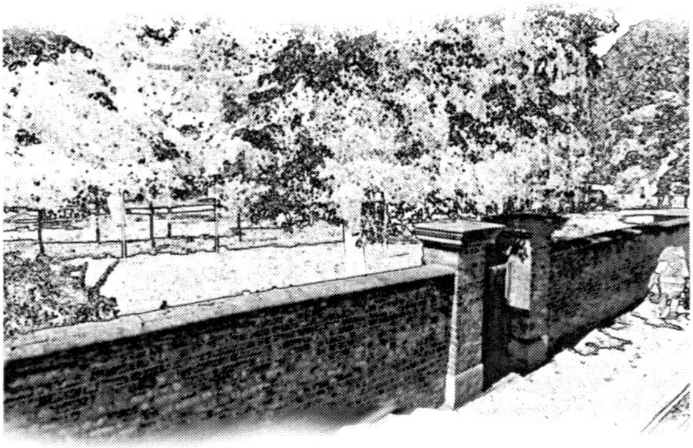

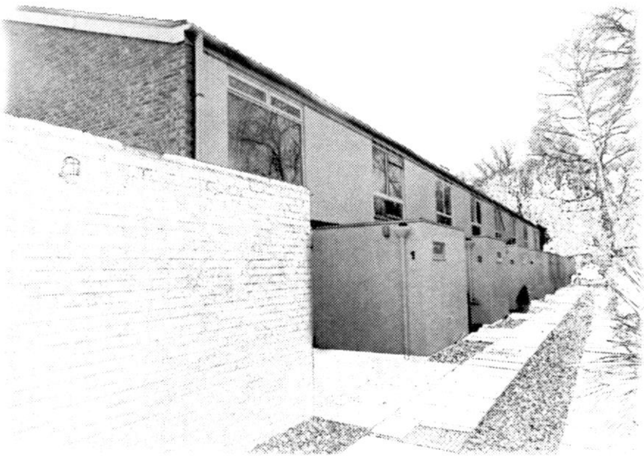

top: 65 - 69 Lower Teddington Road built in 1935
middle: This elegant gate and garden wall is all that remains of *Raeburn House*, built in 1890 and demolished in 1961 to make way for Hampton Wick Infants and Nursery School and later for *Raeburn Close* (bottom) built in 1969.

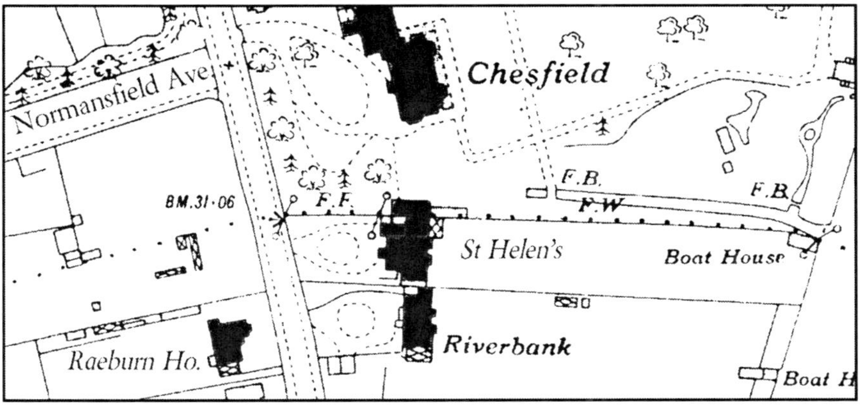

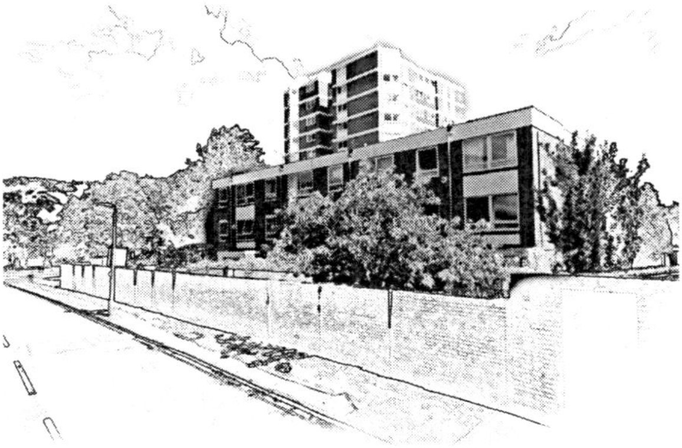

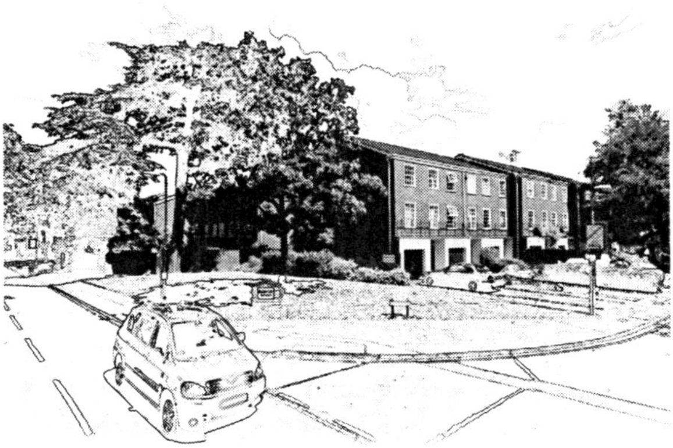

(above top) Four substantial properties were demolished in the 1960's to make way for much needed new development. *Chesfield*, *St Helens* and *Riverbank* disappeared under *Hamble Court* (above middle) and Broom Park (above bottom)

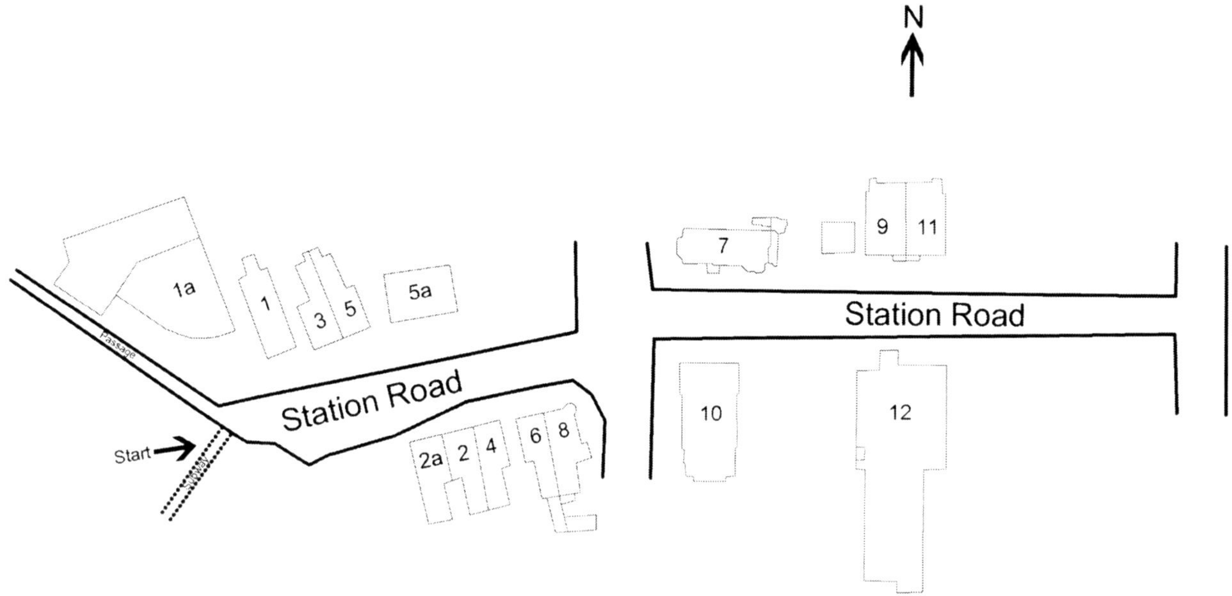
N
Station Road
Station Road
Passage
Start
1a
1
3
5
5a
2a
2
4
6
8
7
9
11
10
12

STATION ROAD

Brick by Brick

Station Road was laid out along existing field boundaries by William Woods around 1863. He needed it to provide direct pedestrian access from his property developments on Lower Teddington Road and the newly arrived railway. The original route to the station passed via the narrow passage that leads out of the north west end of the road - the current back entrance via the subway did not open until the mid-1880's.

The first properties, built in 1864 on the south east section of the road have since been demolished so the oldest original houses are Numbers 1 - 5 on the north west section. These date from 1872, nine years before the building of Numbers 2 - 6 opposite..

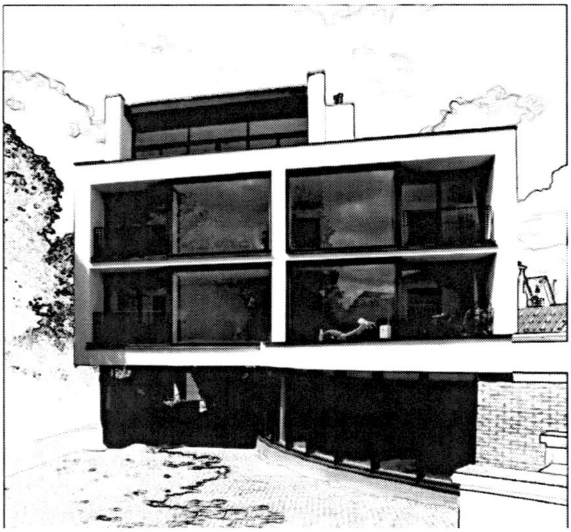

above: *The Sidings*, 1a Station Road

Probably the most visible - and controversial - new development in Hampton Wick, this project was completed in 2011 and consists of commercial space on the ground floor, eight one-bed flats and a two-bed penthouse. The site formerly housed the Infants School up to 1963 after which the buildings were used for warehousing and light industrial activities.

below: *Dalham Villa*, 1 Station Road

This attractive little property (note the unusual ornamentation around the windows) was built in 1873. Originally named Harley Villa, it was renamed in 1905 by the new occupier Jezreel Pleasants after the little village between Bury St Edmunds and Newmarket where he - and his brother and neighbour - were born.

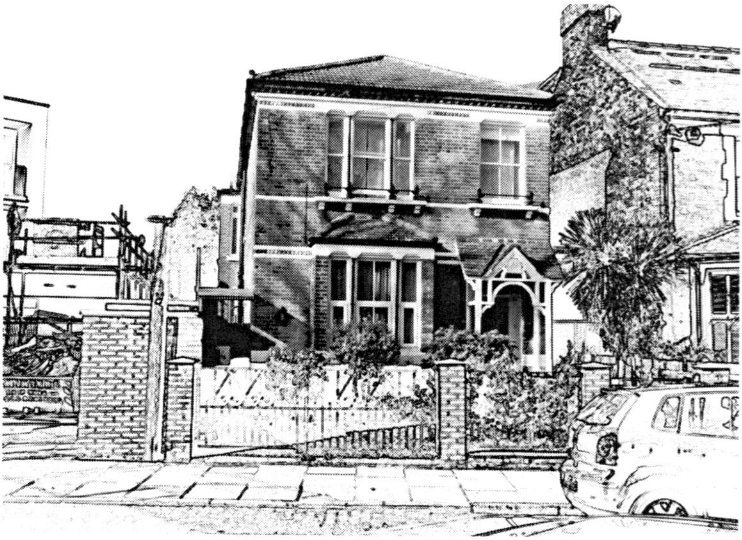

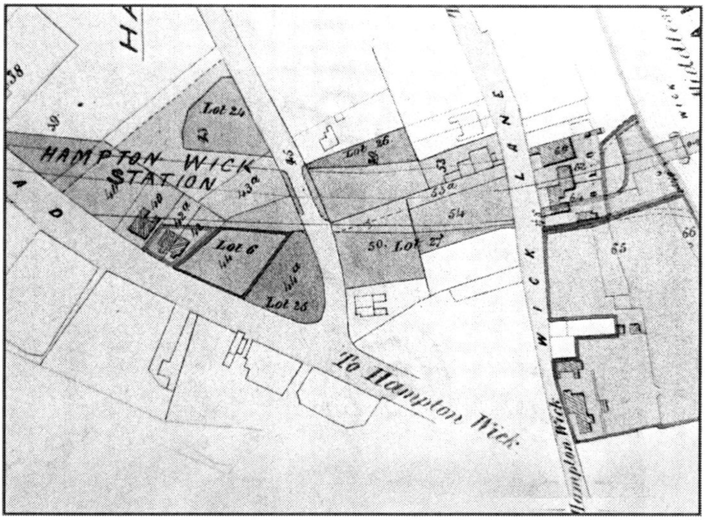

Railway Land

The timescale of the layout and development of this corner of Hampton Wick was heavily influenced by the building of the railway which had opened in 1863. The map (above) shows the parcels of land purchased by the London & South West Railway (L&SWR) around 1861 to allow construction of the trackbed, embankments, station and bridges. In 1866 L&SWR auctioned off the surplus land (below) with Lot 24 becoming the site on which 2 - 8 Station Road and 7 - 9 Seymour Road were finally built in 1881 - why there was a delay of 15 years remains a mystery.

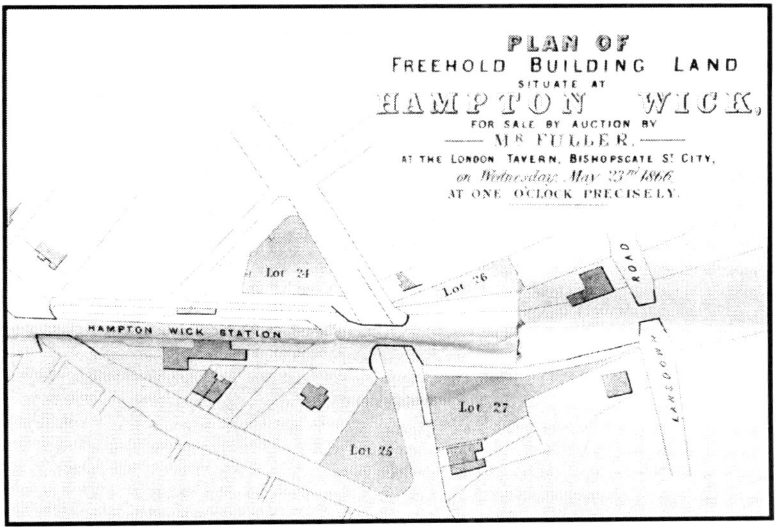

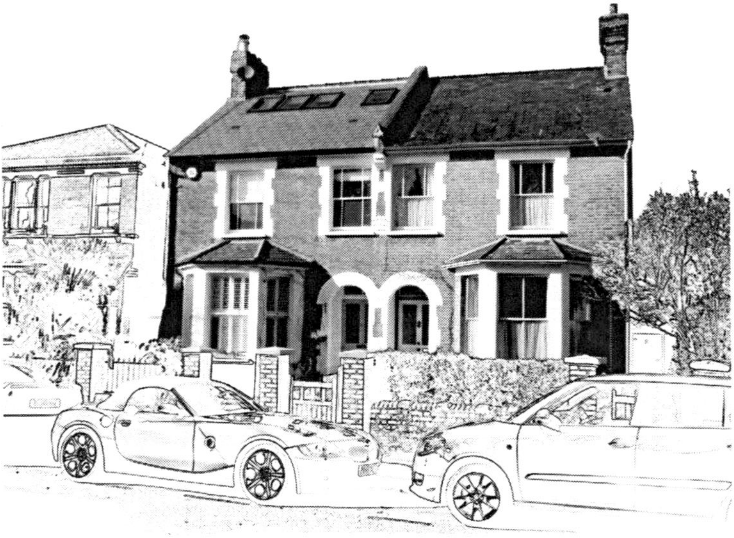

above: *Palmerston Villas*, 3 - 5 Station Road

This property has its own caption clearly - though somewhat crudely - displayed between the upper story central windows. Its first owner was William Henry Pleasants who had been a footman in the service of Lord Palmerston in his last years as Prime Minister.

below: 5a Station Road

Containing four flats, this property was built 1937 in the back garden of Abbotsford (11 Seymour Road) when that property was being converted into flats. Note how out of alignment with the road are Numbers 1 - 5, showing how the line of the road - which originally followed existing field boundaries - was changed, resulting in a dog-leg crossing of Seymour Road .

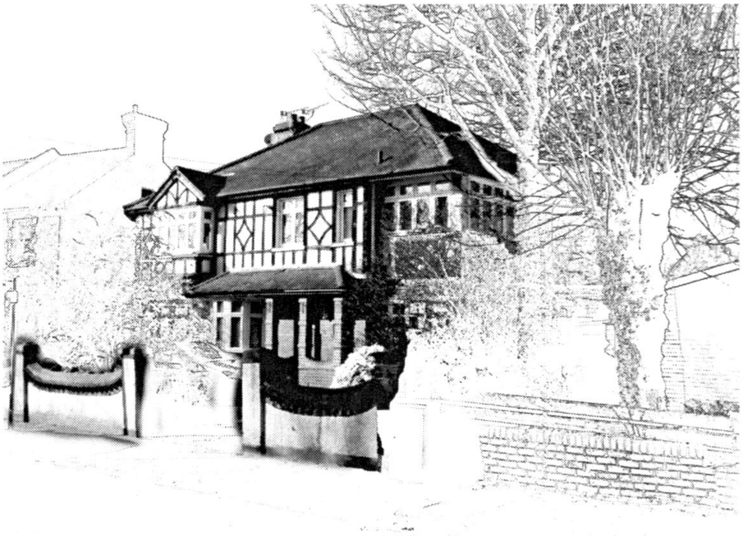

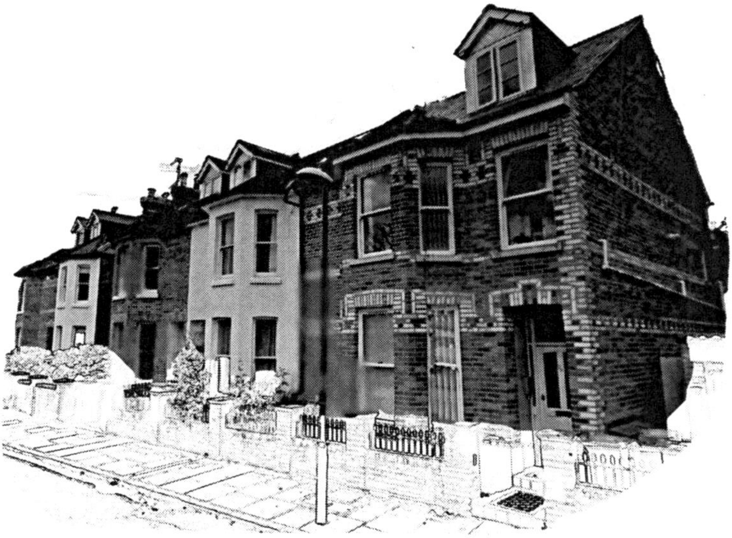

above: **2a - 8 Station Road**

The eight original properties in this development (including those around the corner in Seymour Road) were built in 1881 using a distinctive polychrome brick design and arranged as four pairs of semi-detached dwellings. Number 2a (nearest the camera) was added in 2003 as an exact replica of its predecessors.

below: **8 Station Road**

The original architect capitalised on the corner site of this property by incorporating an attractive two-storey bay with a hexagonal floorplan. Henry Fry who owned both Numbers 6 and 8 elected to live next door and allow his tenant the benefit of the extra space.

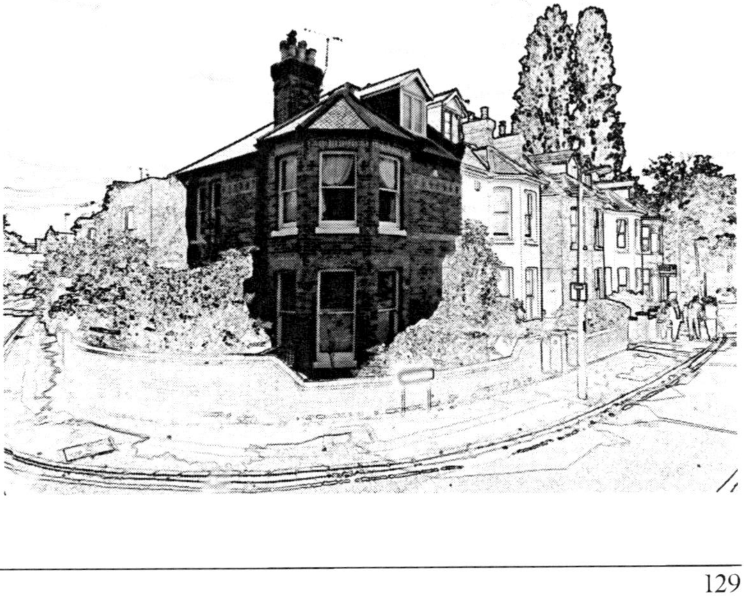

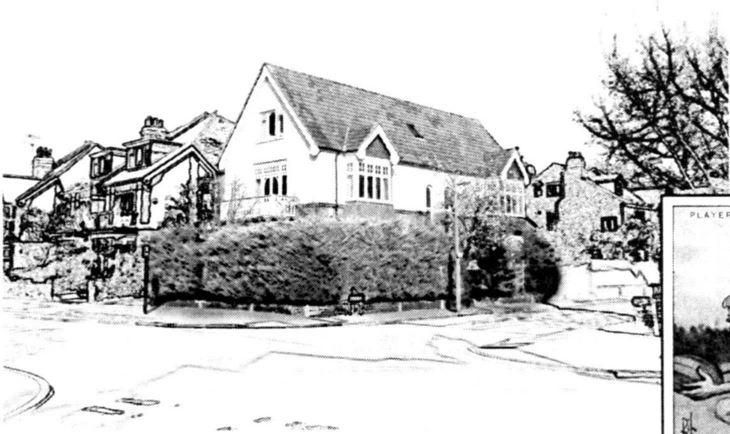

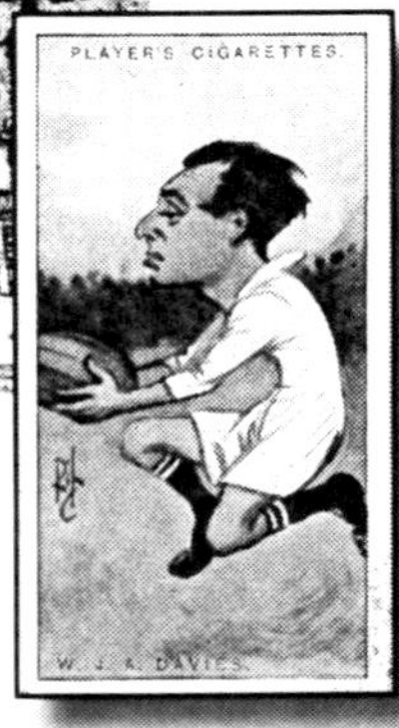

above: **Ludlow House, 7 Station Road**
Built in 1904 by Richard Starkey. WJA "Dave" Davies (inset), England's most capped fly-half until Rob Andrew overtook his record, lived here 1930 - 36. Since 1986 the ground floor has been run as a nursery for 55 children aged from 2 to 5 years.

below: **9 - 11 Station Road**
Built in 1907, the properties retain the attractive hung clay tile cladding and very fine stained glass in the front doors and sidelights. Note the three-plane design of the facade, with the first floor jettied over the ground floor and the central bay projecting even further beyond.

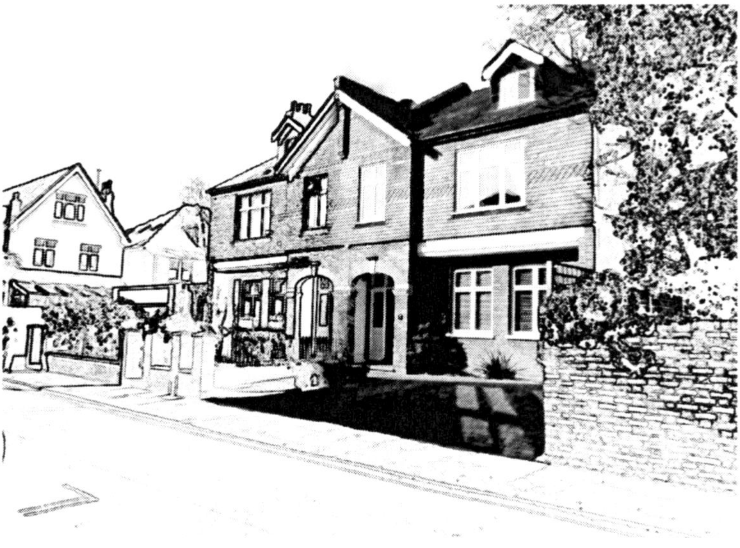

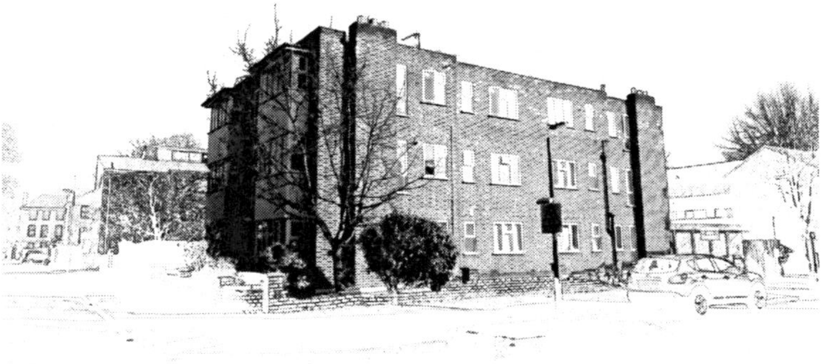

above: Wick House, 10 Station Road

Built in 1939 by Twickenham Council on the site of an 1860's house, the property contains 12 flats. A 2004 plan to convert the flat roof into a mansard configuration to provide an additional pair of flats was never implemented.

below: *Orione House*, 12 Station Road

Opened in 1974 as a care home for older people, *Orione House* now has a capacity for 34 residents. It was extended in 2001. It is run by The Sons of Divine Providence (see page 108).

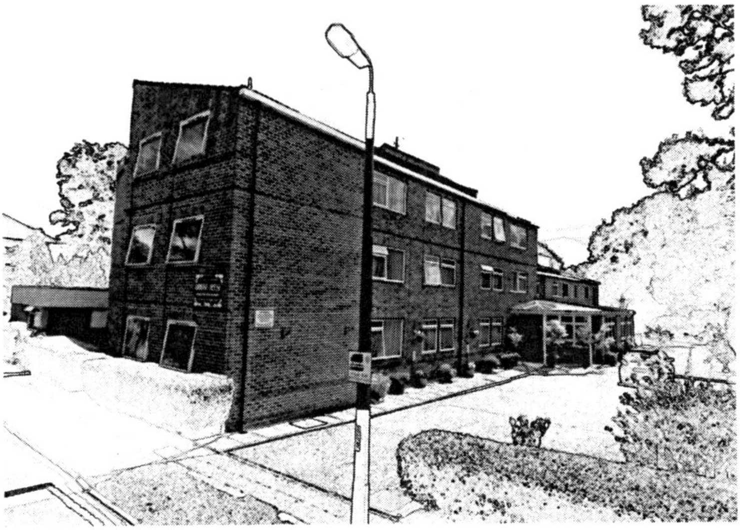

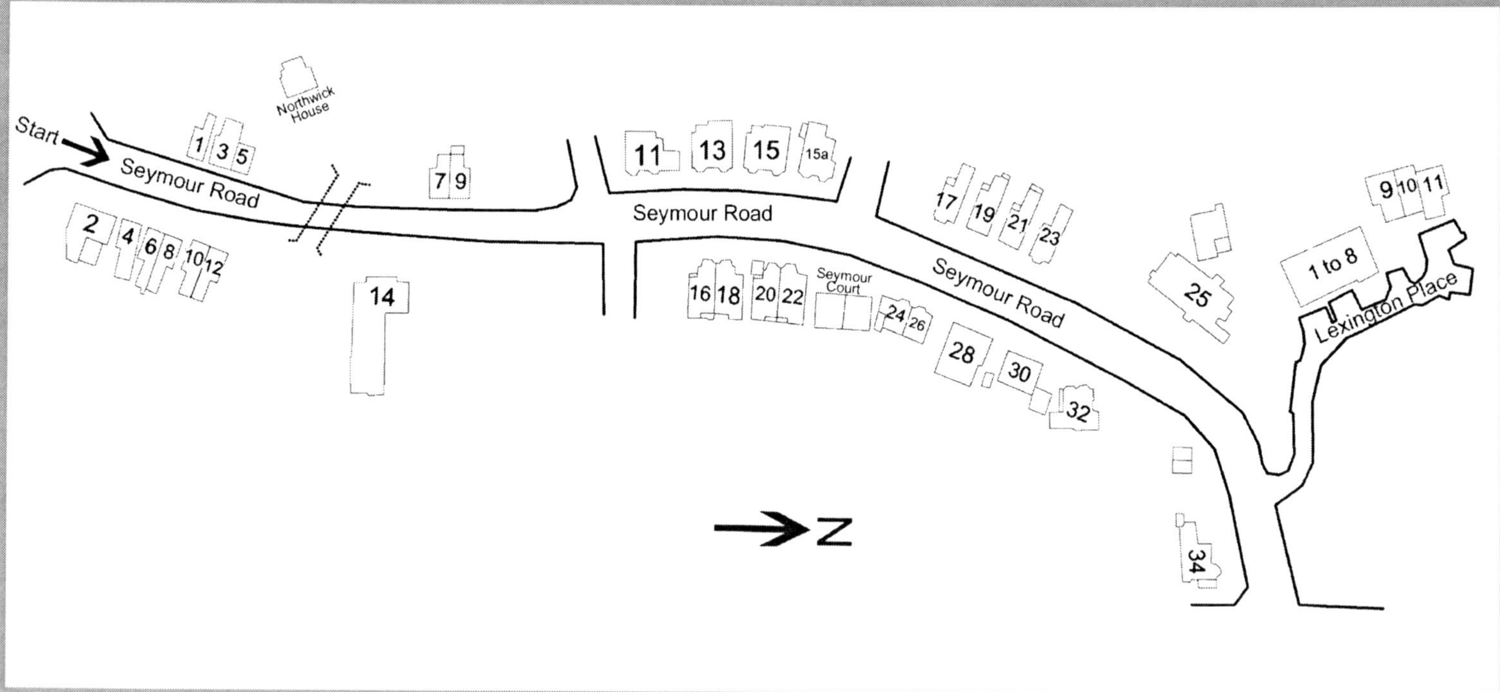
Start
Seymour Road
Seymour Road
Seymour Road
Lexington Place
Northwick House
Seymour Court
1
3
5
7
9
11
13
15
15a
17
19
21
23
25
2
4
6
8
10
12
14
16
18
20
22
24
26
28
30
32
34
1 to 8
9
10
11
N

SEYMOUR ROAD

Seymour Road was laid out around 1860. It probably followed the line of a farm track running across pasture land (known as Seamer's Close) from the High Street to *The Elms* home farm. This latter was located on the west side of Lower Teddington Road on what is now the Junior School playing field. The route was simply known as New Road until named by the Local Board in 1865. Initially there was limited building activity with just four houses erected during the 1860's - including *Fairlea* (Number 25) and *Northwick House*. Numbers 1 - 5 were constructed in the 1870's.

The arrival of Richard Starkey in 1879 marked a change in pace (see page 65). He alone built the whole of the north-western side of the road from Numbers 11 - 23 in 1883, the same year that Numbers 4 - 12 were built at the south east end. Starkey, having then focused his activities on Glamorgan Road, returned to Seymour Road in the early 1900's to add Numbers 16 - 22.

As most of the properties were built on relatively modest plots offering little scope for infilling, Seymour Road has retained most of its original character and includes fifteen Buildings of Townscape Merit.

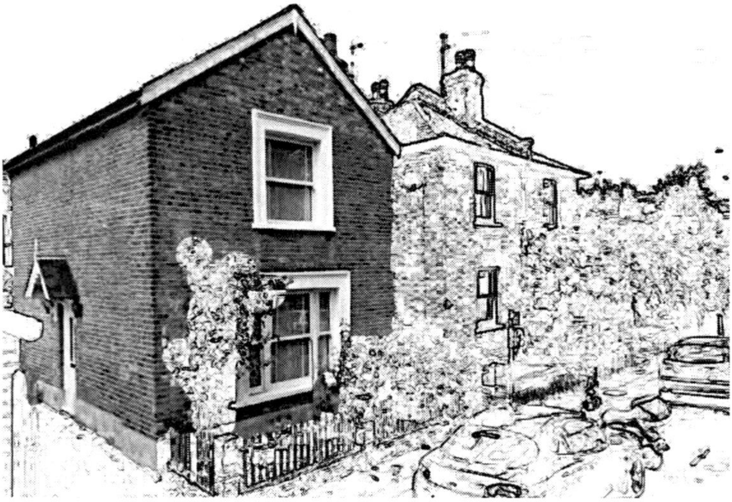

Building of Townscape Merit

above: *Rose Cottage*, 1 Seymour Road
Built in 1871, this modest property was recorded in the 1911 census as having a family of eight living in just four rooms.

below: *Seymour Cottages*, 3 and 5 Seymour Road
Built in 1875 by James Scotcher, a local builder and decorator, for his youngest son Frederick. After Frederick's death in 1906, number 5 was let to Ernest Whenman, another local builder, who built a shop from which he operated an undertaker's business. Both the shop (a) and Whenman's sign-writing on the gable (b) are just visible although largely hidden by the vegetation.

Buildings of Townscape Merit

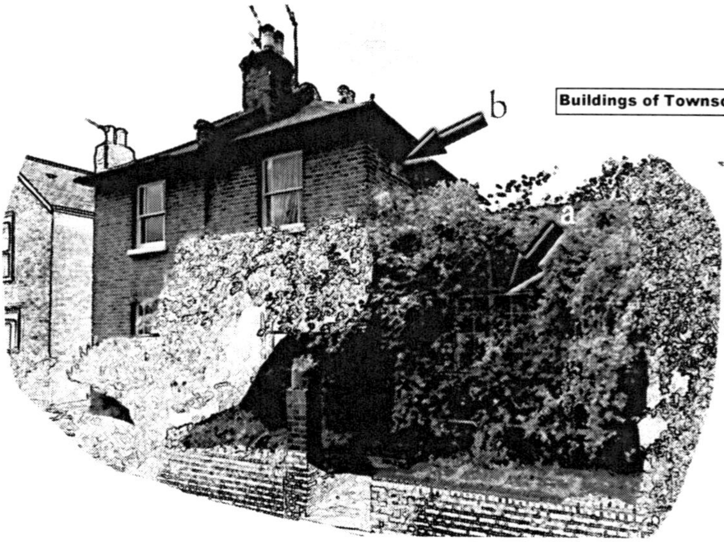

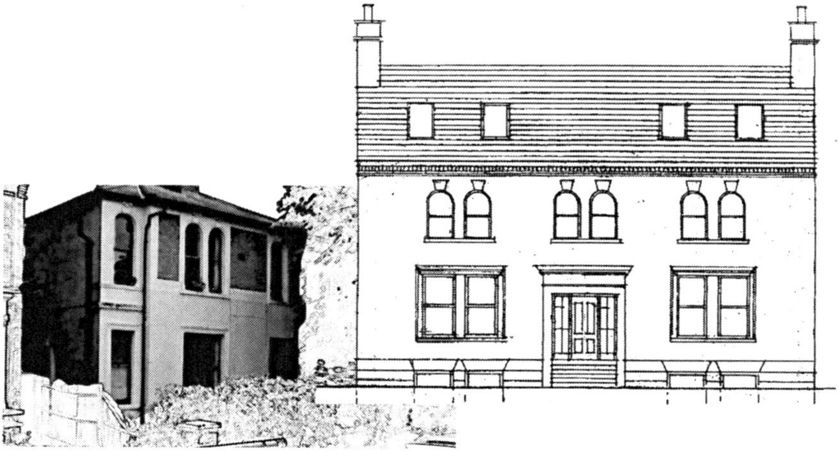

above: 2 Seymour Road

Currently under construction on the site of the first house to be built in Seymour Road (in 1861), the new property will consist of two two-bedroom flats, five one-bed-room flats, one studio flat and six bedsits with shared facilities. The paired round-arch windows mirror the original building (above left)

below: *Merton*, 4 Seymour Road

Built in 1883, over twenty years later than Number 1, its simple design - with pitch roof and single-storey square bay - was upgraded with copious additions of neo-classical ornamentation including pilasters with elaborate capitals on the bay window and porch. Even the house-name plaque is surmounted by an impressive pediment.

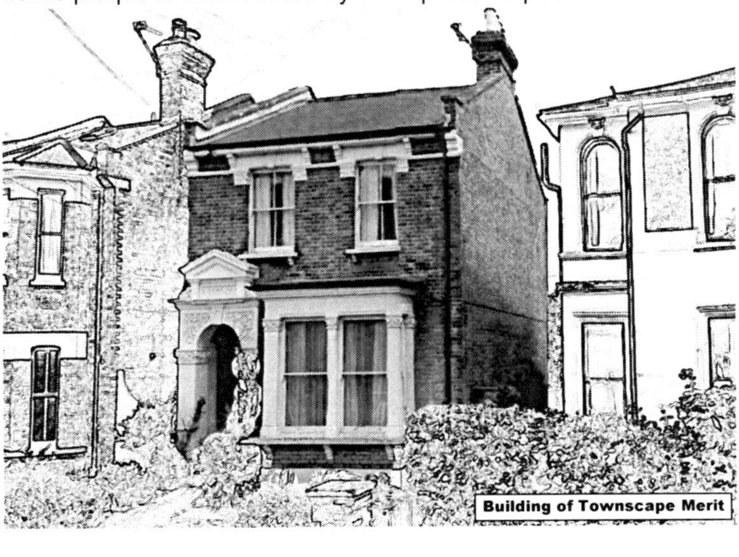

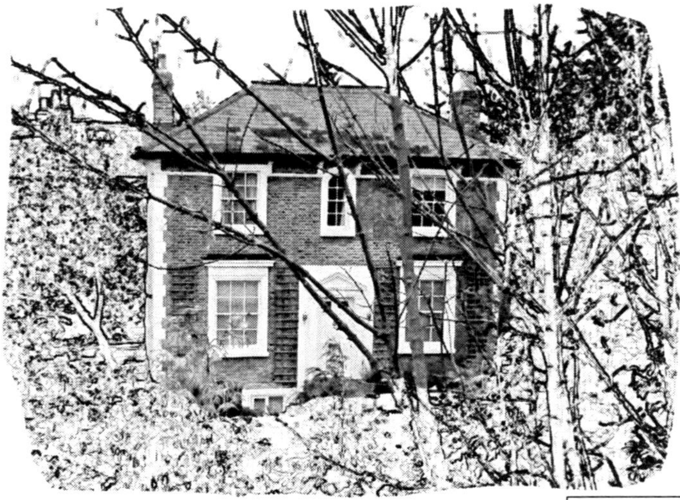

Building of Townscape Merit

above: *Northwick House*

Built around 1862 on land then belonging to the London & South West Railway Company, it is fitting that this attractive property is best viewed from Hampton Wick Station Platform 2! Twenty five years after it was built, its back garden was used as the site for *Northwick Terrace*, 80 - 92 High Street.

below: *Briarly Villa* and *Fernside*, 7 and 9 Seymour Road

One of four pairs of semi-detached houses built in 1881 on land previously owned by London and South Western Railway. At some time in the past, Number 7 had the tiles of the southern roof facet replaced with glass to provide more light into an artist's studio below (arrowed).

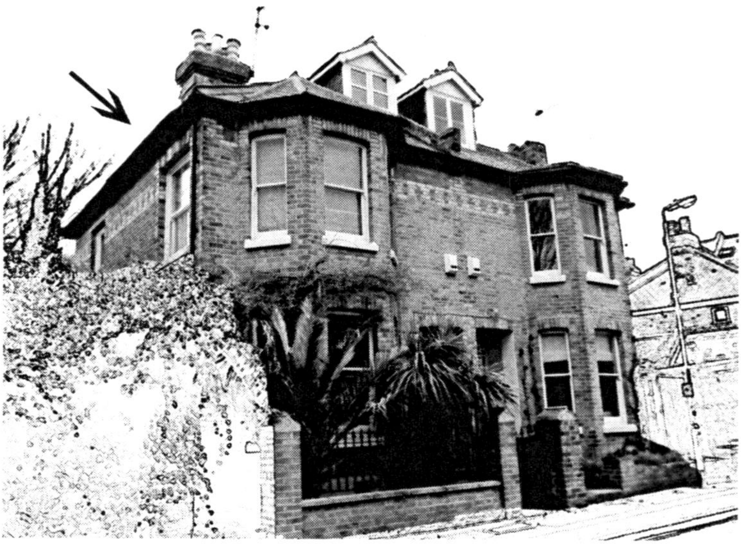

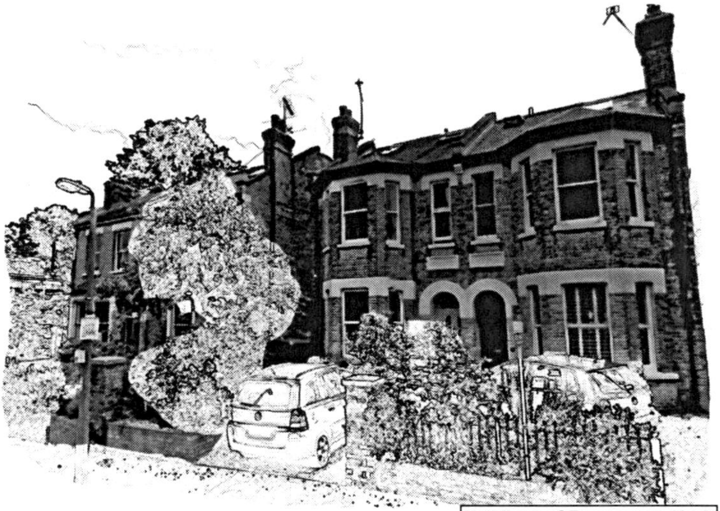

Buildings of Townscape Merit

above right to left: *Nutfield, Cliston, West Bank, West View*, 6 - 12 Seymour Road

Constructed in 1883, this set of properties were not built parallel to the road - but their front fences were. The Local Board chairman accused the owners of stealing land from the community unlawfully to increase the size of their front gardens! The long-running dispute was finally settled by a £10 donation to the Board's funds.

below: *Seymour Lodge*, 14 Seymour Road

The original *Seymour Lodge*, built in 1853, was demolished and replaced by the present structure in 1963. The building contains 15 flats and is run by its own Residents Association, formed in 1965.

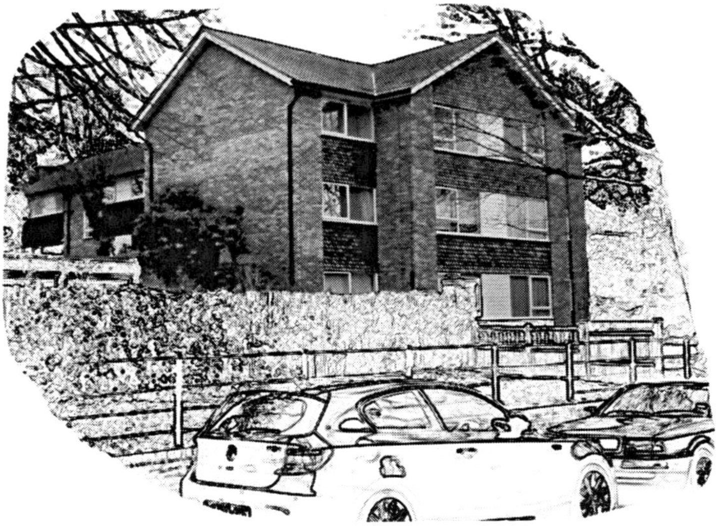

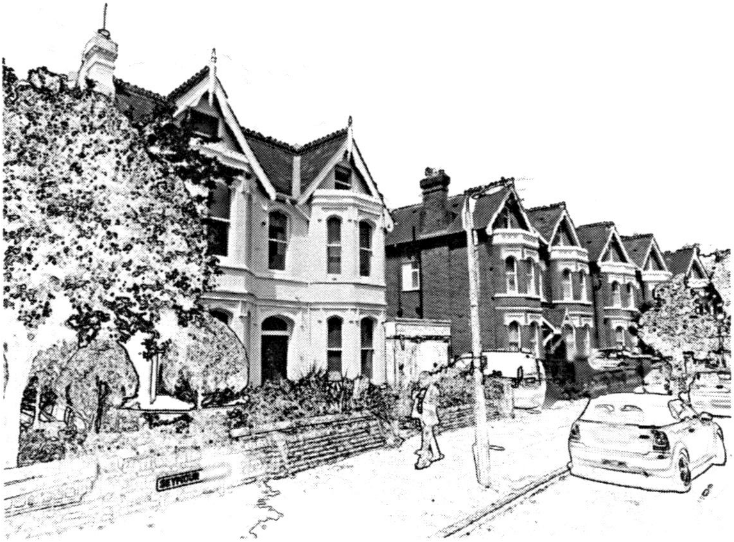

above: **11 - 15c Seymour Road, 1 and 2 Glamorgan Road**
This impressive sweep of houses was built by Richard Starkey in 1883. Though not absolutely identical, the three-bay designs share many common features including gothic-arched windows and upper sashes as well as two-storey canted bays topped with mock battlements on each side of the front door. These 12-room houses were originally built as single-family houses but all have now been converted into flats with, typically, 5 units per block.

Opposite top: ***Ryecroft, Havant House, Stresa*** **and** ***Villette*****, 16 - 22 Seymour Road**
Twenty years on from building the above houses across the road, Richard Starkey erected a further four properties in this lighter and roomier semi-detached Edwardian style. Typical of the period are the balconies, semi-rendered facades and the windows with their multi-pane upper sash/single-pane lower sash. Note also the charming triangular oriel windows above the front doors in the halls-apart configuration.

Opposite middle: ***Seymour Court***
This block, containing four two-bed flats, was built in 1955 on the last vacant plot available in Seymour Road.

Opposite bottom: **24 and 26 Seymour Road**
This pair of three-bed semi-detached houses were built in 1935 in the side garden of Number 28 (*The Croft*).

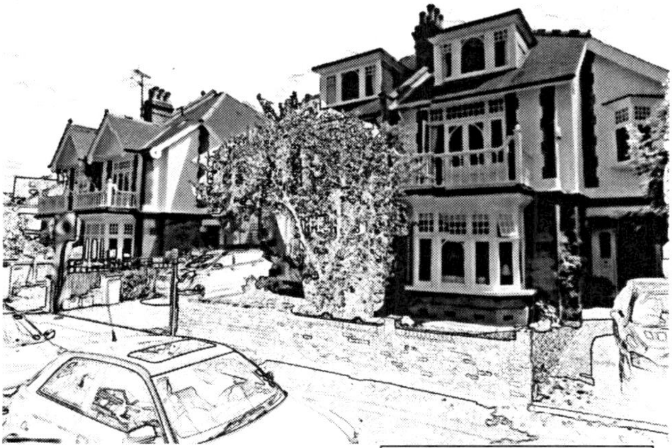

Buildings of Townscape Merit

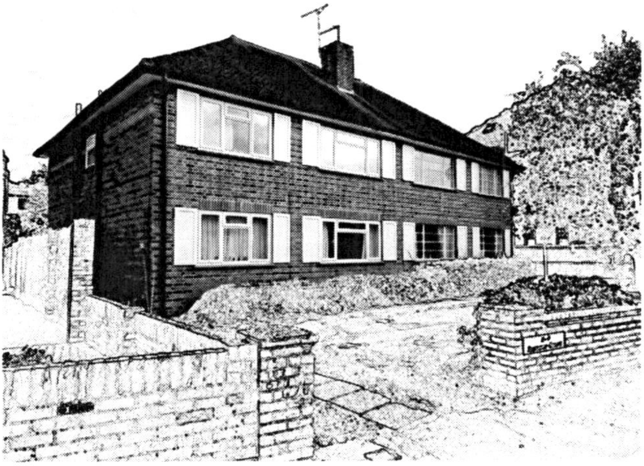

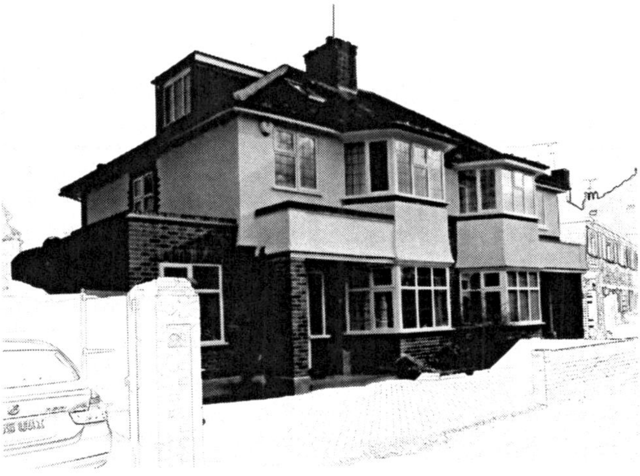

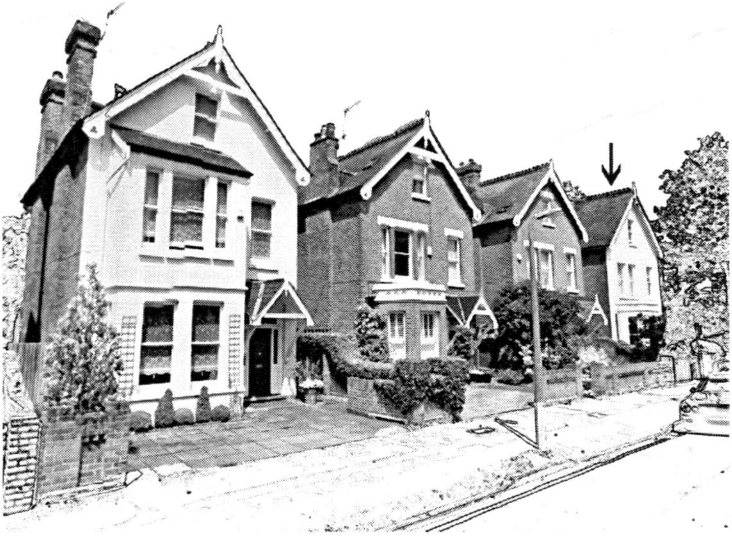

above: *Rosslyn, The Chestnuts, Westwood* and *Penrhyn*, 17 - 23 Seymour Road

This row of houses, built in 1883 at the same time as the grander Numbers 11 - 15, were probably developer Richard Starkey's attempt to offer a more modest eight-room alternative to his less well-heeled clients. The properties nevertheless retained many of the features common to Starkey's designs (see page 65).

Operation Julie

The house known as *Penrhyn* (arrowed, above) appears to be unremarkable and indistinguishable from any of its three neighbours. But from October 1976 it was the subject of an intense under-cover police surveillance operation and on 26 March 1977 Number 23 Seymour Road Hampton Wick hit the headlines around the world in the biggest possible way.

Operation Julie was a UK police investigation into the production of illicit LSD by two drug rings during the mid-1970's. The operation, involving 11 police forces over a two-and-a-half year period, led to the break-up of one of the largest LSD manufacturing operations in the world. It culminated in 1977 with enough LSD to make 6.5 million 'tabs' (with a street value of £6.5million) being seized. 120 people were arrested in the UK and France and over £800,000 discovered in Swiss bank accounts.

Police had originally been monitoring a remote house in Wales which they suspected housed a drug-factory. They had suspected that *Penrhyn* was somehow part of the distribution network and were therefore surprised to find that it too contained a complete LSD production facility - not (as in Wales) located in the basement but in the attic of the house.

Having served his sentence, the one-time resident of *Penrhyn* returned to the house but, after a time, found life "going straight" in Britain was too mundane and he emigrated to Australia.

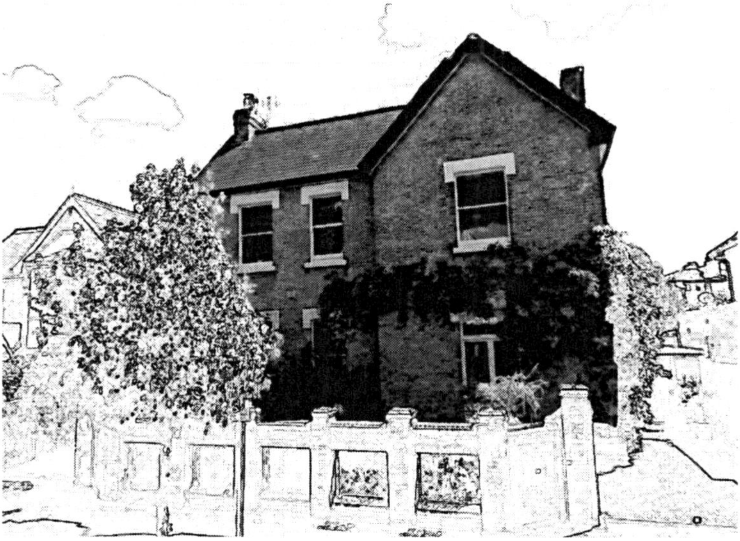

above: **The Croft, 28 Seymour Road**

This (now) seven-bed house was built in 1885 in the midst - both geographically and temporally - of Richard Starkey's developments elsewhere in Seymour Road. The developer and first resident was Edward Alfred Wright, himself a major player in the development of Hampton Wick.

below: **30 Seymour Road**

Built in 1994, the current house replaced a bungalow which had been built in 1935 as part of the same infilling of the garden of *The Croft (above)* as Numbers 24 and 26, and by the same builder.

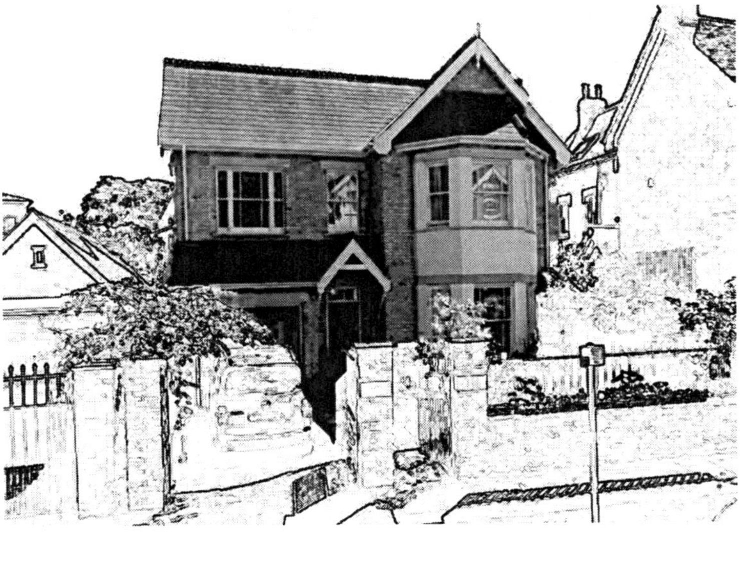

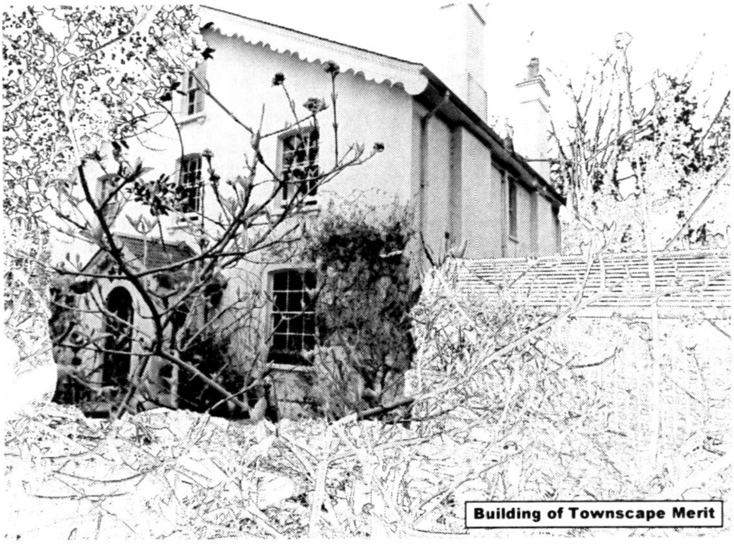

above: *The Old Vicarage*, 25 Seymour Road

Built in 1861 and originally known as *Fairlea Cottage*, Number 25 was the St John the Baptist Vicarage between 1934 and 1984 after the original building on Park Road was replaced by *Ingram House*. The high fence and copious vegetation may mean that the amazing saw-tooth bargeboards are all that can be seen of this elegant house.

below: *Lexington Place*

This development by Laing Homes comprises three three-storey four-bed townhouses and eight flats (four two-bed and four one-bed). It was completed in 2005 on what had been the garden land of *Eversleigh*, 10 Glamorgan Road.

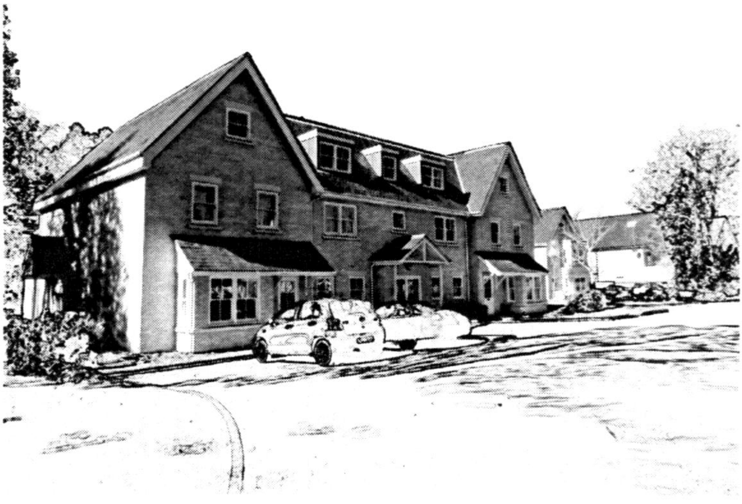

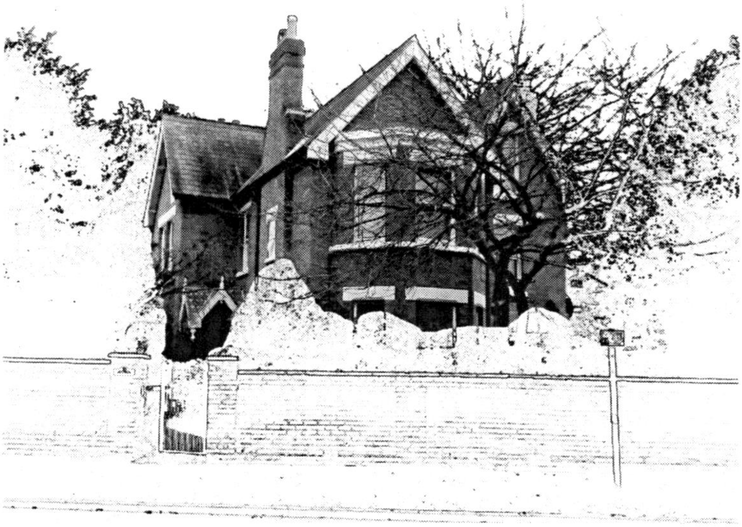

above: *Penmaen*, 32 Seymour Road

This substantial property was built in 1882 by developer Richard Starkey for his own use. The Starkey's had nine children so would have made good use of this 11-room mansion but it is likely that the building was also intended a showcase for Starkey's house-building skills.

below: Richmore, 34 Seymour Road

Another large-scale Starkey house, this one being built in 1892. Charles Preston Minett lived in the house for 50 years and rose to be a very senior, senior civil servant. It was then bought by a developer who converted the property into four flats, three of which are accessed from Lower Teddington Road.

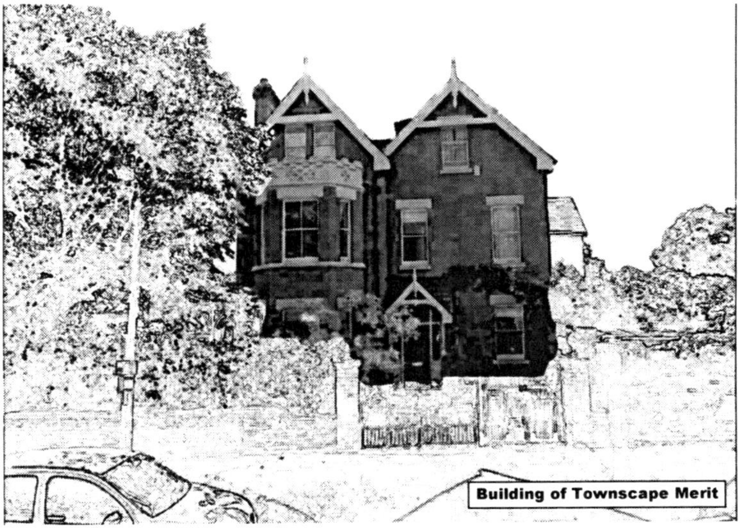

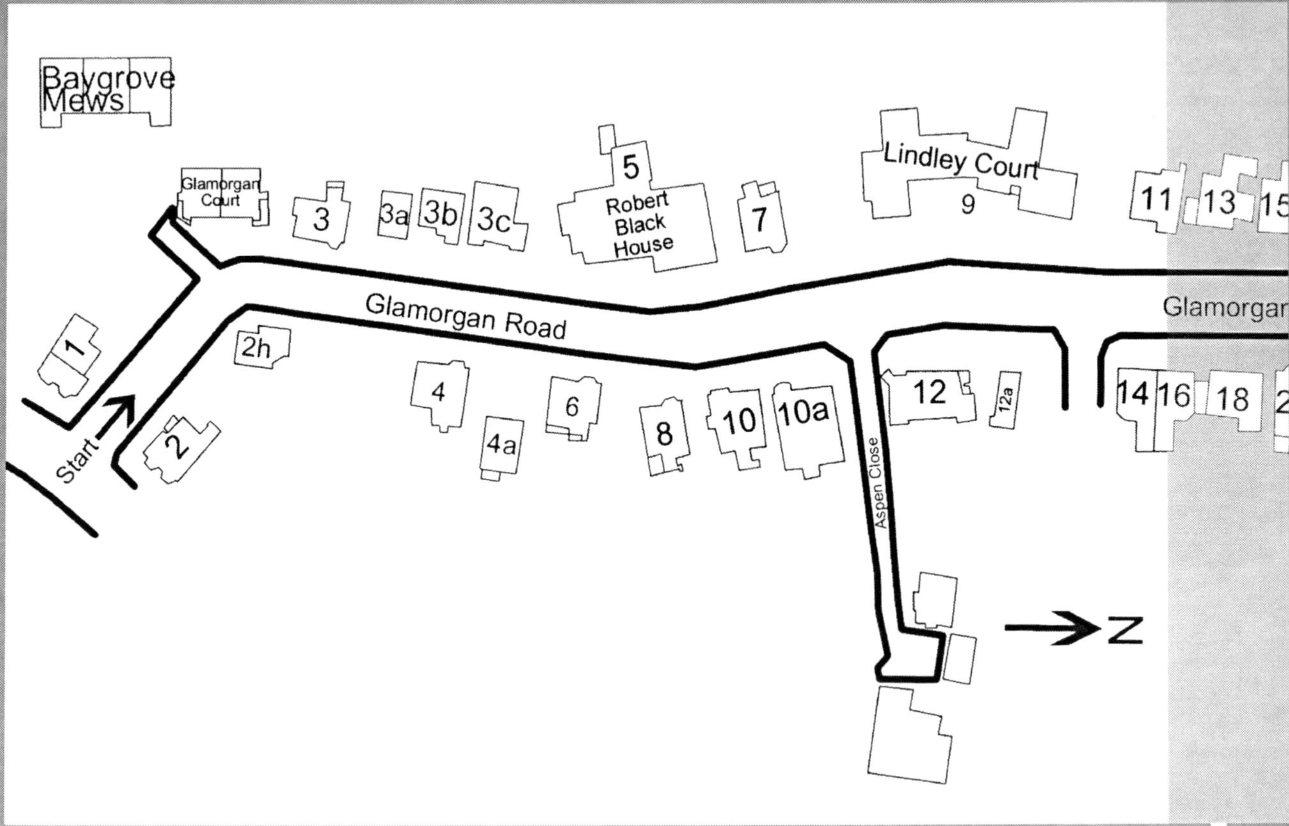
Baygrove Mews
Glamorgan Court
1
2
2h
3
3a
3b
3c
4
4a
5
Robert Black House
6
7
8
Lindley Court
9
10
10a
11
12
12a
13
14
15
16
18
Glamorgan Road
Glamorgan
Aspen Close
Start
N

GLAMORGAN ROAD

Brick by Brick

Created in the 1880's by Richard Starkey (see page 65) and named after his county of birth, the road is typified by large detached and semi-detached Victorian villas set on generous plots away from the pavement edge. The southern part of the road (Numbers 1 to 12) was completed first, all houses being built by Starkey. Most of the properties in the northern part were built in the period 1890 - 1914 with the exception of Numbers 24 - 38 which were built by Henry Bambury in the late 1920's. Major new developments on the sites of Numbers 5 and 9 around 1970 have changed the character of the central area of the road.

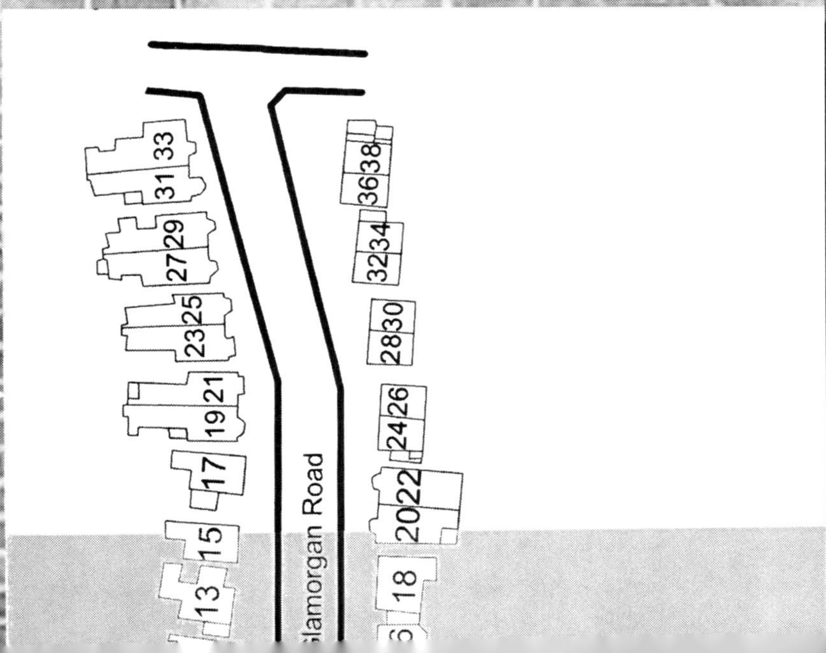

below: *Shardiloes*, 1 Glamorgan Road

One of five almost identical houses built by Richard Starkey around 1883 (see page 65). Built before Glamorgan Road was laid out, *Shardiloes* was originally considered part of Seymour Road. It was later split into two properties, the other half designated as 15c Seymour Road and now converted into flats.

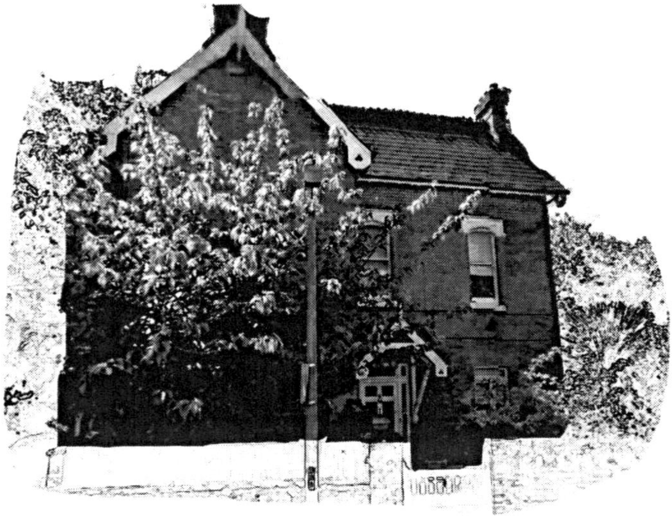

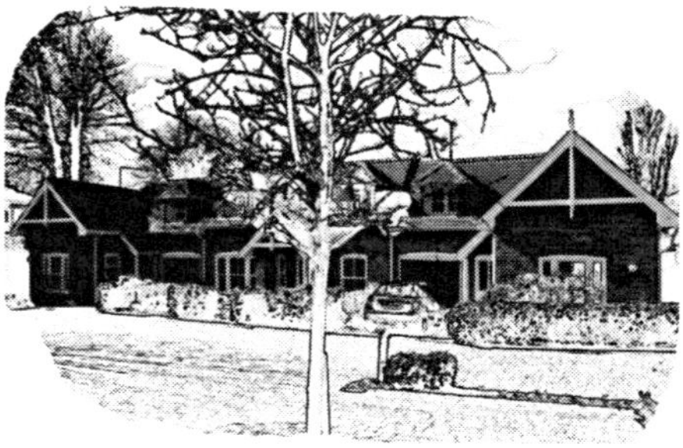

Left:: *Baygrove Mews*

This development by Argrove Properties (with BBA Architects, hence *Baygrove*) was created in 1996 on land at the rear of 2 Upper Teddington Road. It consists of three 3-bedroom Mews Houses. The architects seem to be paying respect to the several neighbouring Starkey-built properties by featuring his prominent white bargeboards with trefoil motifs.

right: *Glamorgan Court*

A block of four flats built in 1959 in the garden of Number 3 to its right.

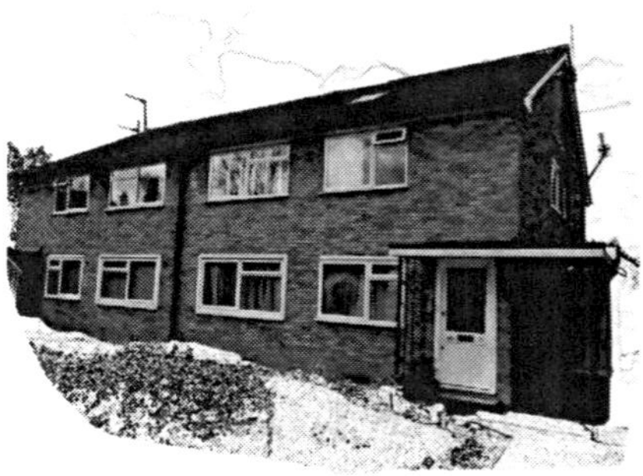

below: *Abermaed*, 2 Glamorgan Road

Unlike its twin on the opposite corner, this property has always been considered part of Glamorgan Road . It differs from the other four similar properties by not adopting the Gothic style for its windows and front door. More recently, its chimneys have been removed. Converted into five flats in 1978

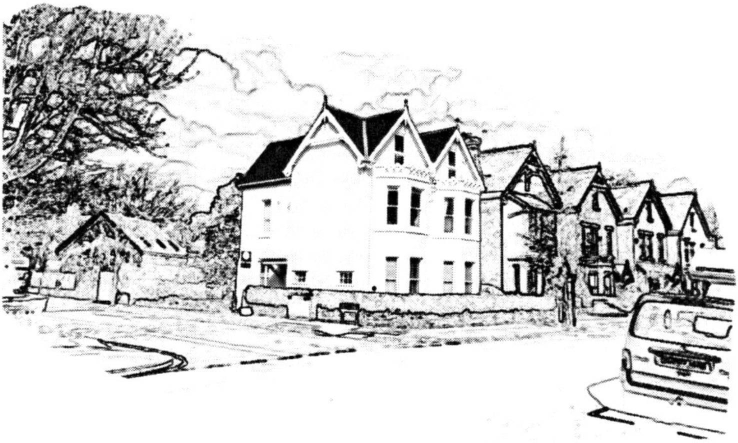

below: 2H Glamorgan Road

This 3-bedroom property was built in 2008. Although most of the plot was created from the rear garden of Number 2 Glamorgan Road, the planning application was made by the occupants of Number 4.

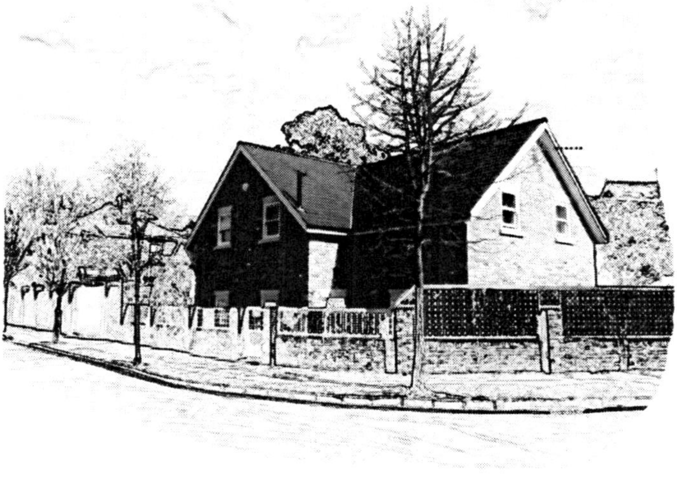

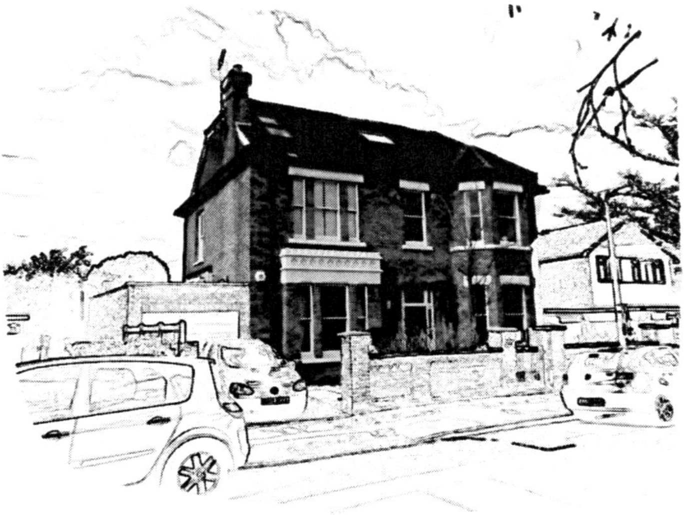

above: *Ravenswood*, 3 Glamorgan Road

One of several almost identical houses built in Glamorgan Road by Richard Starkey around 1885. Although originally designed with a fully hipped roof (see Number 4 opposite) this one has recently been modified to a clipped-gable design to accommodate an additional pair of bedrooms.

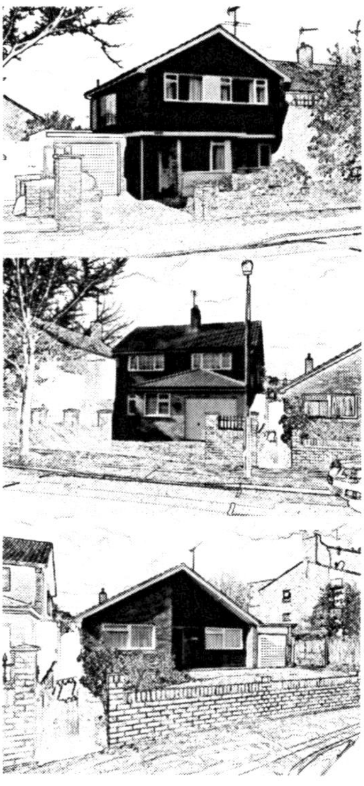

left: *Giltar House*, *The Ridings*, *Baet*
3a- c Glamorgan Road

These three properties were built in 1962 by New Ideal Homes Ltd in the grounds of Number 5 Glamorgan Road and used standard catalogue designs.

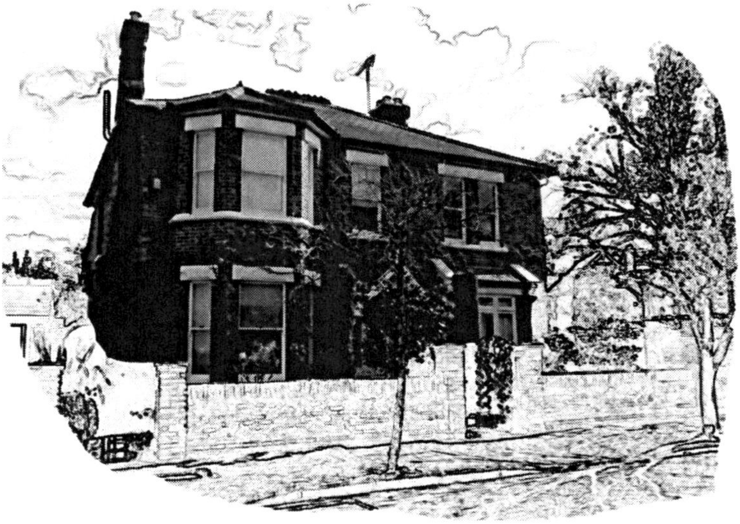

above: *Endsleigh*, 4 Glamorgan Road

One of the most intact of Starkey's standard 9-room three-bay designs. This example has a pent-roof covering the single-storey bay whereas others have the castellated balconets featured in Number 3 opposite.

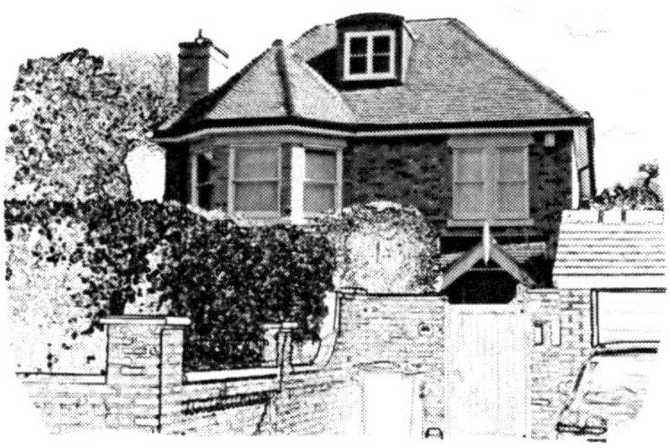

Refused:

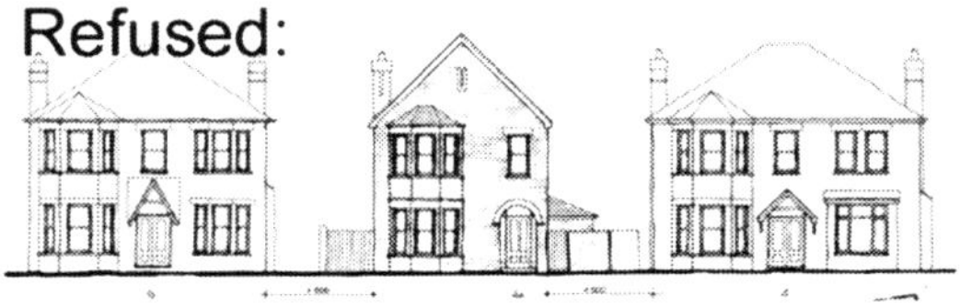

Accepted:

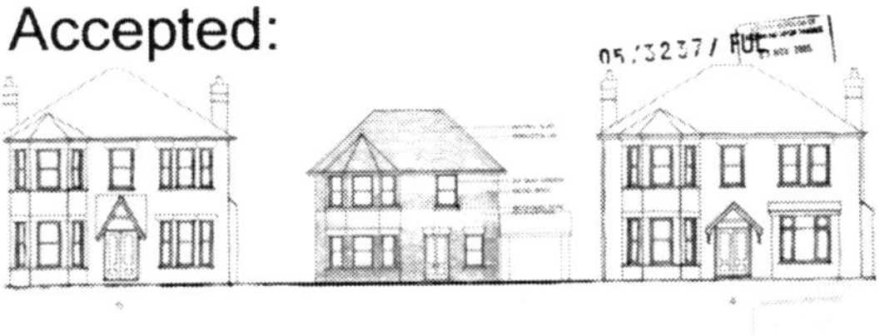

Left:: 4a

Glamorgan Road

The original building on this plot was a bungalow identical to *Baet* opposite and built at the same time (1962). An application to demolish the bungalow and rebuild was refused and the applicants required to reuse the bungalow's foundations. The chimney and dormer were added subsequently.

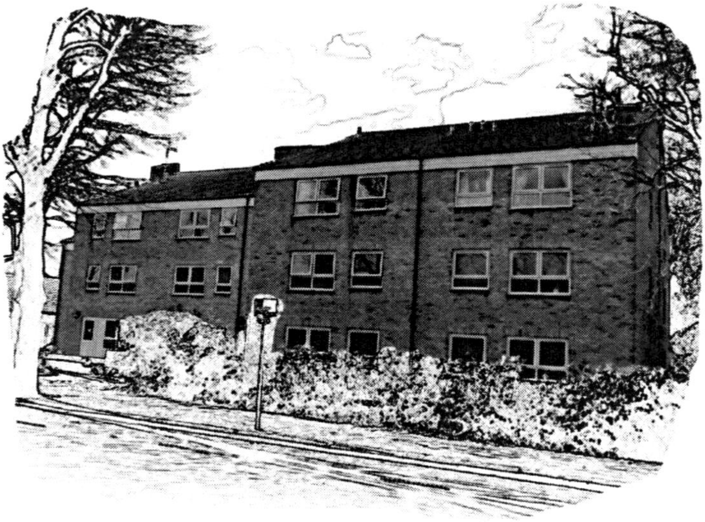

above: *Robert Black House*, 5 Glamorgan Road
This property contains 24 flats purpose-built to provide sheltered accommodation. It was opened in 1979 and stands on the site of a former substantial property (see page 78).

below: *Trethewy*, 7 Glamorgan Road
Built in 1889 by Richard Starkey.

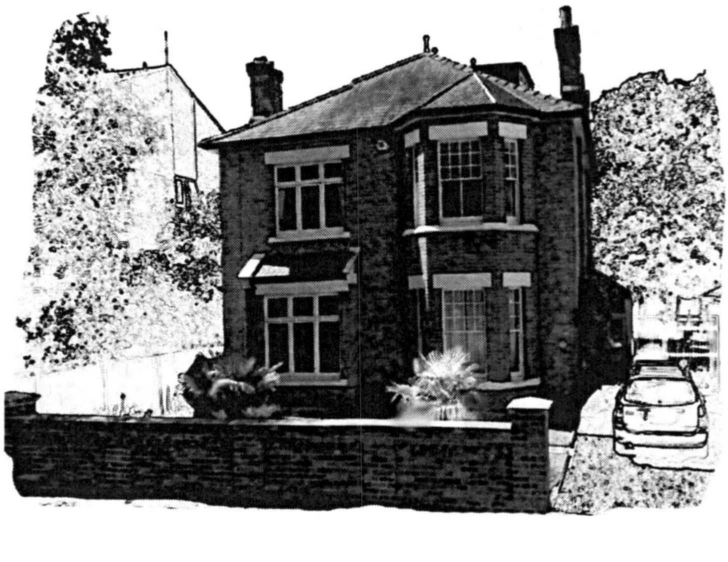

right: *Heathfield*,
6 Glamorgan Road
Built in 1887 by Starkey

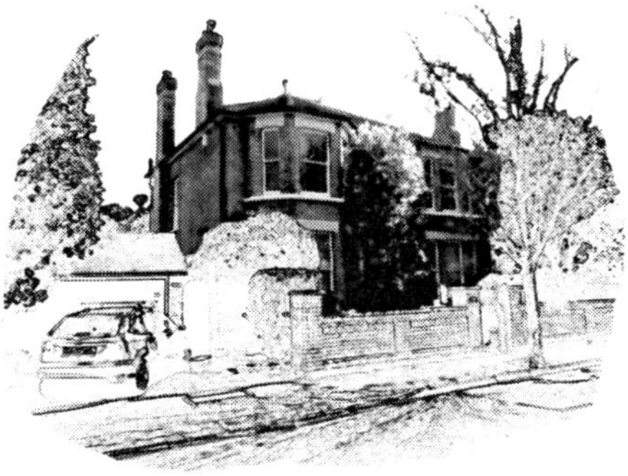

right: *Rosenau*, 8
Glamorgan Road
Built in 1887 by Starkey

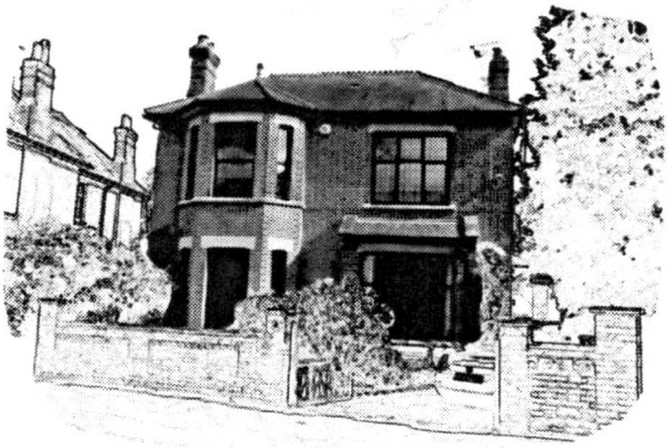

right: *Eversleigh*, 10
Glamorgan Road
Built in 1887 probably by William Horace Hope

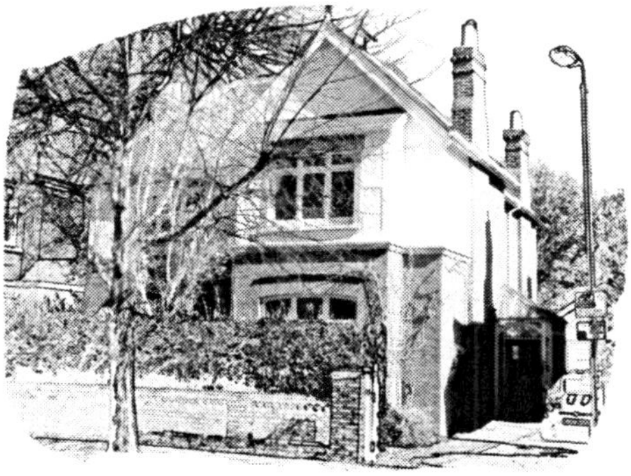

right: 10a Glamorgan Road
This six-bedroom house was built in 2004 after an existing extension to Number 10 had been demolished as part of the overall project to develop *Lexington Place*.

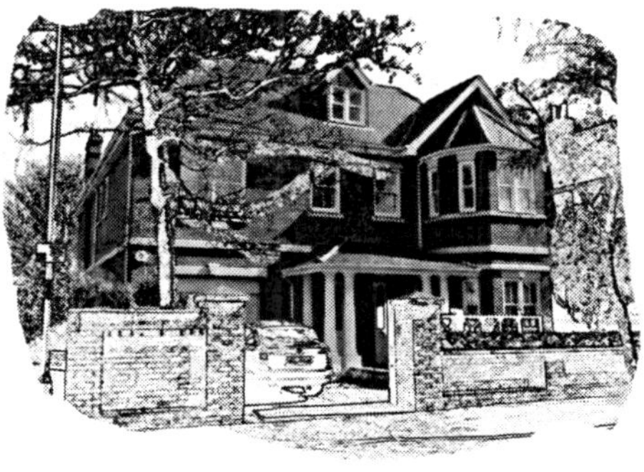

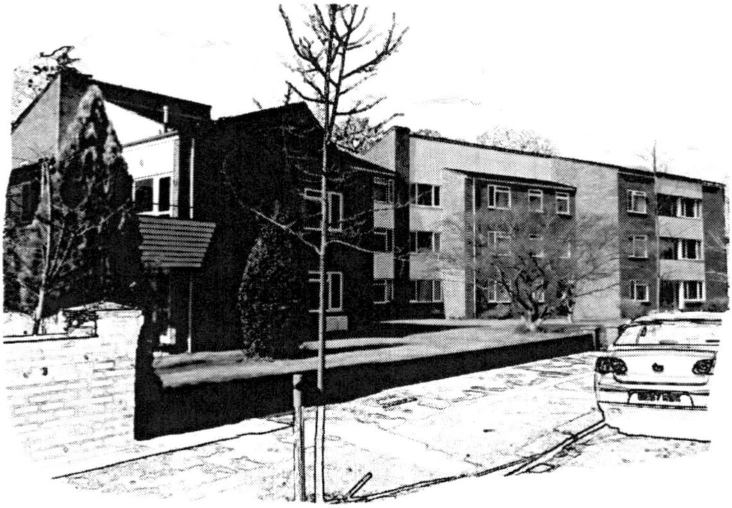

above: *Lindley Court*, 9 Glamorgan Road
Built in 1968, this block of 14 flats was the last of several proposals for redeveloping the site of the original Number 9 (see page 78).

below: Glamorgan Road around 1910
A postcard by Richard Young & Co. of Teddington

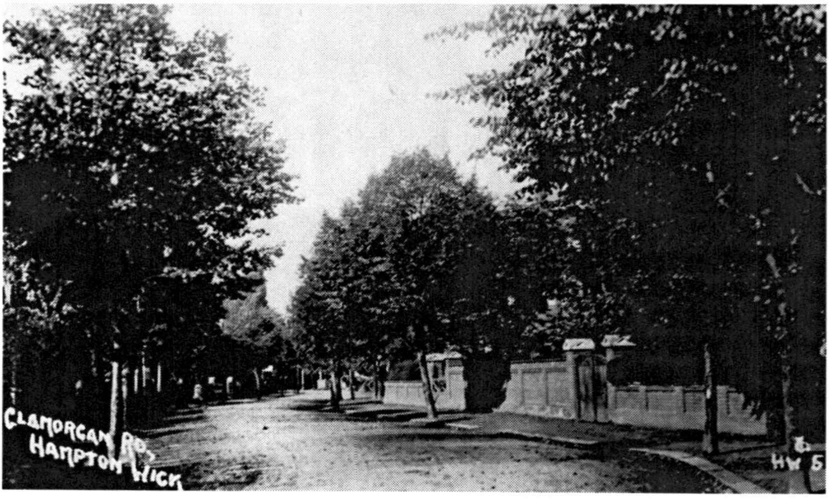

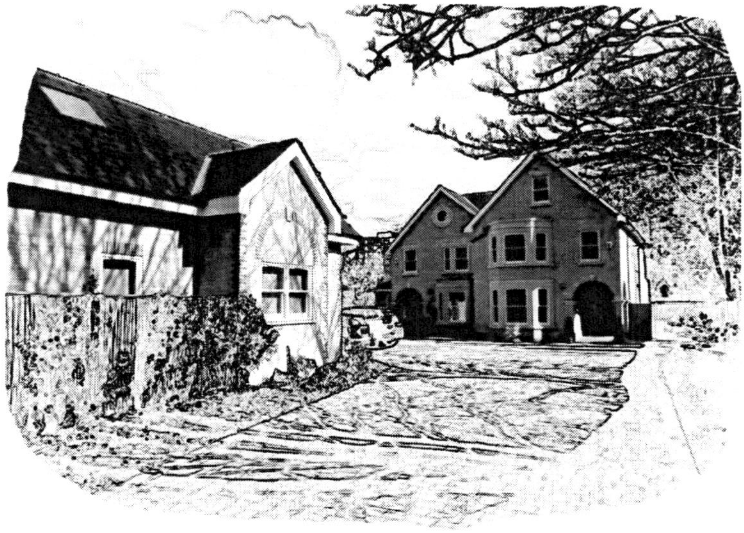

above: *Aspen Close*

This 2008 development by Diadem Homes consists of two three-storey five-bedroom houses and one one-bedroom bungalow. It is sited in the side and rear garden of Number 12 (see below).

below: *St Mary's*, 12 Glamorgan Road

Built in 1896 probably by William Horace Hope, this 15-room mansion remained a single-family home until 1945. After a long phase as a care home for the elderly it was converted back into a single dwelling in 1991. It is currently being re-converted to make two family homes.

inset: The coach house was converted into a separate dwelling in 1992.

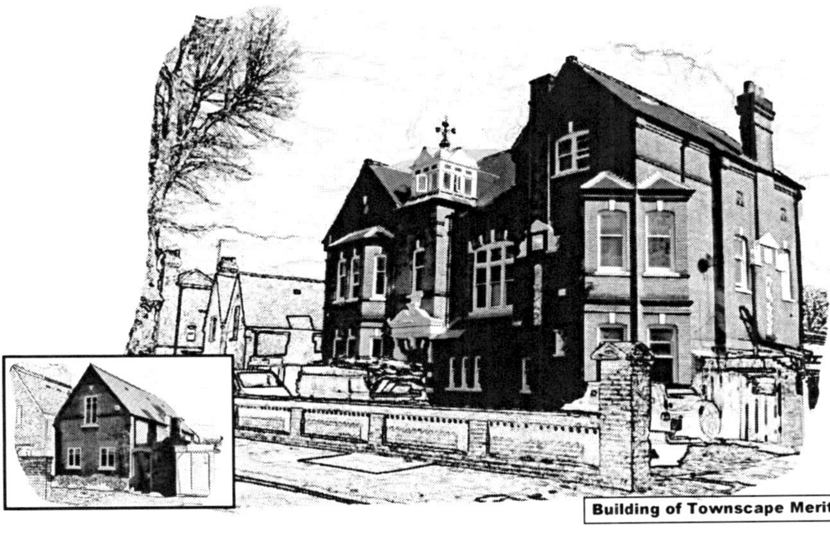

Building of Townscape Merit

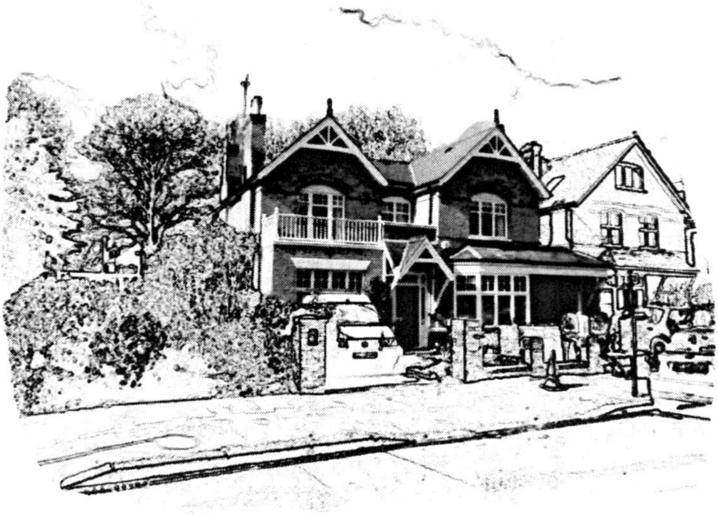

above: *Cotswold*, 11 Glamorgan Road
Built in 1891 by Lee and Lavers-Smith (see below). Although the balcony looks as if it was part of the original design, it was actually only added in 1990.

below left to right: *Mervyn, Durbar House, Cheveley*
13 - 17 Glamorgan Road
These three houses, built in 1889, were the first of many properties to be built on Glamorgan Road by Henry Lee and Charles Lavers-Smith (see above and page 70). The designs were almost identical with the exception of the shape of the brick lintels over the first floor windows. Number 17 has been in the possession of the same family for over 100 years.

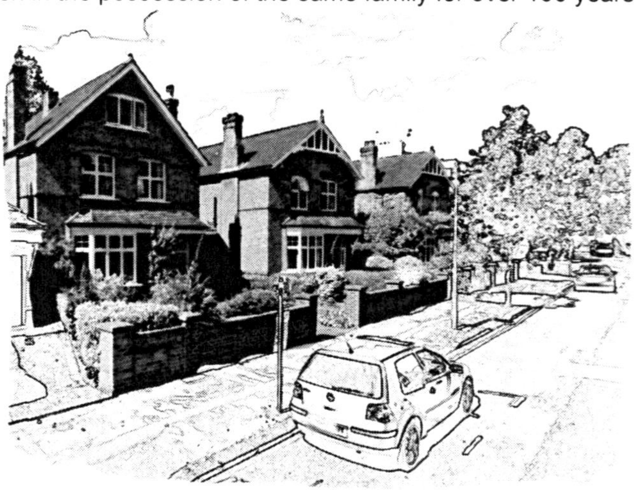

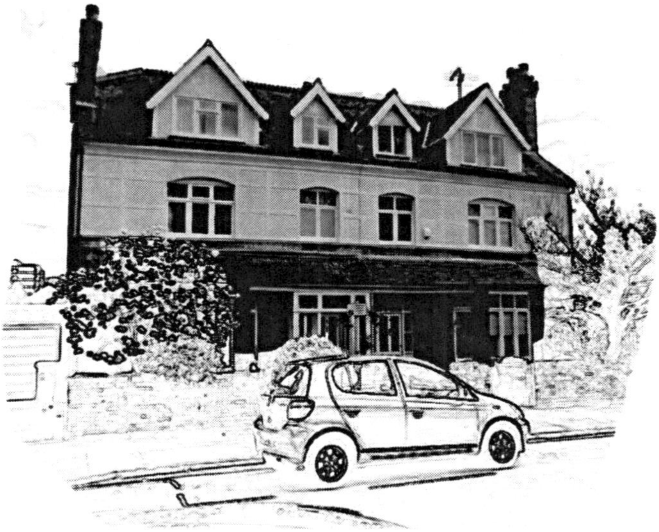

above: *Wood Dalling and St Olaves*,

14 and 16 Glamorgan Road

Built in 1894 by Lee and Lavers-Smith. The owner of Wood Dalling bought extra land to add to his already-extensive garden and sold it off in the 1930's to accommodate Monmouth Avenue see page 74)

below: 18 Glamorgan Road

Built 1914

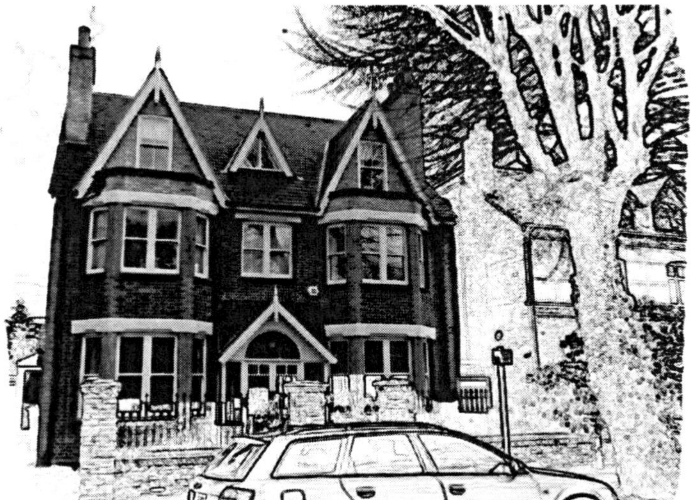

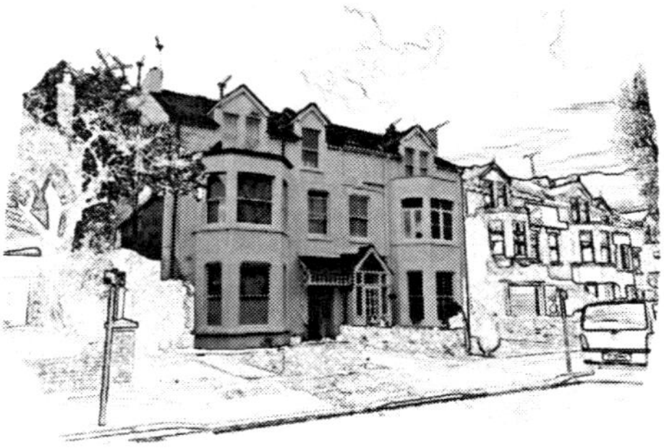

left: *Copsewood* and *Ryall*
19 and 21 Glamorgan Road
Built 1893

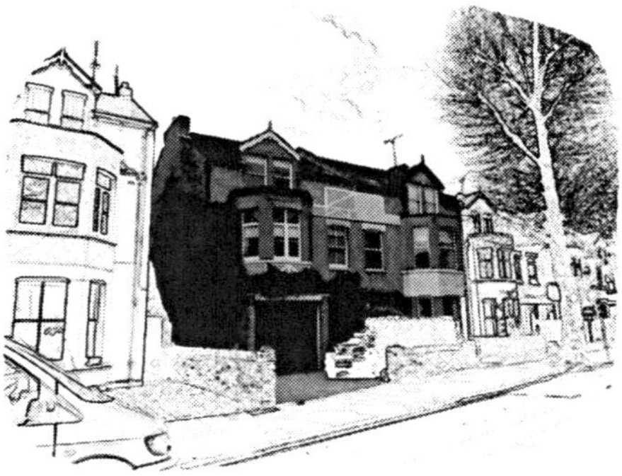

left: *Thirlmere* and *St Brelades*
23 and 25 Glamorgan Road
Built 1900

Henry Lee and Charles Lavers-Smith built four pairs of semi-detached houses on this stretch of Glamorgan Road in the 1890's. An identical design was used for each pair with ten rooms ranged over three floors. Although superficially the properties now look different, the identical barge-boards above the second storey dormer windows confirm their common origins.

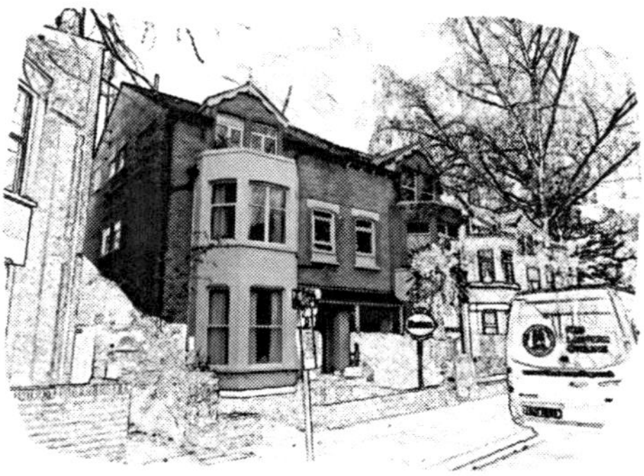

left: *Beaumont* and *Tamerton*
27 and 29 Glamorgan Road
Built 1900

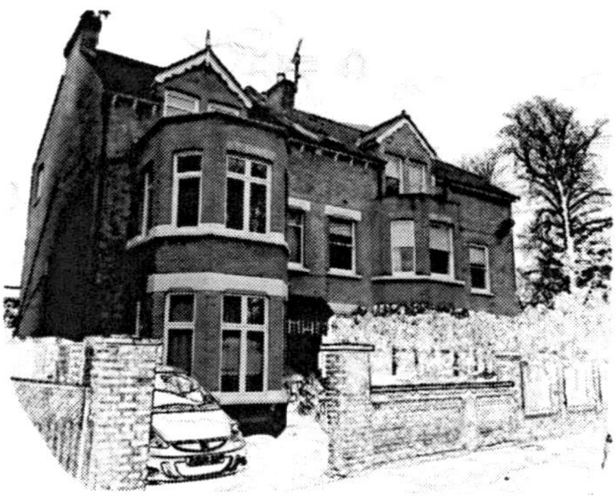

left: *Cibouré* and
St Nicholas House
31 and 33 Glamorgan Road
Built 1893

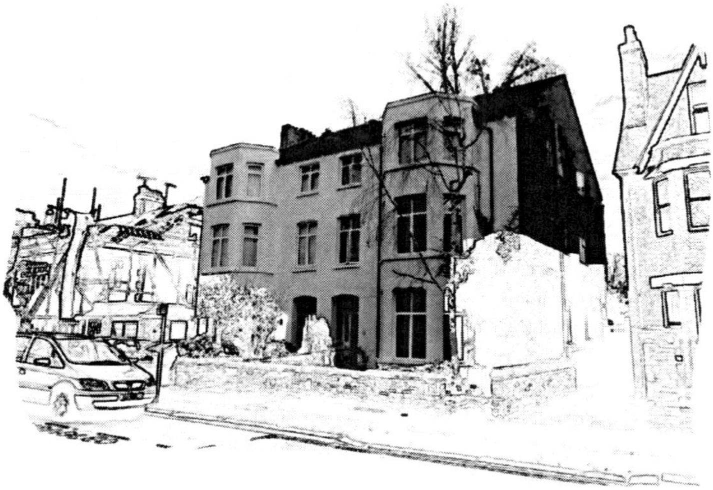

above: *Westgate* and *Glamorgan House*
20 and 22 Glamorgan Road
Built 1906

below: 24 - 38 Glamorgan Road

This row of four pairs of semi-detached houses was built in 1928 by Henry Bambury, a local builder who himself lived in Number 38 for 52 years. Comparing their design with those of the properties opposite shows how dramatically tastes changed over the intervening 30 year period. The houses were constructed with hipped roofs but almost all have been converted to a gabled structure in order to provide third-storey accommodation.

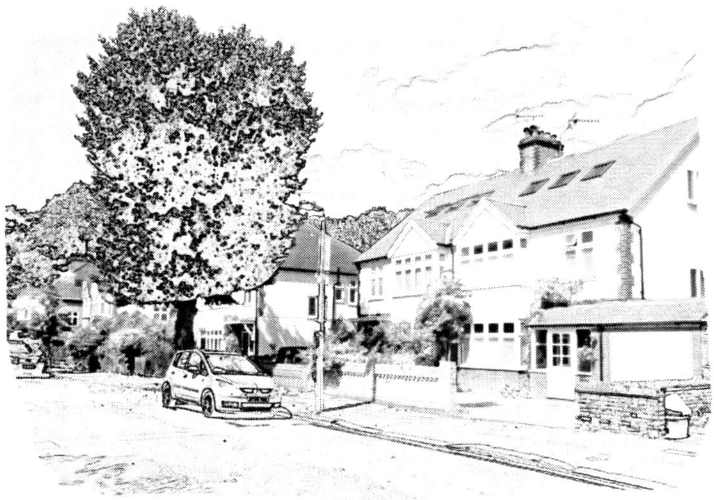

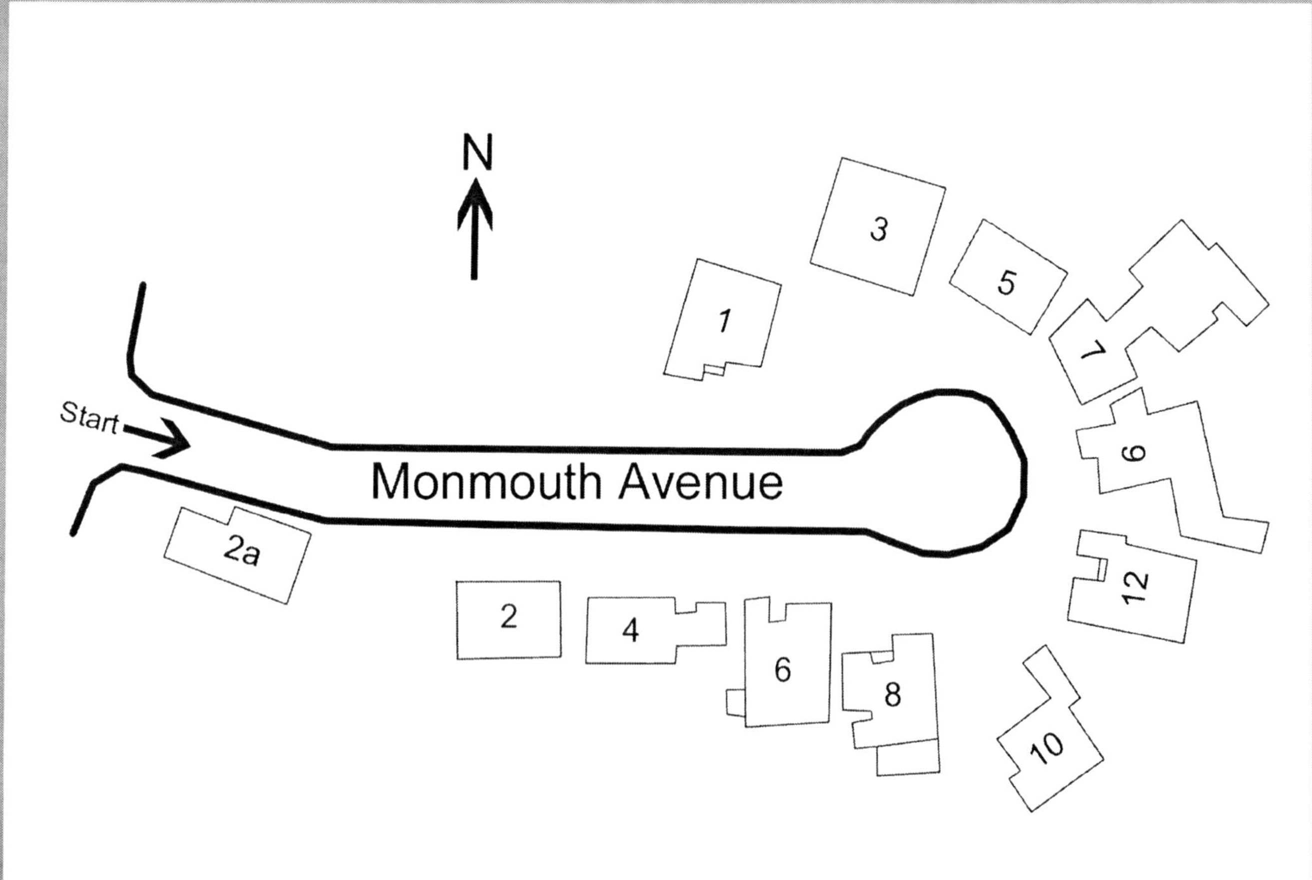
N
Start
Monmouth Avenue
1
3
5
7
9
12
10
2a
2
4
6
8

MONMOUTH AVENUE

Brick by Brick

Monmouth Avenue was created in 1938 by Robert Wake, a local Kingston upon Thames builder. The development was laid out in the side and back garden of Number 14 Glamorgan Road which still stands on the north west corner. Known as a banjo cul de sac, this road layout made excellent use of the space available and allowed eleven plots to be accommodated. World War 2 interrupted the project - six properties were built before and five after the hostilities. All but one were bungalows - these were a first for Hampton Wick.

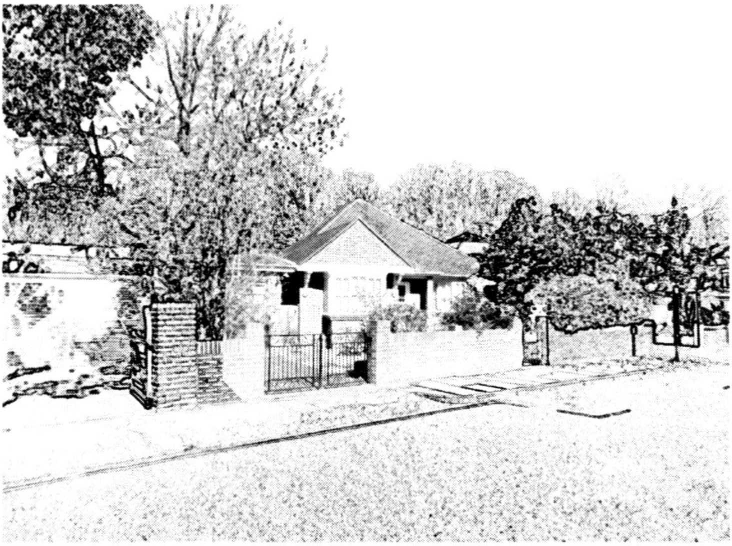

above: 1 Monmouth Avenue
Built in 1939

Opposite top: 2a Monmouth Avenue
This three-bedroom property was built in 1987 at the end of the garden of Number 2.

Opposite middle: 2 Monmouth Avenue
The first property completed in Monmouth Avenue (1938), it was constructed by the scheme's overall developer Robert Wake for his own use.

Opposite bottom: 4 Monmouth Avenue
This three-bedroom house was also built by Robert Wake in 1938 and since extended by a further bay.

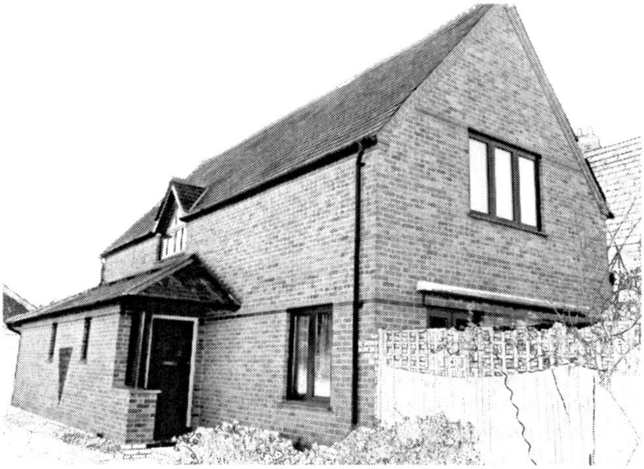

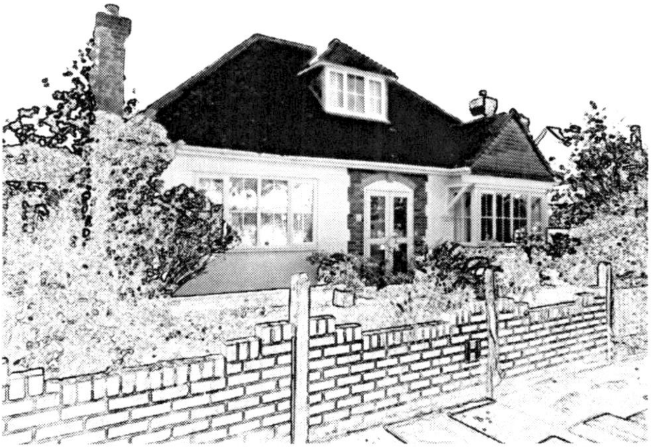

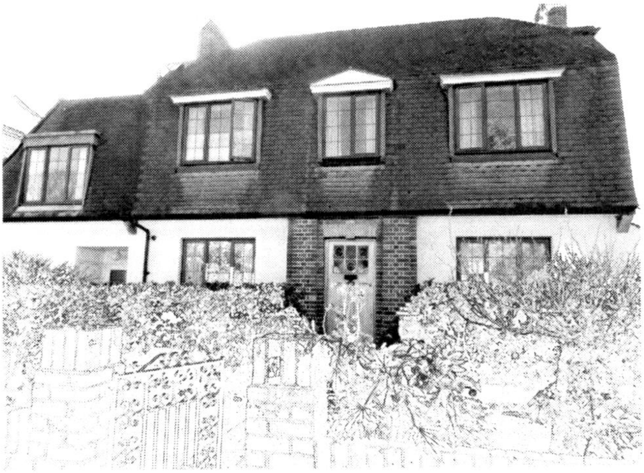

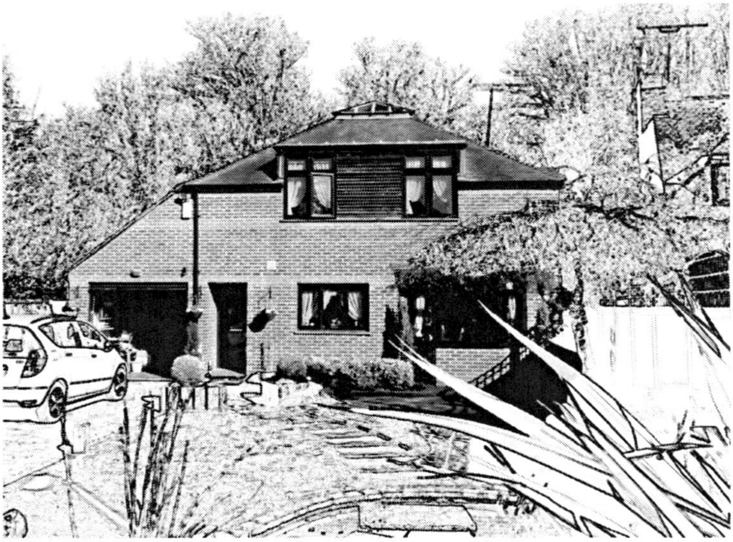

above: **3 Monmouth Avenue**
The original 1954 bungalow was badly damaged by a major fire in 1985. This replacement house was built in 1987.

below: **5 Monmouth Avenue**
Built in 1953 for its current owner/occupier. The chalet bungalow design was approved in place of the originally applied-for two-storey three-bedroom house.

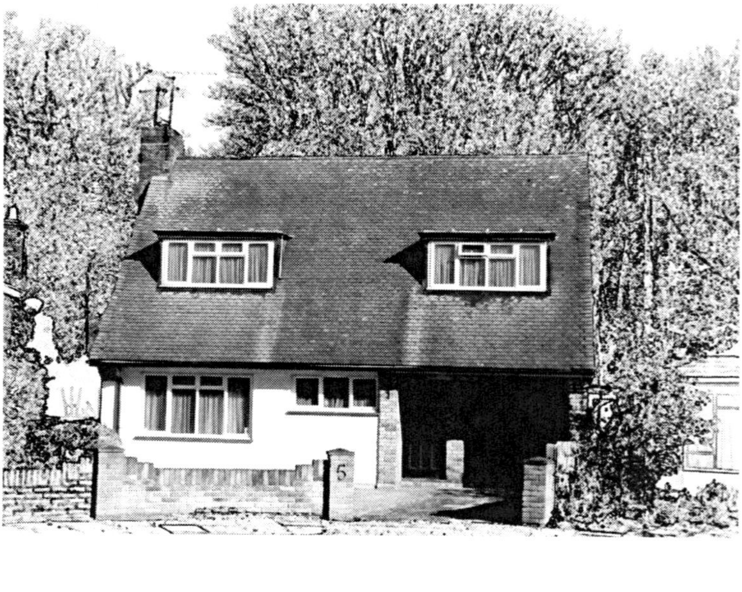

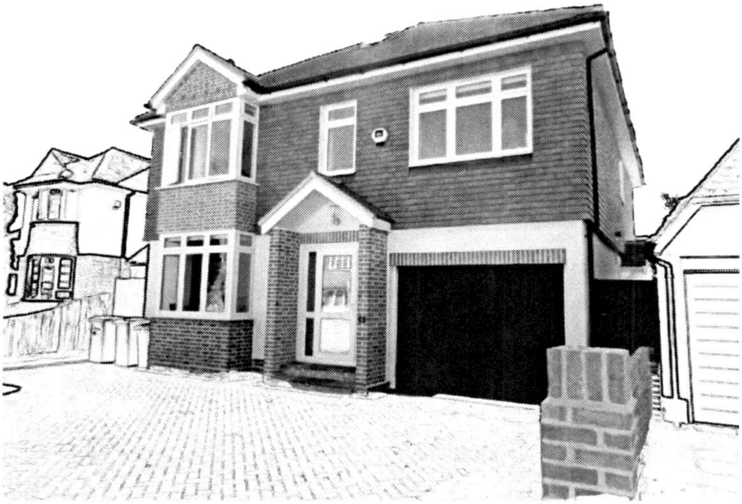

above: **6 Monmouth Avenue**

The original Robert Wake-built 1938 bungalow was built as a mirror image of the plans originally applied for. A second bedroom was later added in the roof but in 2009 the roof itself was removed and a second storey added which, with a further room in the new roof, has converted this into a full five-bedroom house.

below: **8 Monmouth Avenue**

This three-bedroom house appears externally to have remained exactly as it was originally drawn when built in 1939.

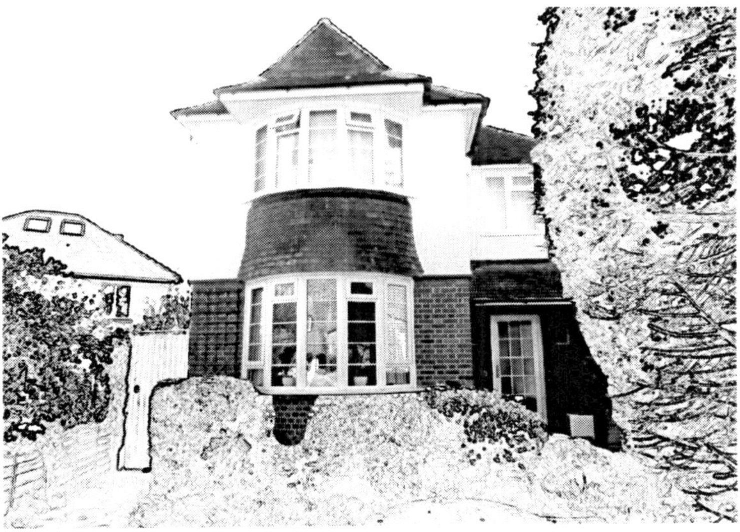

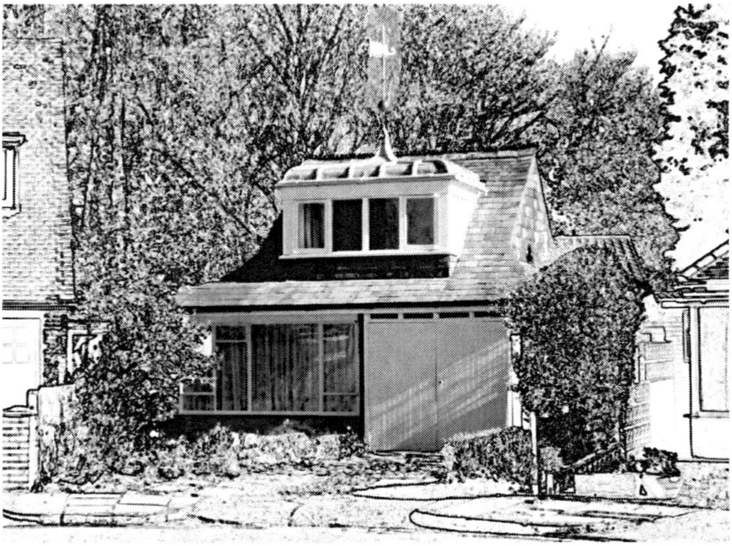

above: 7 Monmouth Avenue

This fascinating property was built in 1959 on land originally owned by Middlesex County Council and ear-marked for the school caretakers house (which was later built at 63 Lower Teddington Road). It was designed by its owner, then a newly-qualified architect. The original design has been progressively extended and makes perfect use of its tight wedge-shaped plot.

below: 9 Monmouth Avenue

Despite its modest-looking exterior, this is now a three/four-bedroom bungalow, originally built in 1953 and since considerably extended.

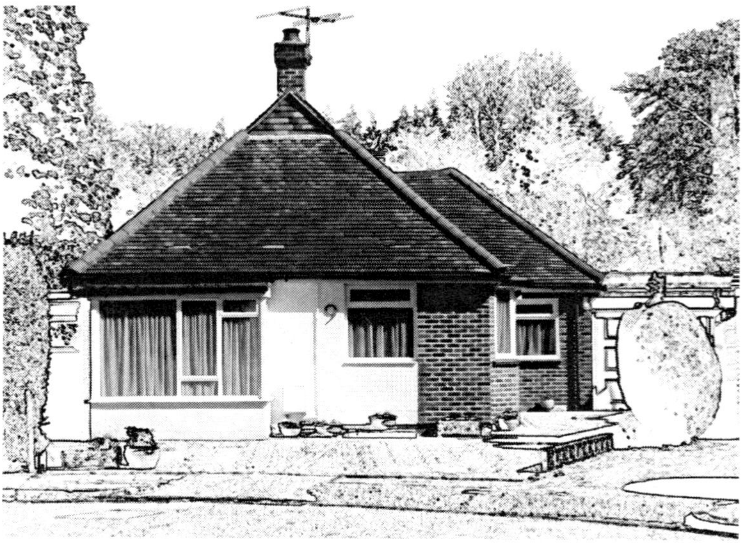

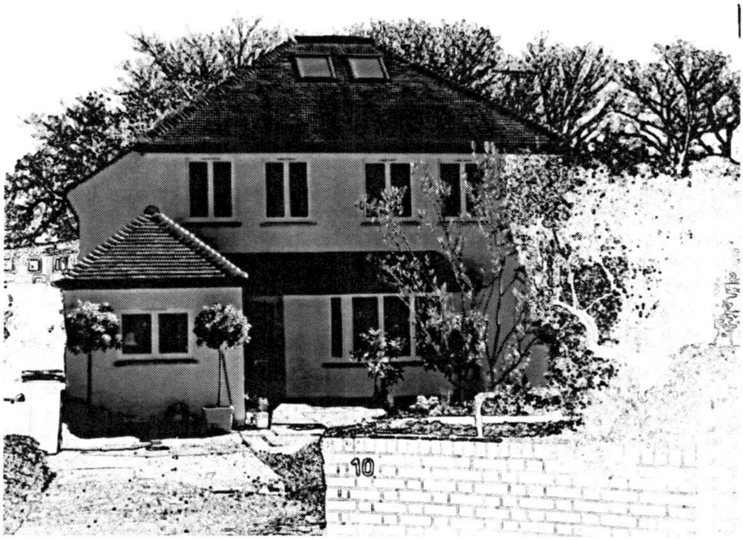

above: **10 Monmouth Avenue**

Although plans for a bungalow on this site were approved in February 1939, it did not get built and ten years later a three-bedroom two-storey house took its place. This was extensively revised in 2005 with a side extension as evidenced by the asymmetrical roof line.

below: **12 Monmouth Avenue**

This is (another) Robert Wake-built bungalow, but one that did get started and finished before the war. The design was the same two-bedroom drawing as previously used at Number 6.

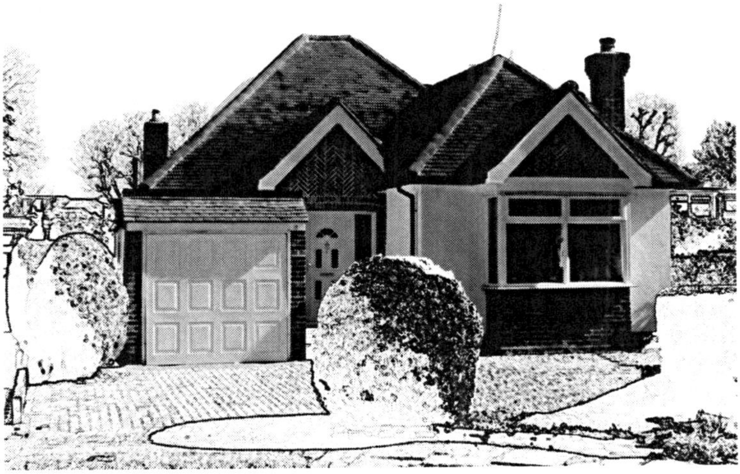

Appendix: ***THE BRICK BY BRICK WEBSITE*** **www.hamptonwickhistory.org.uk**

Before starting to write this book, the author spent many happy hours and days researching in National and County Archives, in Local Study Rooms and on the Internet looking for material - data, maps, images, documents and articles - in fact, anything that would cast light on the development of Hampton Wick. Like any researcher, the task has then been to digest this large volume of material and extract the key facts and images to create this book's content in a (hopefully) interesting and entertaining format.

Normally, a researcher would then "park" the source material with possibly a bibliography and maybe set of footnotes to point to the particular material used. However, it soon became clear that in this project *the source material itself* was potentially of as much value as the conclusions that had been drawn from it. Just as summary Census data tells us about overall population, so also can a particular set of individual Census entries provide snapshots of the occupants of a certain property over time.

The huge popularity of sites like **Ancestry.com** lies in the value that specific items within their vast collections can have for individuals conducting their own particular line of research. From these lines of thought stemmed two additional activities for the current project. First, to create and make available a collection of all the source material relating to the development of Hampton Wick. Second, to construct a mini-website (literally a homepage) *for each residential property mentioned in this book* containing (or pointing to) some of the key source material relating to that specific property. The output from both activities are included in the current website.

The website is an integral part of the overall *Brick by Brick* project. It has the potential to increase the value and enjoyment of this book for those readers who can take a moment to understand the structure and learn how to navigate their way around. The next few pages attempt to provide a brief guide to achieving this.

The diagram opposite shows how, from the **Home Page** of the main site, the user may click (1) to the **Hampton Wick: Brick by Brick** area of the site or (2) through to the **Resource Bank**. The first option, when selected, opens a **Welcome Page**. This presents the user with the contents of all three books as alphabetic lists of the streets covered in each (exactly as shown in the table on page 11). Clicking on an underlined street name (the underline signifies the existence of further information) leads to the **Property List**. From here the user may either (a) scroll down and directly select a property or (b) click on the miniature map for the option to browse and select off the **Property Map**. Either method leads to the **Property Page**.

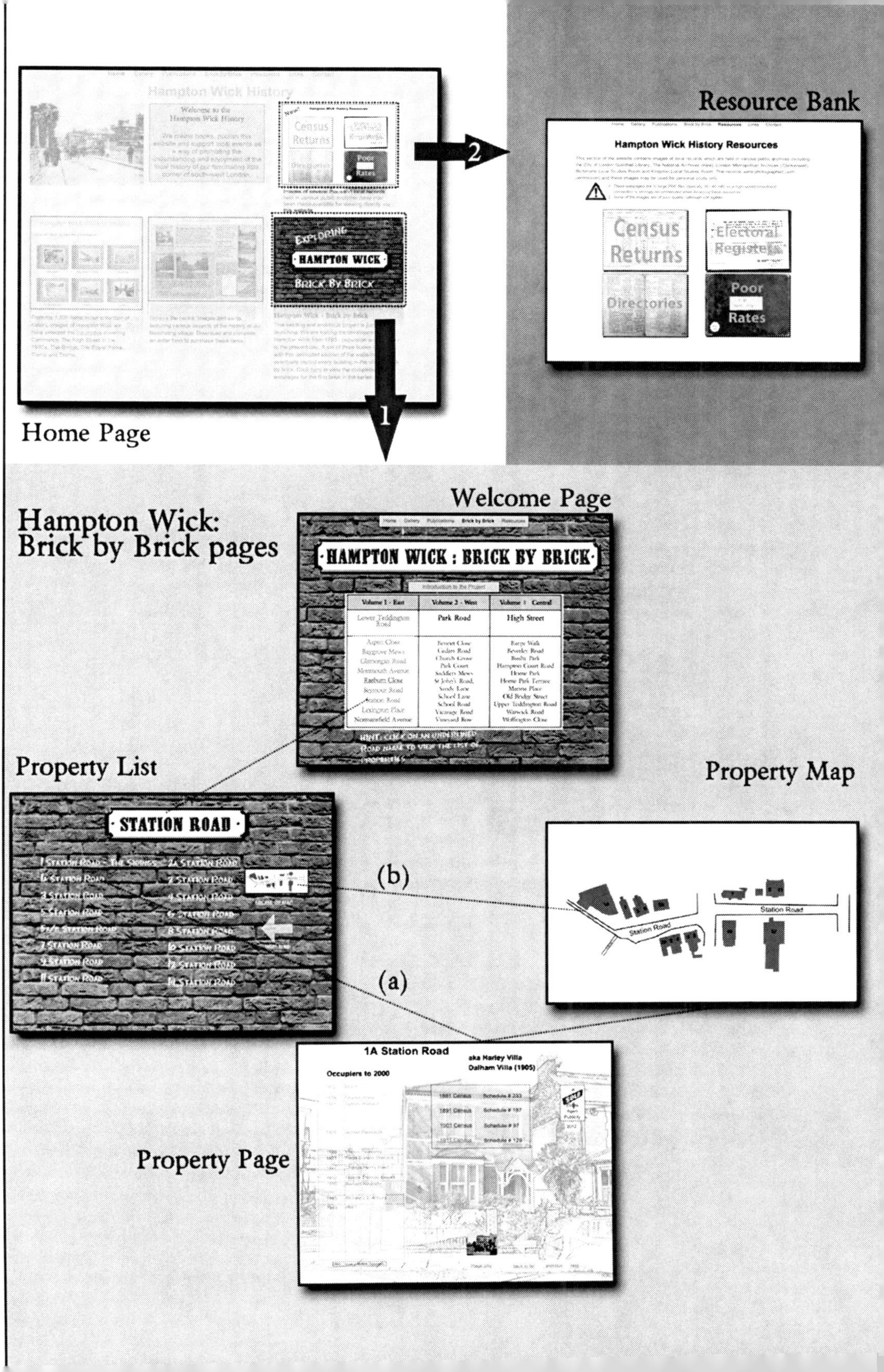
Resource Bank
Hampton Wick History Resources
Census Returns
Electoral Registers
Directories
Poor Rates
2
Home Page
Hampton Wick History
Exploring
HAMPTON WICK
Brick By Brick
1
Hampton Wick:
Brick by Brick pages
Welcome Page
HAMPTON WICK : BRICK BY BRICK
Volume 1 - East
Volume 2 - West
Volume 3 - Central
Park Road
High Street
Property List
STATION ROAD
Property Map
Station Road
(b)
(a)
1A Station Road
Occupiers to 2000
Property Page

Typical Property Page

Individual occupiers of this property (i.e. excluding flat dwellers) from the earliest available records. In accordance with accepted privacy standards, the list does not include householders from the last ten years.

The postal address of the property and whether it is designated as a National Heritage **Listed Building** or a London Borough of Richmond upon Thames Council **Building of Townscape Merit**.

aka: (Also Known As) Alternative names by which this property has been known. Dates of change are approximate and are usually based on the date that changes are noted in Census Return or a Street Directory.

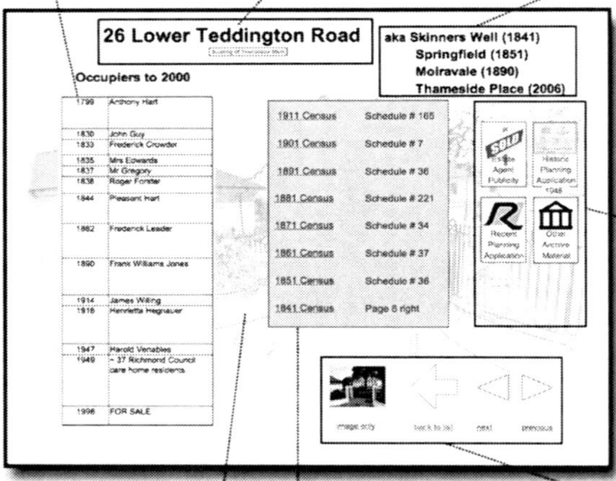

Icons in this area show there is other information available on this property. Typical items include slideshows from Estate Agents' publicity material relating to a recent sale or letting and extracts from planning applications - both historic (1890 - 1960) or recent (last ten years). Double click on an icon to view the available material.

The background image is reproduced from the Brick by Brick section of the book. A full colour version can be viewed by clicking on the "Image only" in the Navigation Area of the screen (bottom right)

Census Returns - click to see the individual entries for this property. Use the schedule numbers to help locate on the Enumerator's sheet. 1911 Census Returns were completed by the occupier.

Navigation Area:
Click these buttons to view a full-screen image of the property, to return to the Property List page or to navigate to the next (i.e. higher numbered) or previous (i.e. lower numbered) property on this same side of the street.

Resource Bank

Clicking in the top right corner of the Home Page leads the user to this section of the website which contains images of local records which are held in various public archives including the City of London Guildhall Library, The National Archives (Kew), London Metropolitan Archives (Clerkenwell), Richmond Local Studies Room and Kingston Local Studies Room. The records were photographed (with permission) and these images may be used for personal study only.

The website carries the following two warnings:

a) These webpages link to large PDF files (typically 20 - 40 mB) so a high-speed broadband connection is strongly recommended when browsing these resources.
b) Some of the images are of poor quality (although still legible)

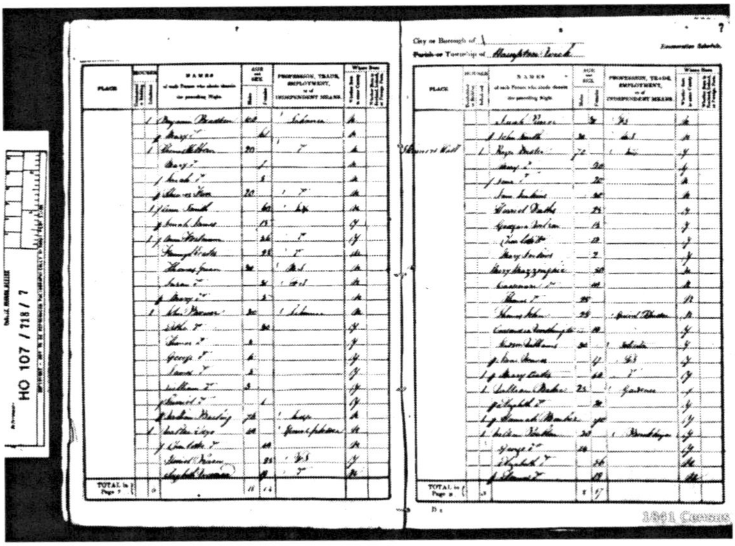

above: **1841 Census - Enumerator's transcription**
The first available census records for Hampton Wick. Information was limited to name, gender, age, occupation. Note the entry for Skinners Hall which was the first recorded name for what is now known as *Thameside Place*.

below: **1891 Census - Enumerator's transcription**
Additional information now includes the address of the property, the relationship to the Head of Family, occupation of all persons together with their place and year of birth.

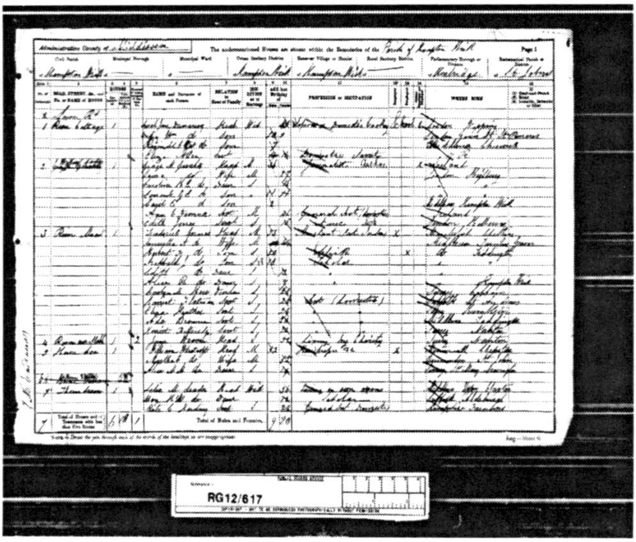

Hampton Wick Census Returns 1841 - 1911

A full UK Census has been conducted every ten years since 1801 (excepting for 1941). The first four censuses (1801–1831) were mainly headcounts and contained little personal information. In 1841, each householder was required to complete a census schedule giving the address of the household, the names, ages, sex, occupations and places of birth of each individual residing in his or her accommodation. From 1851, householders were asked to give more precise details of the places of birth of each resident, to state their relationship to him or her, marital status and the nature of any disabilities from which they may have suffered. Census enumerators then collected the census schedules and these were transcribed into census enumerators' books. Although the original census schedules were destroyed many years ago, the enumerators' books were kept. Census information is subject to a 100-year confidentiality period so the latest information available relates to the Census taken on 2 April 1911.

The Hampton Wick census collection on the website contains complete returns for 1841 to 1901, with currently about one third of the returns for 1911.

below: **1911 Census - Householder's return**
The most recently available census returns, and the first for which the original forms completed by the householder have been retained. Note how much more comprehensive is the information recorded - the inclusion of the number of rooms is particularly useful. This entry for "Rossendale" (Number 2 Seymour Road) includes playwright RC Sherriff, then a 14-year-old schoolboy at Kingston Grammar School.

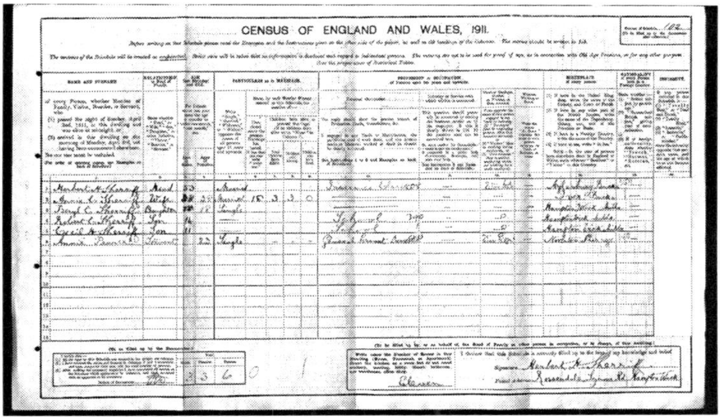
CENSUS OF ENGLAND AND WALES, 1911.

No.	Christian Name and Surname of each Voter at full length.	Place of Abode.	Nature of Qualification.	Street, Lane, or other like Place in this Parish, and Number of House (if any), where the Property is situate, or Name of the Property, if known by any, or Name of the occupying Tenant; or if the Qualification consist of a Rent-charge, then the Names of the Owners of the Property out of which such Rent is issuing, or some of them, and the Situation of the Property.
	PARISH OF HAMPTON-WICK.—[1851-2.]			
190	Ashby, John	14, Old Compton-street	Freehold garden and shed	Occupied by Mrs. Minchin.
~~191~~	~~Babb, William~~	~~99, Upper Wharton-street, Lloyd-square, Pentonville, Middlesex~~	~~Two freehold houses~~	~~Adjoining the Swan public house, in the Lower-road, and in the occupation of Thomas Kelly.~~
192	Beaman, George	Hampton Wick, and 32, King-street, Covent-garden	Freehold house and premises	In the occupation of Alexander Gordon, Esq.
193	Belchamber, Robert	Near the principal street, Hampton Wick, Middlesex	Freehold house and yard, &c.	Adjoining the road leading to Bushey Park, and also adjoining St. John's Cottages, and in my own occupation.
194	Bowyer, Frederick	London-road, Twickenham, Middlesex	Moiety of copyhold malt-house	Near the principal street, Hampton Wick, tenant Thomas Bowyer, jun.
195	Bowyer, Thomas	Guildford	Moiety of copyhold malt-house	Near the principal street, Hampton Wick.
196	Bunce, John	Teddington-row, Hampton Wick, Middlesex	Freehold house and garden	Teddington-road, Hampton Wick, occupied by myself and others.
197	Dale, Thomas	Park-lane, Hampton Wick	Freehold house	Albion House, Park-lane, Hampton Wick, occupied by myself.
198	Earl, John	Kingston-on-Thames, Surrey	Freehold house and yard	Situate in Hampton Wick, Middlesex, occupied by widow Bishop.
199	Elmore, John Richard	27, Harley-street, London	Copyhold estate and freehold held in right of my wife	The Cedars, occupying tenant John Guy, Esq.; and Thorpe Farm, occupying tenant Mrs. Sarah Salter Minchin, being freehold and copyhold estates.
200	Feltham, James	East Moulsey	Copyhold houses	Occupied by Headland.
201	Fenner, Charles James	Hampton Wick	Freehold house	Occupied by himself.

above: **1851-2 Hampton Wick Electoral Register**

The right to vote was restricted to males who owned or leased property worth more than a specified value. A system of registration was administered by the overseers of the poor. Individual's claims for voting rights were entered in a printed register. The entries were then vetted - and could be overruled - by the overseer (as in #191 above). Entry 192 refers to *Rivermead* (6 Lower Teddington Road) and 201 to *Park House* on Park Road. Entry 199 refers to two houses and a large area of land which eventually became the site of Vicarage and Cedars Roads.

below: **1894 Hampton Wick Electoral Register**

From this year, women who owned property could vote in local elections.

Parish of Hampton Wick.

Hampton Electoral Division (part of).

OCCUPATION Electors (other than Lodgers).

DIVISION THREE.—*Persons entitled to vote as County Electors but not as Parliamentary Electors.*

No.	Name of each Elector at full length, the Surname being first.	Place of Abode.	Nature of Qualification.	Description of Qualifying Property.
395	Adam, Emily Eliza (Lady Adam)	Wilderness House, Hampton Court	Dwelling house	Wilderness House, Hampton Court.
396	Adams, Lucy Ann	Park-road, Hampton Wick	Dwelling house	Park-road, Hampton Wick.
397	Anderson, Caroline Frances	Bay lodge, Hampton Court	Dwelling house	Bay lodge.
398	Arnold, Julia	Park-road, Hampton Wick	Dwelling house	Park-road, Hampton Wick.
399	Barker, Maria Louisa	Cambridge House, Hampton Wick	Dwelling house	Cambridge House.
400	Baron, Mary Eliza	Mayfield cottage, Park-road, Hampton Wick	Dwelling house	Mayfield cottage.
401	Beauchamp, Hannah	Park-road, Hampton Wick	Dwelling house	Park-road.
402	Beauchamp, Mary Ann	Park-road, Hampton Wick	Dwelling house	Park-road, Hampton Wick.
403	Bedford, Maria	Old Bridge-street, Hampton Wick	Dwelling house	Old Bridge-street.
404	Bolton, Alice	Lucerne House, Hampton Wick	Dwelling house	Lucerne House.
405	Bolton, Abigail	"Merton," Seymour-road, Hampton Wick	Dwelling house	"Merton."
406	Bolton, Mary	Upper Teddington-road, Hampton Wick	Dwelling house	Upper Teddington-road.
407	Bush, Isabella	Old Bridge-street, Hampton Wick	Dwelling house	Old Bridge-street.
408	Chamberlain, Ann	Upper Teddington-road, Hampton Wick	Dwelling house	Upper Teddington-road.

Hampton Wick Electoral Registers

Electoral registers are lists of voters able to vote in parliamentary and local government elections. They are arranged by constituency and divided into polling districts. Electoral registration was introduced by the Reform Act of 1832 and, since then, registers have been compiled annually with the exception of the years 1916, 1917 and 1940 to 1944. The original Act directed parish overseers to prepare the electoral registers which were compiled from returns. Rules for who was allowed to vote were defined in the various Representation of the People Acts significant amongst which were the Acts of 1918 (all men over 21 and women over 30 allowed to vote), 1928 (women over 21) and 1969 (voting age reduced to 18).

The website collection of Electoral Registers for Hampton Wick includes the Overseers' Returns from 1847 - 1882 (complete with their handwritten corrections and deletions) together with the actual registers from 1883 - 1899 and from 1945 - 2000. The image quality of some of the registers from 1940 on is marginal.

below: **1945 Hampton Wick Electoral Register**
The modern register is a simple listing of eligible voters with their postal addresses.

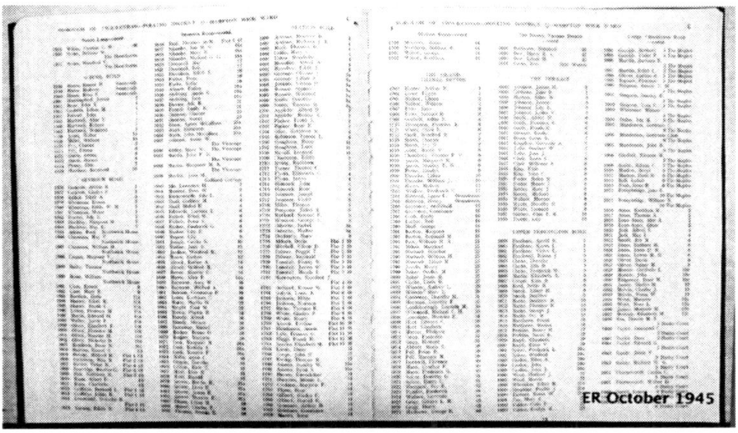

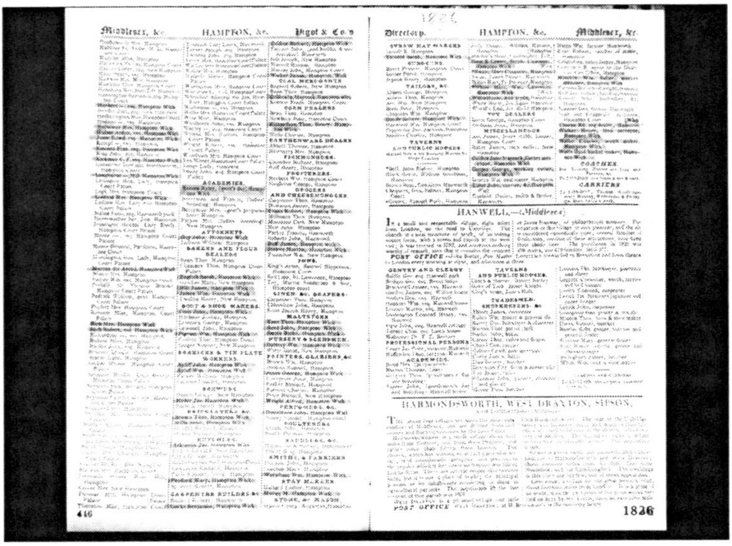
Middlesex, &c. HAMPTON, &c. Pigot & Co's

Directory. HAMPTON, &c. Middlesex, &c.

HANWELL,—Middlesex.

446

1826

above: **Pigot's 1826 Middlesex Directory**

At this time, individuals and Traders paid for their entries in the directory. The academy listed as being run by Ryley Barnes was in Number 3 Lower Teddington Road.

below: **Green's 1888 Directory of Hampton Wick**

This unique local directory was produced by R Green, printer, stationer and bookbinder of Caxton House (now 47 High Street) Hampton Wick.

(Transcription courtesy of Paul Barnfield)

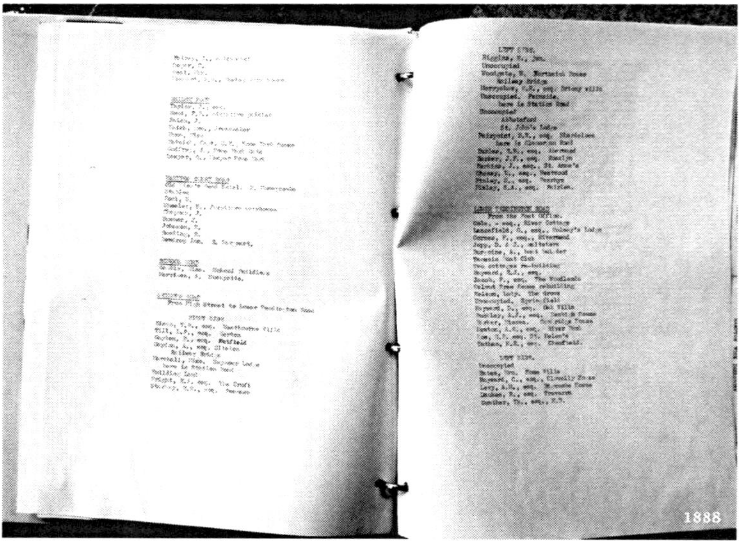
1888

Hampton Wick Trade and Street Directories

Directories are an invaluable primary source for historians. They provide first hand data about local communities, their infrastructure and the individuals inhabiting those communities. Published more frequently than the census, directories can also help fill in any missing gaps. Early directory compilers often relied on people sending in their names together with a small payment if they wanted to be included in the directory. By growing links with the Post Office, the compilers were able to use information originally gathered for mail-delivery purposes. Best known was Frederick Festus Kelly whose eponymous directories first appeared in 1845. They continued in production until the early 1970's, at which time the Kelly's HQ was in Tudor House, Hampton Wick.

This current website collection includes twenty Trade Directories covering the period 1826 - 1886. A one-off locally-produced directory was published by E Green of 47 High Street in 1888 (thanks to Paul Barnfield who has painstakingly transcribed it). There also is a complete set of Kelly's Directories covering the period 1892 - 1940 when Hampton Wick was dropped from Kelly's coverage.

below: **Kelly's 1938 Directory of Hampton Wick**
One of the last directories covering Hampton Wick.

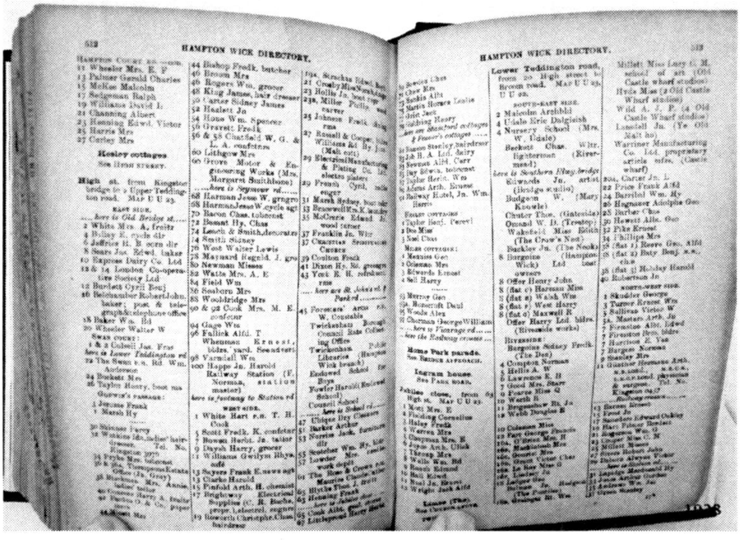

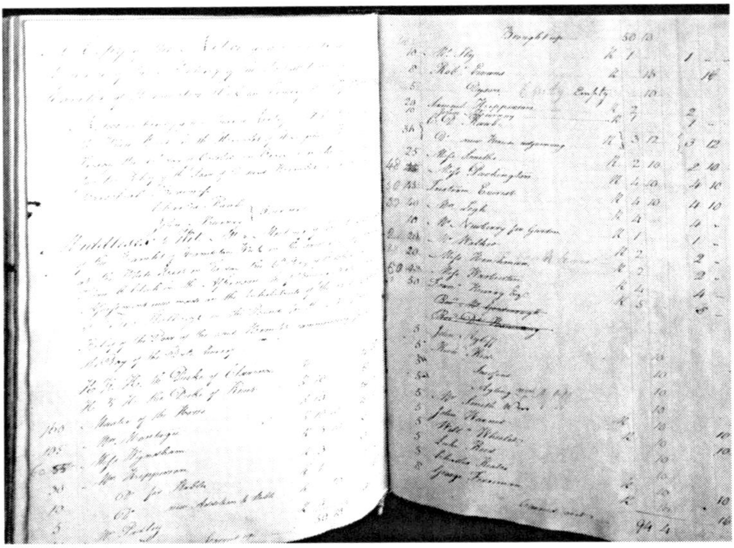

above: **Hampton Wick Poor Rate Book 1808**
This image from the earliest Poor rate Book available shows the minimalism in the accounting system. Almost all payments were identified just by name, with only an occasional note of the property to which it referred.

below: **Hampton Wick Poor Rate Book 1868**
By this date, the records included the name of the occupier as well as owner together with brief description of the property. The entries were in street order although no street numbering was yet in existence.

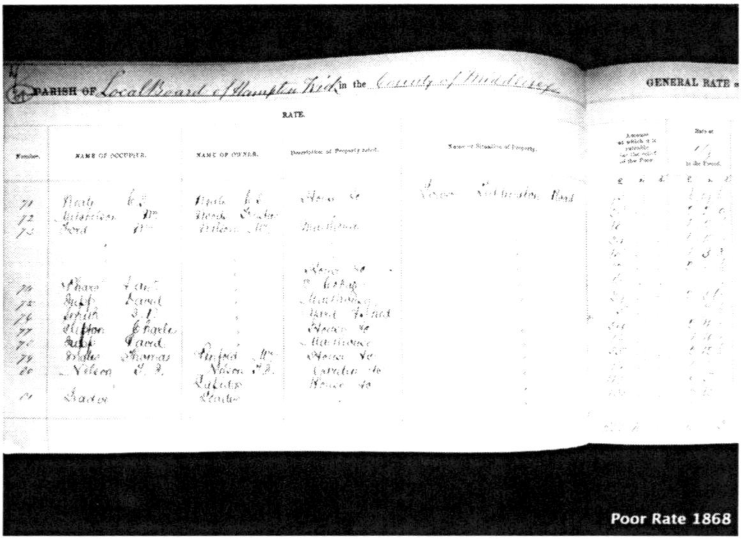

Hampton Wick Poor Rate Books

The Poor Law - originating from the reign of Elizabeth I - created a system for the relief of the Poor, administered at parish level and paid for by levying local rates on property owners and middle-class occupiers. Each Parish elected two Overseers of the Poor annually who were responsible for setting the Poor Rate, collecting the dues and distributing the proceeds to the Poor. They were answerable to two Justices of the Peace for the County for the correct administration of the system. The combination of skills and attributes needed to be an effective Overseer meant that in practice the same limited group of individuals performed the task in rotation.

The rates as collected were recorded into Poor Rate Books, the earliest available for Hampton Wick being a standard format accounts book dating from 1808 and listing names, rateable values and amount collected. A comprehensive reform and centralisation of the Poor Law System in 1834 created standardised books which recorded both occupier and owner and included a description of the property. When the Hampton Wick Local Board promulgated street names in 1864, this was added to the information recorded in the Poor Rate Books, greatly increasing their value to the researcher. Roughly one-third of the original set of Hampton Wick Poor Rate books survive from the period 1808 to 1915 and are included on the website.

below: Hampton Wick Poor Rate Book 1915
The last book that has survived, all entries now include street addresses.

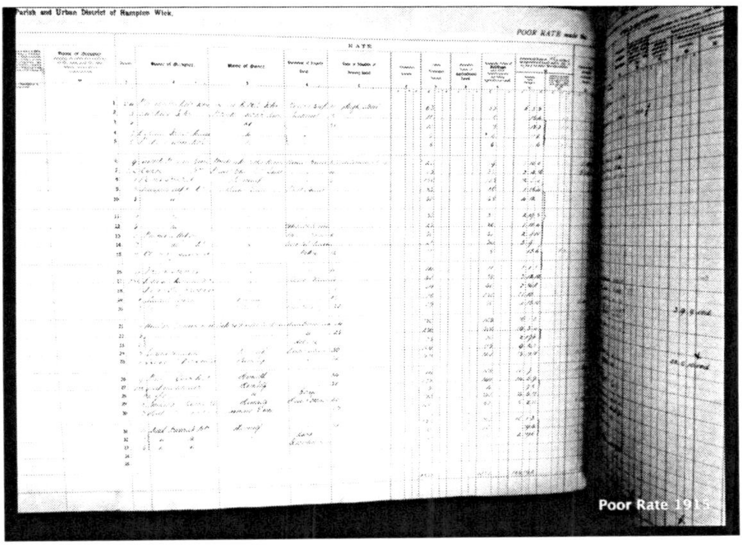

A Hampton Wick Timeline - from Domesday to Current Day (November 2010)

A collection of thirty-one images from photographs, postcards, maps and news-cuttings telling the illustrated story of this historic village in south west London. Each picture is provided with a caption that sets the historic context and which, collectively, provide a brief but thorough history of Hampton Wick.
Available in two editions:

- standard 66pp (150 x 230 mm) perfect bound b&w £6.99
- de luxe 40pp (250 x 200 mm) perfect bound full colour £19.99

The High Street Traders of Hampton Wick (May 2011)

A fascinating study of Hampton Wick High Street which, although less than 400 metres long, has in its time been host to more than seventy shops and pubs. In this comprehensive review of the period from 1826 to the current day, the author has traced every retail establishment, listing the shop-keepers and their trades and providing a series of reminiscences and anecdotes extracted from several sets of local memoirs as well as the more than twenty five interviews he has conducted during his research. Illustrated with over 500 photographs, maps and contemporary adverts.

178 pp (150 x 230 mm) perfect bound black and white £9.99

The Grove - The story of a house and a home (August 2009)

On the banks of the River Thames at Hampton Wick stands *The Grove*, a relatively modest mansion built in 1750 by the Earl of Halifax. Quite why this wealthy philanderer needed it when his - very grand - family residence was only just over a mile away is a matter of conjecture.
However he sold it when his wife died and the house passed into the hands of a family of landscape gardeners and architects. It remained in their ownership for 150 years although it was let for most of that period - to a succession of interesting and colourful tenants including several lawyers, a gentleman soldier, an author, an artist and a dish-washer inventor. The author tells the story with the passion and warmth you would expect from someone writing about their own home.

38 pp (180 x 180 mm) perfect bound full colour £19.99

For more information and to order go to www.hamptonwickhistory.org.uk or write to:
1 *The Grove*, 24 Lower Teddington Road, Hampton Wick, Surrey KT1 4HJ

Lightning Source UK Ltd.
Milton Keynes UK
UKOW040507031112

201634UK00003B/3/P

9 780957 167933